CW00589967

PROJECT ANALYSIS IN DEVELOPING COUNTRIES

Project Analysis in Developing Countries

Steve Curry
Lecturer, Development and Project Planning Centre
University of Bradford

and

John Weiss
Senior Lecturer, Development and Project Planning Centre
University of Bradford

St. Martin's Press

© Steve Curry and John Weiss 1993

All rights reserved. No reproduction, copy or transmission of this publication may be made without written permission.

No paragraph of this publication may be reproduced, copied or transmitted save with written permission or in accordance with the provisions of the Copyright, Designs and Patents Act 1988, or under the terms of any licence permitting limited copying issued by the Copyright Licensing Agency, 90 Tottenham Court Road, London W1P 9HE.

Any person who does any unauthorised act in relation to this publication may be liable to criminal prosecution and civil claims for damages.

First published in Great Britain 1993 by
THE MACMILLAN PRESS LTD
Houndmills, Basingstoke, Hampshire RG21 2XS
and London
Companies and representatives
throughout the world

A catalogue record for this book is available
from the British Library.

ISBN 0–333–49450–4

Printed in Great Britain by
Antony Rowe Ltd
Chippenham, Wiltshire

First published in the United States of America 1993 by
Scholarly and Reference Division,
ST. MARTIN'S PRESS, INC.,
175 Fifth Avenue,
New York, N.Y. 10010

ISBN 0–312–09432–9

Library of Congress Cataloging-in-Publication Data
Project analysis in developing countries / Steve Curry and
John Weiss.
p. cm.
Includes bibliographical references and index.
ISBN 0–312–09432–9
1. Economic development projects—Developing countries–
–Evaluation. I. Curry, Steve. II. Weiss, John.
HC59.72.E44P76 1993
338.9'009172'4—dc20 92–38983
CIP

For Aran, Asha and Lisa (S.C.)

For Francisca, Alfred and Antonio (J.W.)

Contents

List of Figures

List of Tables

Preface

Project analysis has grown up in the last thirty years and has been widely adopted particularly in the external funding of public sector projects. Analyses are undertaken from different points of view, the scope varying according to different applications.

The focus of this book is on economic project analysis in developing countries, and is complementary to financial and more recent environmental or social analyses. There are several reasons for concentrating only on the economic analysis of projects. First, there is a relatively coherent body of economic theory to rely on. Secondly, existing texts on the economic analysis of projects are too theoretical in their approach. Here we have tried to combine the application of project analysis methods with their theoretical underpinnings. Finally, in recent years there has been considerable progress in the estimation of national parameters for use in the economic analysis of projects, which gives a firmer base to their application in developing countries. In addition, it is the authors' view that the identification of projects that are economically worthwhile is the appropriate basis for their selection, to which the analysis of other project effects must be related.

Some of the developments in this area have been facilitated by the development of microcomputing. The ways in which microcomputing techniques can be used for project analysis is again a subject in its own right, and although it is not dealt with here the application of the methods we discuss can be done most accurately using microcomputers.

This book arises not only from the consideration of developments in the economic analysis of projects of the last few years, but also from a sizeable period of applying and teaching the methods described. Several groups of postgraduate and post-experience students at the Development and Project Planning Centre of the University of Bradford have been subjected to expositions of the material in different forms, and their reactions to it have been much appreciated. The authors have benefited also from the general interest in the subject by several colleagues.

What follows, however, should not be attributed to students or colleagues. The joint authors have discussed and revised all the chapters of the book, but there has also been a division of labour with chapters 1–4 and 8 being principally the work of Steve Curry and chapters 5–7 and 9–11 being principally the work of John Weiss. Chapter 12 was written jointly.

The authors take this opportunity to acknowledge the patient and excellent work of Jean Hill, who produced the manuscript despite her other responsibilities.

STEVE CURRY
JOHN WEISS

1 Introduction

Project analysis involves estimating and comparing the beneficial effects of an investment with its costs. Such a comparison is done within a broader economic framework that provides the basis on which full costs and benefits are identified and valued. Project analysis originated more than fifty years ago, the main ideas developing simultaneously in different places. The last thirty or so has witnessed an extensive application of project analysis methods, particularly in developing countries. This introductory chapter provides a brief outline of the basic ideas of project analysis, and the way in which their application has developed. These basic ideas are also situated in the broader process of project planning.

BASIC IDEAS

The basic ideas of project analysis have a long history, but they became clear only with the first applications. These occurred simultaneously in different economic contexts. In the United States in the 1930s a problem was formulated in relation to water resource investments. The costs of investing in and running such projects were relatively straightforward to estimate; what was not so straightforward was an estimate of the benefits water resource investments would generate. The beneficial effects distributed between many different types of user first had to be identified and then valued. Moreover, there was no market in water provision which could yield an appropriate price to value water. At this time, guidelines were established for estimating the benefits and costs of water resource projects. In the context of a capitalist economy in recession, this use of project analysis can be described as extending quasi-market criteria to an area of infrastructure services where the full characteristics of a competitive market could not be established.

This can also be viewed from a closely related but different perspective. It is no accident that this application was in the provision of services within the public sector. In a capitalist economy there is competition for resources between the public and private sectors; investments in the public sector often need to be resourced from incomes generated in the private sector. To justify public sector investments, it is useful to show that they also have productive effects. Project analysis can be used, therefore, not simply to analyse the effects of a project, but to justify it in relation to the alternatives available.

In the 1930s also the first use of project analysis was made in the Soviet Union. The introduction of central planning at the end of the 1920s provided the investment framework; the overall rate of investment and its distribution between sectors was determined through the central planning mechanism. The emphasis was placed on expanding material production rather than social service sectors. However, within this context of planned investment several choices still had to be made at the sector and project level. For example, there were choices to be made about the best transport mode to meet a forecast demand; about the appropriate location for priority heavy industry investments; about the type of technology to be used in new investments; and about the scale of individual investments. Investment criteria were devised that allowed comparison not of the costs and benefits of specific investments but the alternative costs of generating given outputs.

These forms of project analysis therefore differed. Whilst one form sought to analyse and justify the provision of infrastructure services the other sought the best alternative means of achieving productive effects. However, there was a similarity in the theoretical basis of project analysis developed in both contexts. The reference point was a competitive equilibrium that markets would produce either in a capitalist economy or under market socialism. The prices obtaining in such an equilibrium would indicate the marginal or additional value of resources and thus would be the appropriate ones to use in project analysis. Project analysis could therefore be rationalised as a means of formalising the best choice of investments by simulating a competitive market framework.

The prices at which to value the benefits and costs of an investment have been a major concern in project analysis. An alternative basis for arriving at a set of prices for project analysis was proposed in the 1960s. Rather than relying on an abstract notion of competitive equilibrium, it appeals to trade opportunities. For many countries, especially developing countries, trade opportunities are an important issue. A decision to develop domestic economic activities should take into account the possibility of relying on trade to obtain resources, possibly more cheaply. From this reasoning, international prices have come to be used in project analysis, not because they represent a competitive equilibrium but because they represent the terms upon which countries can participate in foreign trade or what can be termed trade opportunity costs.

APPLICATION OF PROJECT ANALYSIS

Project analysis has been applied in several contexts in the period since the Second World War. The form it has taken has been influenced by underlying changes in the world economy. Only a brief summary of the main applications can be given here relating particularly to developing countries.

Within the industrialised countries, project analysis generally has been confined to large scale infrastructure projects like water systems, airports, transport investments, and educational institutions. These applications have continued the original focus on indirectly productive investments – identifying and estimating the full cost, especially the beneficial effects, for services that are not generally sold. In developing countries initial applications of project analysis were of a similar nature. In the 1950s, the assistance programmes of the International Bank for Reconstruction and Development (IBRD) concentrated on public sector investment in infrastructure such as roads, railways, ports, schools and colleges, and water resources, to complement private foreign investment in industry and agro-processing. In this context, the methods of measuring costs and benefits developed in the industrialized countries found a ready application. At the same time, project analysis became a condition for the release of funds to assisted projects.

Since the early 1960s, project analysis in developing countries has continued to be applied to both indirectly and directly productive projects. The extension to the latter was enhanced by the growth of the public sector in developing countries, and by the broader economic role of the state. The release of finance for new investments by large international financial institutions, in support of government investment plans, has come to depend on a demonstration through project analysis that the investments will prove viable from a national perspective. At the same time, many developing countries lacked a capitalist class and financial institutions necessary for the growth of new sectors. The alternative to relying on foreign investment was for the state to step in and establish investment programmes in directly productive sectors. Project analysis became a means of exerting some control over public sector investments where enterprises were required to demonstrate that new investments could generate a minimum return to the economy. In addition, where private and especially foreign capital were investing in the domestic economy, project analysis was sometimes used by governments as a means of testing the viability of investments before the issuing of production licences, the granting of protection or concessionary finance.

The involvement of international institutions was also crucial in the major theoretical development of project analysis in developing countries in the 1960s: namely, the introduction of methods of shadow pricing through use of trade opportunity costs. These methods were intended to assess the viability of new investments from the national point of view, especially within the public sector. The idea of using an alternative set of prices to actual prices, and the methods of applying it in project analysis, were developed virtually simultaneously within the Development Centre of the Organization for Economic Cooperation and Development (OECD) and the United Nations Industrial Development Organization (UNIDO). Although these institutions were not the only sources of ideas for developing operational methods of national economic analysis, their involvement illustrates the connection between project analysis and international development agencies.

The growth of project analysis from a national point of view was connected to critiques of development policy. The application of project analysis to new productive investments in developing countries found a theoretical base in an area of development economics, specifically debates over the choice of technology. It was argued that developing countries needed to adopt recent technologies in some sectors, to raise productivity as fast as possible and to become internationally competitive. Others argued that developing countries should adapt the choice of technology to what was seen as an abundance of cheap labour and a shortage of domestic investment funds. Although this debate could not be resolved simply at the project level, project analysis, by systematically outlining the costs and benefits of different alternatives, could indicate the technology choice for different sectors that would generate the greatest economic surplus for reinvestment.

Studies of the industrial import substitution process also concluded that protection of new investments had created profitable but high-resource-cost industries that would never be internationally competitive. As an alternative to removing protection it was recommended that new investments should be analysed as if there were no protection. Such an analysis conformed to using trade opportunity cost as the basis of shadow pricing. A similar approach derived also from a consideration of domestic price policy. Where governments set many domestic prices especially for agriculture and food, production patterns did not necessarily conform to the international cost advantages of the economy. Again, use of an alternative set of prices based on trade possibilities was advocated as a means of planning resource allocation in agriculture.

PROJECT ANALYSIS AND NATIONAL PLANNING

Applications of project analysis in developing countries have depended on the size and role of the public sector and the level of external assistance. India provides an example where project analysis has been applied over a long period. The role of the public sector has been significant both at the federal and state level in India; project analysis became institutionalised in the government investment process as a means of assessing the effects of both indirectly productive investments and the viability of commercially oriented public projects. At the same time, the extensive system of licensing and controls placed on private sector development, especially in the industrial sector, allowed further applications in the assessment of private investment proposals.

In some smaller countries, application of project analysis has developed later and on a smaller scale. In Jamaica, for example, major project proposals are given preliminary assessment by a committee encompassing planning, finance and sectoral interests. More detailed analyses are reviewed subsequently, prior to actual investment. However, the process only covers those projects reliant on external funding, either directly in the form of project loans or indirectly through lines of credit. In these circumstances, the application of project analysis methods is concentrated in development finance institutions as much as the government sector directly. In Sri Lanka, similarly, the application of project analysis is linked to the process of external funding. Assistance agencies themselves carry out the bulk of the analysis work, which is subsequently reviewed by national planning staff. Again, the process of project analysis is linked to the larger public sector projects and programmes, and is applied through financial agencies as much as the government sector itself.

The extent to which project analysis is used in a particular country changes over time. In recent years, some countries have relaxed controls over internal prices and the exchange rate, and have witnessed a growth in private sector investment, whilst largely abandoning project analysis as a means of controlling investment. Other countries are now more dependent on foreign investment inflows than they were, and have a greater need to ensure such inflows are used to their most productive effect. Moreover, socialist developing countries such as China and Mozambique have adopted project analysis as part of a process of reform. In both, recent economic reforms have addressed the problems of inadequate investment returns; improvement in the productive effects of investments can be enhanced by greater attention to the choice and design of new projects. Project analysis provides a means of implementing this process, within the context of substantial international trade, on the one hand, and some decentralization of investment funding and decision-making, on the other.

THE PROJECT PLANNING PROCESS

Project analysis forms part of the broader process of project planning, which focuses on discrete, new activities, involving a substantial commitment of investment resources. It consists of a set of procedures and techniques that can be applied, first, in the process leading up to a decision whether or not to invest and, secondly, in the implementing and organizing of the new activity. Project planning is frequently conceived as a series of stages: the identification of investment possibilities; their preliminary investigation through a pre-feasibility study; a more detailed investigation and implementation plan through a feasibility study; and a decision process accepting or rejecting the project. Once a project has been accepted further stages involve detailed design and finance negotiations, construction and commissioning, and full operation of the new activity. Project analysis plays a major role in those stages leading up to a decision whether to invest or not.

Project analysis involves the comparison of those benefits and costs of an investment that can be quantified. At each stage of the project planning process, a decision is required whether to commit planning resources to the subsequent more detailed stage. The prospect of a project's benefits exceeding its costs should be a major influence on such decisions. This can be briefly elaborated in relation to the first four stages outlined above.

Project identification involves outlining the main characteristics of proposed new activities, including the scale of investment and the main economic and financial resources required to implement it. It also involves outlining the main costs of the project and the benefits that are likely to ensue. A preliminary analysis of the project's costs and benefits at this stage would be based only on the simplest of forecasts and estimates.

Projects that appear viable can be carried forward to the pre-feasibility stage where a small team of people can investigate the technical basis of the proposed project and define the main alternatives – of scale, technology, location – that are worth investigating. These alternatives need to be compared and the overall project viability assessed. At this stage, project analysis should investigate the economic costs and benefits of all alternatives, without going into the details of financing and organization; it is the overall viability of the project that matters here, regardless of how it is financed or organized.

The feasibility study stage involves a full assessment of viability, based on the chosen technical alternative and an implementation plan. An organizational and legal basis has to be defined for undertaking the investment and managing the operations. Sufficient financial resources have to be brought together on terms that can be met. However, the estimates of project benefits and costs, now defined in more detail, still provide a crucial element. The project analysis should now extend beyond the basic economic characteristics to include assessment of financial viability, leading to a detailed financing plan and the distribution of benefits and costs between different participants. The comparison of costs and benefits will also have to be repeated from the viewpoint of different participants, for example, from the point of view of the project owners in particular, as well as the investment as a whole.

Typically, investments require cooperation between a number of participants – owners, operators, lenders, workers or producers, government and even output users. An analysis, beginning from the same basic project description and statements, can be carried out from the point of view of each participant, recording their particular costs and benefits. A precondition for a successful and productive project is that all participants should share in the additional resources the project produces, at a sufficient level to justify their participation. Sometimes the relative shares will have to be resolved by negotiation; the government often plays a crucial role in resolving differences over relative shares, which can affect the surplus any project produces.

A final decision on whether to proceed with a project will depend on a range of factors. An essential component of the decision is a comparison of a particular project with alternative investments. It is not sufficient that project benefits should exceed project costs: they must do so by more than in other feasible investments. Project analysis techniques must incorporate this comparative element so that the appropriate decision can be taken.

OUTLINE OF THE BOOK

After this brief introduction to the basic ideas of project analysis, the sequence in which they are presented in the rest of the book can now be given. Chapter 2 provides a definition of the investment problem project analysis addresses, describes the conventions used in drawing up project statements upon which such analysis is based, and introduces the technique of discounting which is required for decision-making purposes.

Decision-making requires clear criteria. Chapter 3 outlines the main measures of project worth which project analysis offers for this purpose. These are applied both in the case of decisions on a single project and in the choice between project alternatives. These measures of project worth involve comparing the returns from a project with returns from other investments in the economy.

There are different sets of prices at which project analysis can be conducted. Chapter 4 introduces the concept of shadow prices and the means by which they can be applied. It outlines the consequences for decision-making of introducing an alternative system of valuation of project inputs and outputs.

Application of shadow prices can be based on the same principles but applied in different ways. Chapter 5 presents a much more detailed description of the application of shadow prices using what is termed a world price numeraire. The means by which shadow prices are derived for different types of project inputs is combined with a case study of their application. Chapter 6 repeats this process for a set of shadow prices using a domestic price numeraire, also including a case study application. The simplifications often adopted in domestic price applications are compared with more detailed approaches.

For some types of project the range and extent of beneficial effects are difficult to measure. Chapter 7 deals with two categories of projects in more detail; those indirectly productive projects where benefits cannot be directly measured through shadow pricing methods; and those where a project has substantial external effects upon other activities. In both cases the analysis is more complex than for directly productive projects which have no significant effects on other projects, and greater care has to be taken in identifying benefits and costs, and greater ingenuity used in measuring them.

The application of project criteria at any set of prices involves forecast information of both quantities and prices. There will be considerable uncertainty attached to such estimates. Chapter 8 discusses means of estimating the possible effects of such uncertainty, and the risk that project decisions might be wrong because of it.

The costs and benefits of a project will accrue to different participants. It is often not obvious what the resulting distribution of net effects will be. In Chapter 9 a method is presented for drawing out the effects of a project on the distribution of net benefits to different groups. These additional project effects can be incorporated into the project decision if an appropriate set of weights are devised and applied to the savings and consumption components. In Chapter 10, the procedures used for calculating these weights, and their effect on the project decision, are presented.

The information required to apply shadow prices in project analysis can be extensive. A large part of it can be collected and processed by a central projects agency. Methods exist for estimating consistent sets of economic parameters at the national level. These methods are outlined in Chapter 11, together with the range of values found in past studies.

Finally, project analysis has its limitations. Some of the main limitations of project analysis and the associated approaches described in this book are discussed in Chapter 12.

2 Main Features of Projects, Project Resource Statements and Financial Statements

A project involves the commitment of resources now to obtain extra resources in the future. Projects can be analysed from different points of view. This chapter begins by explaining some basic differences between project resource statements and project financial statements, and the prices used in drawing them up.

A project statement includes all the inflows and outflows of a project according to the time-period in which they occur. It involves the use of certain conventions about the valuation of resources and the time-frame into which they are put. These conventions can be applied to different types of project. This chapter also includes a brief outline of different types of project and the conventions used in drawing up the corresponding project statements.

For decision-making purposes, the net effects of a project need to be added up. These net effects will occur in different years; adding them together involves defining the value of net effects in different years relative to a base year. This chapter also introduces the technique of discounting, and indicates how a discount rate for project statements might be derived.

PROJECT VIEWPOINTS

Any commitment of resources now to obtain extra resources in the future will involve different groups. A project can be analysed from different points of view. For example, a project to raise agricultural production in a particular area can be analysed from the point of view of the farmers who will produce the output and their households, the supplying and marketing agencies who will handle the inputs and outputs, the lending agencies involved in financing the project, and the government that stands to lose or gain revenue and commit expenditures through the project. Again, a factory project can be analysed from the aspect of the workers who will be employed there, the banks who will assist in funding, the government that will gain or lose from associated revenues and expenditures, and the owners of the project who will retain any net profits that are made. Whilst each point of view can be made explicit, two project viewpoints carry particular significance – capital as a whole or total capital, and the project owner or equity capital.

Regardless of the range of participants, it is important to look at a project as a whole, the aspect of total capital. An analysis from the viewpoint of total capital must include all the resource costs – investment, operating, and working capital costs – as well as the resource benefits. These are combined in a project resource statement, showing the economic effects of the project. Such a statement allows assessment of the project with reference to its overall economic impact regardless of how it is financed and regardless of the project's effect on the government budget.

The underlying philosophy behind a project resource statement is that if projects can be demonstrated as beneficial as regards total capital, then the economy as a whole will benefit from their implementation. How the beneficial effects are distributed between owners, producers, lenders and government will depend on financial arrangements, but a worthwhile project overall will be able to meet its financial commitments whilst generating additional resources for the economy.

However, the financial arrangements cannot be ignored. In particular, no project, however worthwhile, will be implemented unless there is a sufficient return to the owners, or in the case of some projects where there are many who contribute their land assets as well as labour to production, the producers. On the owners' side loan inflows and outflows affect their returns; so do tax or subsidy payments. These financial transactions need to be taken into account in a project financial statement so that the net effects of a project for the owner can be calculated. Although the resource costs and benefits form the basis of all project statements, they are supplemented by financial transactions to complete the financial statement. These are open to negotiation, about loan terms and interest rates and sometimes about tax and subsidy rates; they can be varied to influence the return to equity capital in a way which the underlying resource costs and benefits cannot. In essence, the financial transactions are transfer payments which redistribute the benefits a project produces.

This basic difference in perspective can be stated more elaborately as in Table 2.1 where four aspects are compared. Total capital (number 2i) requires a resource statement drawn up at market prices. However, it has been argued that market prices may not reflect the opportunity cost of resources from the national angle, the contribution to national production if inputs were used in other uses, or the costs of alternative supplies of outputs. If this argument is accepted, then an alternative set of prices known as shadow prices will have to be applied in the resource statement to obtain a project statement regarding the national economy (number 1).

Table 2.1 Project perspectives and statements

Perspective	*Project statement*
1. National economy	Resource statement at shadow prices
2. Total capital	
i Pre-tax	Resource statement at market prices
ii Post-tax	Resource statement at market prices adjusted for net taxes
3. Owner: Equity capital	Financial statement = resource statement at market prices adjusted for net taxes and financing

For the owners, it is also useful to draw up a project statement independent of financing arrangements, which takes account of net taxes payable to the government (number 2ii). This will indicate the consequences of the project for private capital. It can form the basis of a judgement as to whether there are alternative projects which are better from the private viewpoint, independent of how any net benefits would be distributed between owners and lenders. The effect of specific financing arrangements for equity capital can be included in a separate statement from the owner's viewpoint (number 3).

The perspectives of total capital and the owner, or equity capital, are illustrated later in this chapter. The perspective of the national economy forms the basis of Chapter 4 and subsequent chapters.

PRICES

Both resource statements and financial statements can be drawn up using different prices. Both types of statement involve estimating the effects of a project in the future. There is a choice as to whether these estimated effects should be valued at a specified set of prices – at constant prices – or whether an attempt should be made to forecast prices in future years – current prices.

Using constant prices to value the economic effects of a project is appropriate for decision-taking. The basic decision in project analysis is whether to invest in the project or not. The alternative is to assign the resources to other investments. Moreover, it is convenient for resources to be valued at present prices, which define their value in different uses when the investment decision is being made. If constant present prices are used throughout the project analysis – for future years as well as the initial year – then resources will be consistently valued at prices reflecting their value in alternative uses now. Future economic effects will be measured in the same units as present effects. This use of constant prices is both in relation to total capital and equity capital. In both cases the basic question is, is the project worthwhile? The answer depends upon a project statement with effects valued at constant prices, whether from the economic or the owner's viewpoint.

The use of constant price project statements requires two qualifications. The first relates to resource statements which are usually drawn up initially at constant market prices. However, as indicated above, they can also be drawn up at constant shadow prices, to better reflect project effects from the national point of view.

The second qualification relates to changes in relative prices. Over the life of a project it may be foreseen that some prices will rise or fall relative to others. For example, it may be foreseen that wages will fall relative to the present price for outputs and other inputs; or it may be foreseen that the price of essential components in an assembly operation may rise relative to the present prices of other resources including labour. Where a particular price is expected to change in real terms, that is, relative to other items in the project statement, then the constant price analysis can be adjusted for this relative price change.[1] This supplements the use of constant prices to value project statements for decision-making purposes, but may be difficult to apply in practice.

For projects to be implemented, a financial plan will need to be prepared. This must identify the total cash requirements of a project and the sources from which they will be met. For this purpose, a financial statement at current prices will be required, incorporating forecasts of general price increases and the specific rate at which prices will change for major inputs and outputs. It is easier to incorporate such price changes if the period for detailed financial planning is not too long. However, the use of current prices, although necessary to the implementing of a project, should make no difference to the decision whether to commit resources or not. A project statement at current prices, if discounted by a rate at current prices, will lead to the same decision as a project statement at constant prices discounted by a rate adjusted to constant prices. The effect of discounting is discussed below. It is sufficient to make the point here that constant prices are sufficient for project decision-making. The construction of financial plans for implementing a project lies outside the scope of this book.

TYPES OF PROJECT

Basically, three types of project can be identified depending upon how new resources committed to them relate to existing economic activities. First, the largest type of project, around which project analysis grew up, involves new investment. New investments are designed to establish a new productive process independent of previous lines of production. They often include a new organization, financially independent of existing organizations. Secondly, there are expansion projects which involve repeating or extending an existing economic activity with the same output, technology and organization. Thirdly, there are updating projects which involve replacing or changing some elements in an existing activity without a major change of output. Updating projects involve some change in technology but within the context of an existing, though possibly reformulated, organization.[2] With changing economic circumstances the balance between these types of project may change. New investments predominated in developing countries in the 1960s and 1970s. However, with declining investment resources and limited access to operational inputs, the proportion of expansion and updating projects has increased.

Whatever type of project is being analysed, the effect of using new resources has to be distinguished from the effect of existing operations. The incremental resource costs have to be identified, that is, the resources that will be committed in a project over and above what would otherwise have been used. Similarly, the incremental benefits, the additional benefits over and above what would otherwise have occurred, have to be identified. Both incremental costs and incremental benefits have to be valued. For a new investment the whole of the output and the whole of the costs will be incremental; for expansion and updating projects, the effects of the new resources have to be separated from the effects of existing resources.

The figure below illustrates the three types of project. Figure 2.1a simply traces the total costs and total benefits of a new investment. Figure 2.1b traces the costs and benefits with and without an expansion investment. It is the difference between these two streams of costs and benefits which describes the effect of the investment. Figure 2.1c does the same for an updating investment; the difference here is that the costs and benefits from existing operations will have a downward trend unless the new investment is undertaken.

Project costs are generally easier to identify and estimate than project benefits. Costs may be met directly by a particular institution; benefits are frequently more diverse. A distinction can be drawn between directly productive and indirectly productive projects. The former are those where the immediate costs and benefits accrue to a single organization; a consequence is that this organization is able to calculate and commit any resulting surplus to new activities. Indirectly productive projects, broadly speaking, are those where the benefits derived from new resources do not accrue to the organization responsible for carrying the costs. In these circumstances, any resulting surplus is not concentrated in the hands of a single organization. Most infrastructure projects, such as roads, are indirectly productive; the benefits accrue to users and producers whilst the costs are met by government. Of course, several projects, especially large ones, may be a mixture of directly and indirectly

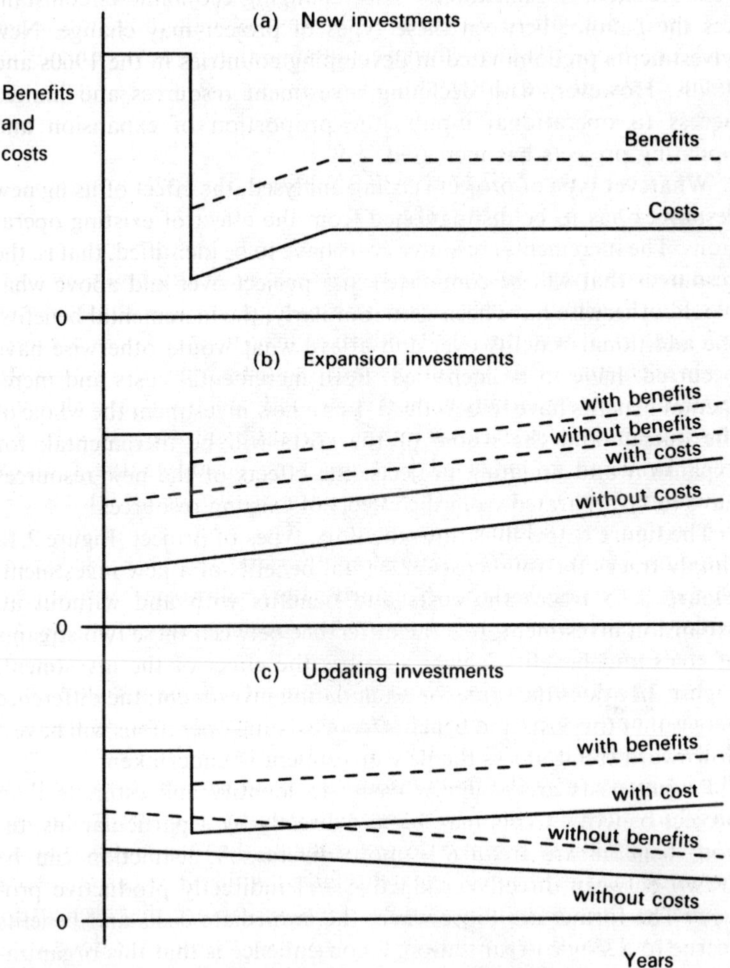

Figure 2.1 Project benefits and costs: different types of project

productive activities, for example, a rural development project involving both increases in agricultural output through farmer investment as well as roads, schools and other infrastructure facilities. The importance of the distinction between directly and indirectly productive projects is that the benefits from new resources are more difficult to estimate in the case of indirectly productive projects. None the less, whenever possible they should be incorporated in the project statement.

CONVENTIONS USED IN DRAWING UP PROJECT RESOURCE STATEMENTS

The main conventions used to describe the scale and timing of costs and benefits in a project resource statement will be illustrated in relation to a new directly productive investment. There are four main elements of a project resource statement: investment costs, operating costs, working capital costs, and benefits. These elements are frequently broken down into several different items. A value for each needs to be included in every time period in the resource statement, but to start with a convention must be established for separating the different time periods. The usual convention is to draw up a resource flow using annual time periods; for discounting purposes (which will be explained later), all costs and benefits within a particular time period are treated as occurring at the end of the time period.[3]

The time-frame for a resource statement will then consist of a series of consecutive annual periods; the investment costs of a project will normally occur in the earlier periods. There is some choice about the nomination of the first period. If it is anticipated (generally for small investments) that the investment process could begin immediately a decision to accept a project is taken, then the first period can be nominated as period 0, and items falling within it can all be treated as though they occur immediately. If it is anticipated that even after a favourable decision it will take some time to organize the design and funding, and hence the investment expenditures themselves will occur some time after the decision-making, then it is appropriate to nominate the first annual period as period 1, as if items falling within it occur at least one year after the decision to invest.[4]

Investment Costs

The items included under investment costs have to be broken down into three components – initial expenditures, replacement expenditures and residual values. Initial expenditures refer to the costs involved in establishing and commissioning a project.[5] Replacement expenditures refer to the costs of equipment and other investment items in the operating phase of a project, to maintain its productive capacity. Residual values refer to the value of all these investment items at the end of the project's life, when production is expected to cease (or be substantially changed); it is unlikely that any residual value will be large enough to have a major impact on decision-taking.

Initial investment expenditures will be one of the largest items in most project resource statements. For relatively small projects these expenditures may all occur in the first time-period; for larger projects the expenditures will be spread over two or more years. Moreover, some projects may be explicitly designed in phases so that initial investment expenditures are spread over several periods. Where several periods are involved, land preparation works expenditure has to precede construction activities which in turn have to precede the purchase of machinery and commissioning activities. There will be an overlap between these different items within the time periods, but they will follow this general sequence.[6]

Investment items each have a different operating life. Land preparation works will be permanent and do not need to be repeated. However, other investment items such as buildings, machinery and vehicles have a limited life. Often buildings will last longer than the anticipated operating life of the project as a whole and will need maintaining but not replacing; however, machinery and vehicles will normally need replacing at fixed intervals. This is illustrated in Table 2.2 where machinery replacement costs are entered in the resource statement as an additional investment eight years after operations begin, and vehicle replacement costs are entered every three years. The replacement period will differ from item to item; the replacement cost is entered in the resource statement in the year before the replaced asset will be required in order to ensure continuous operation. Such replacements will be repeated as often as necessary within the overall length of time anticipated for project operations.

The project life will differ from case to case and will affect the number of times replacement costs are incurred and the residual values of different assets. There are three bases upon which the project life can be determined (Figure 2.2). The first is the technical

Table 2.2 Project investment costs (000)

Items	*Replacement period (years)*	*Years* 0	*1*	*2*	*3*	*4*	*5*	*6*	*7*	*8*	*9*	*10*	*11*	*12*	*13*	*14*	*15*	*16*	*17*[1]
Land preparation		20																	
Building	40	60	40																(60)
Machinery	8		40								40								(0)
Vehicles	3		12			12			12			12			12			12	(8)
Other Items			18																

[1] Brackets indicate negative values: a negative cost is a benefit.

life of the major replaceable assets, generally machinery. It may be assumed that the project ends when the machinery is worn out. Within the life of the machinery, as in the example of Table 2.2, other items like vehicles will have to be replaced every three years and may not be worn out at exactly the same time as machinery, thus retaining a residual value.

Alternatively, the project life may be determined by the market life of the output or, where benefits are not a marketed product, the period for which the benefits will satisfy a need.[7] In the case where this exceeds the technical life of the major assets (*M*1, Figure 2.2), these assets also will need replacing and will have a residual value at the end of the project life. Where the market life is shorter than the technical life of major assets (*M*2, Figure 2.2), the latter will have a residual value without replacement.

However, as a third possibility, the project life may be determined by the economic life of the major replaceable assets (*E*, Figure 2.2) and this requires closer consideration of the replacement decision. Within the market life of the output, and with ageing machinery, it may be more economic to close a project down, or to replace the machinery before the technical life has been completed.

Maintenance costs for an investment may evolve in two ways. Those associated with one alternative may continue at a normal level which remains constant each year, but another alternative involves increased maintenance costs over time associated with longer down-time or increased operating costs per unit of output. At some time, maintenance and operating costs may increase to the

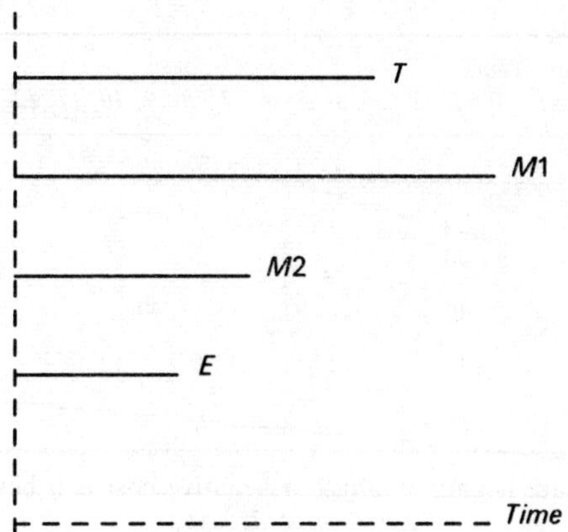

Figure 2.2 Project life: Technical (*T*), Market (*M*) and Economic (*E*) life

point where it becomes economic to replace old machinery with new, not because it is fully worn out but because the maintenance and operating costs associated with a new machine are now sufficiently low to justify replacement. In this way, the economic life of major assets may differ from the technical or market life and involve an earlier replacement.

This can be illustrated through Figure 2.3 in which the line *AA* represents the operating costs per unit of output which increase over time with the age of the machinery. This increase is even more marked when maintenance costs per unit of output are added to operating costs as in line *BB*. The line *BB* has to be compared with line *CC* which, for the same level of output, represents the operating, maintenance and capital costs per unit of output of replacing the old machinery with new. Where *T* represents the technical life of the old machinery, *E* will represent its economic life; the point *D* shows the point at which the operating, maintenance and capital costs of replacement are worth incurring by comparison with the increasing operating and maintenance costs of the old machinery. In many cases, the point *D* will lie within the technical life of the original investment. Thus economic life of an investment depends on determining the best year in which to replace the main assets.[8]

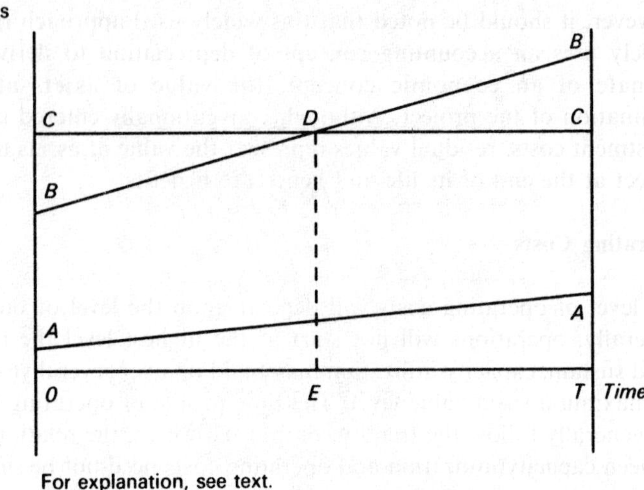

For explanation, see text.

Figure 2.3 Economic life of a project

Only where the project life is determined exactly by the technical life of the major replaceable assets will these have a residual value of zero at the end of the project; other assets will still have a residual value even in these circumstances. Residual values for each investment item need to be entered as a resource benefit at the end of a project and can be given two interpretations. The first is that they represent the salvage value of remaining assets, the amount they would be worth if they were sold off. The process of selling assets may take some time and so this salvage value can be recorded in the year after operations cease. Alternatively, residual values can be interpreted as the accumulated value of net benefits to be generated in the future from the remaining assets if they are adapted for other purposes rather than being sold off; these can be written into the final year of project operations, as representing the value at that moment of a stream of returns in subsequent years.

Whichever interpretation is given to residual values, a value has to be estimated. In practice, this is generally derived by allowing for the process of physical depreciation rather than by estimating salvage values or future net benefits directly. Hence, residual values are often estimated as the difference between the initial cost of an asset and the accumulated depreciation up to the end of the project. However, it should be noted that this widely used approach rather crudely uses an accounting concept of depreciation to derive an estimate of an economic concept, the value of assets at the termination of the project. Although conventionally entered under investment costs, residual values represent the value of assets to the project at the end of its life and hence are benefits.

Operating Costs

The level of operating costs will depend upon the level of output. Generally, operations will not start at the highest level the assets could sustain; capacity utilization may build up over several years to the maximum sustainable level. The time profile of operating costs will generally follow the trend in output. However, the relationship between capacity utilization and operating costs need not be simple. Some operating cost items may not vary with the level of output. Operating costs may be a combination of fixed and variable costs as illustrated in Figure 2.4.

Fixed operating costs will be incurred whatever the level of output; the variable costs will change as output increases, becoming constant when maximum sustainable output is reached.[9] Finding total operating costs involves adding these two elements

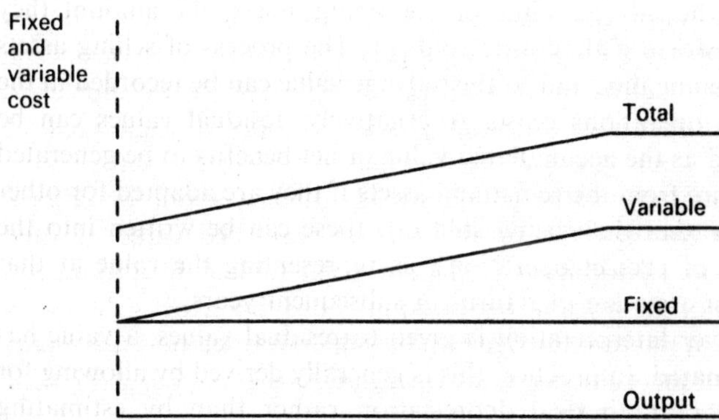

Figure 2.4 Operating costs

together. Hence, total operating costs usually fall as a proportion of the value of output as higher capacity utilization rates are reached.

Working Capital

Working capital refers to the physical stocks needed to allow continuous production. These stocks have to be built up at the beginning of operations and may have a residual value at the end of the project's life. There are three components of working capital-initial stocks of materials, final stocks of output, and work in progress (Table 2.3). Initial stocks of materials are required at the beginning of production and the level will depend upon planned annual production levels. For example, stock requirements may be defined as one month's worth of materials. If initial stocks are to be maintained at one-twelfth of annual requirements, they will have to be increased each year as production rises to its highest sustainable level. Hence, when production rises after the first commitment of stocks, further incremental commitments will need to be recorded in the project resource statement (Table 2.3 rows 6 and 7). Initial stocks need to be purchased in advance of production increases, and so are recorded in the year before the output level to which they refer.

Similarly, the production process will give rise to final outputs that will be stored for a period before distribution. Again, the level of final stocks will be estimated as a proportion of annual production and will involve annual increments until the highest sustainable output level is reached. It may be that the investment process involves a commissioning period in which final stocks can be built up before normal production commences; however, subsequent increases in final stocks will occur each year as production levels are increased. Final stocks embody the initial materials and the value of resources such as labour or energy, committed through the production process. The value of final stocks before distribution is therefore determined by production costs and not the price of final output. Thus final stocks should be valued not at the revenue that will be achieved when they are finally sold but at the value of total operating costs embodied in their production (Table 2.3 rows 8 and 9).

Working capital also involves work in progress. At any point in time some materials will be passing through the production process.

Table 2.3 Working capital calculation[1]

Capacity utilisation (%)		*60*	*70*	*80*	*90*	*100*	*100*	*100*	*100*	*100*	*100*
Years	*0*	*1*	*2*	*3*	*4*	*5*	*6*	*7*	*8*	*9*	*10*
Operating costs											
1. Fixed		100	100	100	100	100	100	100	100	100	100
2. Semi-variable[2] – Power		60	65	70	75	80	80	80	80	80	80
3. Variable[3] – Materials		120	140	160	180	200	200	200	200	200	200
4. Variable[3] – Labour		60	70	80	90	100	100	100	100	100	100
5. Total operating costs		340	375	410	445	480	480	480	480	480	480
Working capital											
6. Initial stocks[4]		10.0	11.7	13.3	15.0	16.7	16.7	16.7	16.7	16.7	16.7
7. Change over previous year	10.0	1.7	1.8	1.7	1.7	0.0	0.0	0.0	0.0	0.0	0.0
8. Final stocks[5]	0.0	28.3	31.3	34.2	37.1	40.0	40.0	40.0	40.0	40.0	40.0
9. Change over previous year		28.3	2.9	2.9	2.9	2.9	0.0	0.0	0.0	0.0	0.0
10. Work in progress[6]	0.0	0.4	0.4	0.4	0.4	0.5	0.5	0.5	0.5	0.5	0.5
11. Change over previous year		0.4	0.0	0.0	0.0	0.1	0.0	0.0	0.0	0.0	0.0
12. *Total Working Capital Change*	10.0	30.4	4.7	4.6	4.6	3.0	0.0	0.0	0.0	0.0	(57.3)[7]

Notes

1 Some discrepancies owing to rounding.
2 Varies with half of the difference in capacity utilisation.
3 Varies with the full difference in capacity utilisation.
4 One-twelfth of annual materials for subsequent years.
5 One-twelfth of output valued at production cost.
6 In this case the production period is 10 days, and operations are for 250 days per year so that work in progress is ((row 8 – row 6 of previous year)/2) × 10/250.
7 Residual value shows all working capital recovered in last year, as production is closed down.

Such working capital is valued at the average of the initial stocks and the final stocks for the same year. The quantity of working capital to be valued like this depends upon the production period, that is the time it takes for initial materials to be transformed into a finished product. For many processes the production period is short meaning that work in progress is usually a small proportion of annual output. For example, in Table 2.3, the production period is ten working days out of an annual level of 250 working days, so that the working capital tied up in work in progress will be small both in relation to total annual output and to initial and final stocks (Table 2.3, rows 10 and 11).

The three components of working capital will generally have a residual value. This will be the total value of working capital at the highest sustainable level of output. The residual value of initial stocks, work in progress, and final stocks will accrue in the final operating year as stocks are reduced with the ending of production.

Benefits

There can be several benefits even of a directly productive project. Such a project may produce different types of output which are sold. These will be aggregated together to give the direct benefits of the project. Direct benefits are generally fully variable with respect to capacity utilization; they are generally taken as equal to annual production less any increase in final stocks that is required as production builds up. The level of direct benefits will depend on factors outside the project, such as incomes and competing products, as well as factors determined within the project such as quality and, in most cases, price.[10]

In addition, there can be indirect benefits which accrue outside the project organisation. For example, an expanded supply may reduce the price of existing supplies, bringing a benefit to those who purchase it. Such indirect benefits also ought to be included in a resource flow from the economic point of view although they will not appear in the financial statement from the owner's point of view (for a fuller discussion of indirect or external effects see Chapter 8). These types of benefit are more difficult to estimate and will not necessarily be variable in relation to production

SOME PROJECT RESOURCE FLOWS

The figures in a project statement can be represented as a set of annual cost and benefit flows. Different types of project will have different resource flows, depending upon their technical and economic characteristics. An essential step in project analysis is to derive an accurate resource flow for the project being analysed, understanding not just the technical features which lie behind it but the assumptions on which the resource flow is based. The following illustrations show a series of resource flows for different types of project. Table 2.4 is a resource flow for a light manufacturing plant. It involves a short construction period followed by a build-up of production to a stable level. Operating costs are largely variable and so working capital is built up incrementally along with production. The net resource flow shows a pattern typical of manufacturing projects, with negative net resources in early years, including the first two years of operation, followed by a stream of positive net resources.

Figure 2.5 illustrates in outline the cost and benefit time profiles of several other types of project. Illustration A shows a continuous production chemical plant; operations begin at full capacity, there is very little replacement investment, and the proportion of fixed operating costs is small relative to the flow of materials through the plant and the physical stocks of inputs and outputs this requires.

Illustration B is a typical holiday hotel project. There is large initial investment in landscaping and buildings and high fixed operating costs where staff are employed round the clock, full time, in the face of an uncertain occupancy level. Variable operating costs, largely food and cleaning materials, are small, as is working capital. The net resource effects are very sensitive to the occupancy level. The investment requires regular replacement of operating assets and renewal of furnishings and equipment to sustain quality standards.

Illustration C is of a nuclear power plant. The significant features of this time profile are that the construction period is very long, eight years here, with a lengthy operating period as well. The fuel rods are purchased at the beginning of operations, and are subsumed under investment. There is hardly any working capital as this is a non-storable product. Finally, the residual value of the nuclear power plant is negative since there are substantial costs of dismantling and disposal of materials at the end of the plant life.

Illustration D also shows a project with a long gestation period, a tree-crop project combined with a processing plant. However, the investment is not continuous. The first four years involve the phased planting of trees in a cleared area; because the trees do not start yielding fruit for six years after propagation, the processing plant does not need to be constructed until the sixth year. In addition, full bearing of the trees takes ten years from propagation; the full

Table 2.4 Carton project – resource flow statement ($000)

Years	*0*	*1*	*2*	*3*	*4*	*5*	*6*	*7*	*8*	*9*	*10*	*11*	*12*	*13*	*14*	*15*	*16*
% Capacity utilization		*30*	*40*	*50*	*60*	*70*	*80*	*80*	*80*	*80*	*80*	*80*	*80*	*80*	*80*	*80*	
Capital costs:																	
Land	100																
Buildings	1400																(525)[1]
Plant & equipment	4500																(1125)
Vehicles	100				100				100				100				
Working capital		1329	365		366	363	364									(2787)[2]	
1. *Total capital costs*	6100	1329	365	365	466	363	364		100				100			(2787)	(1650)
Operating costs																	
Material		3157	4210	5263	6315	7368	8421	8421	8421	8421	8421	8421	8421	8421	8421	8421	
Labour		200	220	240	260	280	300	300	300	300	300	300	300	300	300	300	
Fuel & water		70	75	80	90	95	100	100	100	100	100	100	100	100	100	100	
Maintenance		25	30	35	40	45	50	50	50	50	50	50	50	50	50	50	
Overheads[3]		900	900	900	1000	1000	1000	1000	1000	1000	1000	1000	1000	1000	1000	1000	
2. *Total operating costs*		4352	5435	6518	7705	8788	9871	9871	9971	9871	9871	9871	9871	9871	9871	9871	
3. *Total costs 1 & 2*	6100	5681	5800	6883	8171	8788	10235	9871	9971	9871	9871	9871	9871	9871	9871	7084	(1650)
4. *Revenue*		4275	5700	7125	8550	9975	11400	11400	11400	11400	11400	11400	11400	11400	11400	11400	
5. *Project net resource flow 4–3*	(6100)	(1406)	(100)	242	379	824	1165	1529	1429	1529	1529	1529	1429	1529	1529	4316	1650

All values at constant prices.

1 Buildings have a forty-year life; plant and equipment have a twenty-year life; vehicles are replaced every four years.

2 Working capital all recovered in last operating year.

3 Overhead costs increased once only when 60 per cent capacity is reached.

Source: Adapted from COMSEC (1982), p. 18.

benefits of planting will not accrue until ten years after the completion of planting, that is year thirteen. By that year all trees will be fully bearing for thirty years per tree. Without replacement of trees, benefits will start decreasing over the last four years of the project life.

Illustration E involves an infinite life project. It relates to a cattle project on vacant land. An initial purchase of cattle stock is reinforced by extra purchases of stock over the years. The extent to which cattle are slaughtered and used builds up in a series of steps to an approximately stable level by the fifteenth year. The project operations are potentially infinite, since the investment – the cattleherd – reproduces itself.

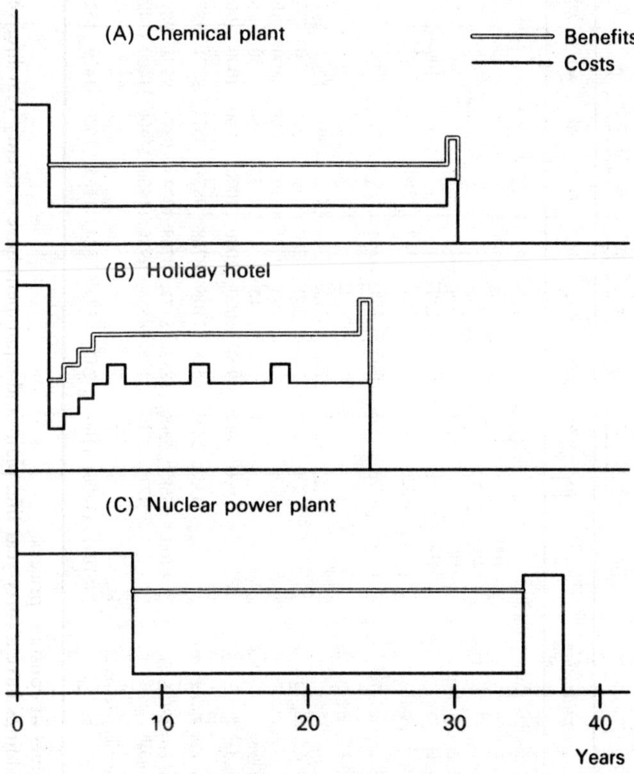

Figure 2.5 Project resource profiles (A – C)

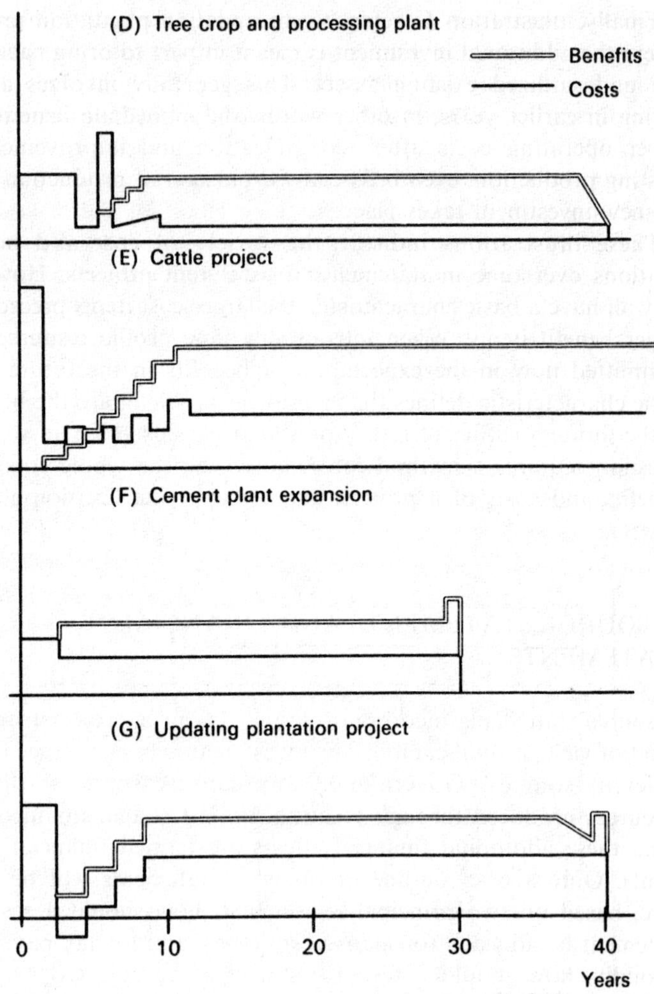

Figure 2.5 Project resource profiles (D – G)

Illustration F relates to a cement expansion project based on an existing site and using existing distribution channels. The additional capacity investment utilizes some of the same overhead facilities on site, so incremental costs are largely the variable costs in production. The joint use of existing facilities allows a low level of additional costs when production is building up to full utilization.

Finally, illustration G refers to an updating plantation project, where the additional investment is meant in part to bring back into use underutilized existing assets. This generally involves a cost saving in earlier years; in other words, the immediate benefits are lower operating costs after reorganization and improvement of existing production, even before any expansion of production from the new investment takes place.

These illustrations indicate the variety of cost and benefit relations over time in statements for different projects. However, they all have a basic characteristic; the larger cost items precede the larger benefit items. When set out in a time profile resources are committed now in the expectation of benefits in the future. This basic characteristic defines the investment problem; are the benefits in the future a sufficient return on the earlier costs? To answer this question requires a method for summarising the whole stream of benefits and costs of a project, and for applying decision-making criteria.

RESOURCE STATEMENTS AND FINANCIAL STATEMENTS

Resource statements incorporate the effects of a project from the point of view of total capital. The investment may be financed from different sources. Government may capture some of the net resources produced through taxation. Project statements incorporating these additional financial effects are termed financial statements. Only a brief outline of financial statements will be given here, based on two principal issues: first, how should a resource statement be adjusted for loans of all types, and for tax payments; secondly, how should a resource statement be adjusted when an investment is financed through foreign loans and equity, resulting in corresponding outflows from the economy.

The financial statement from the point of view of the project owners may differ considerably from the resource statement from the point of view of total capital. This is illustrated in Table 2.5 where a project involving an investment cost of 5000 is financed in part through a loan of 3000. This loan inflow requires a series of loan repayment and interest outflows. The financial statement (before tax) differs from the resource statement; the net expenditure in the investment period by the project owners is smaller because of borrowing, whilst the net annual inflows after loan repayment and interest repayments are smaller also.

Table 2.5 Project financial statement

Year	*0*	*1*	*2*	*3*	*4*	*5*
Outflows						
Investment cost	5000					
Working capital	50					(50)
Operating cost		1000	1000	1000	1000	1000
Loan repayment		600	600	600	600	600
Interest		360	288	206	144	72
Inflows						
Revenue		2500	2500	2500	2500	2500
Loan inflow	3000					
I. Resource flow[1]	(5050)	1500	1500	1500	1500	1550
II. Financial flow before tax[2]	(2050)	540	612	684	756	878
Calculation of tax						
Profit after interest[3]		1140	1212	1284	1356	1428
Depreciation		1000	1000	1000	1000	1000
Taxable profit[4]		140	212	284	356	428
III. Tax at 40%		56	85	114	142	171
IV. Financial flow to owners (II–III)	(2050)	484	527	570	614	707

1 Revenue minus investment cost minus working capital cost minus operating cost.
2 Inflows minus outflows.
3 Profit after interest is revenue minus operating cost minus interest.
4 Profit after interest and depreciation.

An additional feature of any project is the tax that has to be paid on profits. The government allows profit to be calculated after interest payments and after a depreciation allowance related to the project's stock of fixed assets. This taxable profit is the basis of an additional tax outflow, reducing the financial flow to the project owners.

The financial statement is the basis for calculating a return to equity, that is the return to the project owners for the funds they have put in. The simple illustration of Table 2.5 has the same basic characteristic as the resource statements presented earlier; the large negative items appear at the beginning followed by the positive items. The investment problem for the owners is the same as from the point of view of total capital; are the benefits in the future a sufficient return on the earlier costs?

Project financial statements can be very varied. They will deviate between different projects because of differences in financing arrangements and in the way that the tax and subsidy system affects each project. The return to owners can vary substantially for the same type of project because of such differences. Although it is essential that a project generates a sufficient return to owners for investment to take place, nevertheless the return to owners is not necessarily a good guide for investment decision-making when it comes to choosing between different types of project. The financial and tax arrangements influence the distribution of benefits between lenders, government and project owners, but do not reflect the productiveness of the underlying investment with reference to total capital or the national economy.

A particular problem in the use of financial and resource statements is the treatment of foreign loan and equity transactions. Foreign loan and equity inflows increase the command of a project over investment resources. Usually they will be spent on investment items or working capital. However, the consequent interest and loan payments, and remitted profits, will reduce resources available to a project. Like other financial transactions, these should be included in the financial statement for the project.

Whether such inflows and outflows should be included in a project resource statement depends on the specific circumstances. Foreign loan and equity inflows can only be regarded as adding to total resources of the economy as a whole if they were attracted by a specific project. Where such inflows would not take place without the specific project in question, they can be included in the resource statement for that project. Here, the consequent interest and loan payments, and remitted profits, should also be recorded as outflows.

If such foreign inflows and outflows are included in the project resource statements, the effects of the project on the national economy may be changed substantially. Where the interest rate on the foreign loan is higher than the return on the project, the resources available to the national economy will be reduced. However, where the interest rate on the foreign loan is lower than the return on acceptable projects, the resources available to the national economy will be increased. Again, where remitted profits represent a rate of return to foreign owners in excess of the return on acceptable domestic projects, the resources available to the national economy will be reduced; where remitted profits represent a lower rate of return, resources available will increase. The treatment of foreign terms and investment is discussed further in Chapter 6.

However, it is not often the case that foreign flows should be included in a project resource statement. Where projects are dependent on multilateral or bilateral funds, the funding agency may have an investment budget from which it draws; allocation of funds to a specific project will not increase the total resources available to the economy. Similarly, directly productive projects using private capital inflows may not induce an additional inflow of resources to the economy, where there is a corporate investment budget that would be spent in the country anyway. Only where there is a clear case that foreign loan and equity inflows can be regarded as incremental resources available to the economy because of a particular project, should they be included in the resource statement.

DISCOUNTING

The total costs and benefits of a project can be added up over the full project life; however, this would assume that all resources used up or generated in different years are valued equally so that the investment resources committed in the first year are of equal value to the benefits generated in the twentieth year, for example. Conventionally, resources used up or generated in earlier years are valued more highly than resources in later years. The process of discounting applies a weight to the resources in different years to convert them to a common basis. Usually, the base year to which they are related is the period in which the investment decision is being made, denoted year 0 at the beginning of the project statement.

The weight applied in different years is known as the discount factor, and it depends upon a chosen rate of discount which measures the fall in value of net benefits over time. If the same level of costs will be incurred in two successive years, then the costs incurred in the second of the two years will be given a lower value relative to the same costs in the first year. This lower value can be specified by multiplying the second year's costs by a factor of the following form:

$$\text{Discount factor} = 1 / (1 + r) \tag{2.1}$$

where r is the rate of discount expressed in decimals. For example, if it were appropriate to value the second year's costs at a level 10 per cent below that of the first year then r would be set at 0.10 and the discount factor would become 1/1.10 = 0.909 (Table 2.6).

Table 2.6 Applying a discount factor as a weight

	First year	*Second year*
Costs	200	200
Discounted costs	200	200 × 0.909 = 181.8
(Discount rate 10%)		

This comparison between two years can be extended to comparisons between many. The costs and benefits of a project can be weighted to give an equivalent value in the base year. Costs and benefits in subsequent years are weighted by the discount factor relevant to each year, where the

$$\text{General Discount Factor} = 1 / (1 + r)^t \tag{2.2}$$

and t is the number of years after year 0. The weight to be applied to the costs and benefits of different years then depends not just upon the rate of discount, r, but also on the number of years, t, over which the discounting is conducted. This is illustrated for the following project net benefit stream for two different rates of discount (Table 2.7)

Table 2.7 Discounting a net benefit stream

Years	*0*	*1*	*2*	*3*	*4*	*5*
Net benefit stream	0	100	100	100	100	100
Discount factor at 10%	1.000	0.909	0.826	0.751	0.683	0.621
Discounted benefits	0	90.9	82.6	75.1	68.3	62.1
Discount factor at 7%	1.000	0.935	0.873	0.816	0.763	0.713
Discounted benefits	0	93.5	87.3	81.6	76.3	71.3

The discounted benefits are smaller in later years and for a higher rate of discount. This follows from the character of the General Discount Factor. The discount rate has to be only moderately high, say 15 per cent, for the discount factor to become very small after a few years, and hence for discounted costs and benefits to be reduced to a negligible value. When discounting is applied so that all resources are revalued relative to year 0, the revalued resources are called present values.

Discounting as applied in Table 2.7 involves two assumptions which it is necessary to make explicit. The first is that there is a constant rate of decline in the value of resources from year to year; thus the discount rate is the same for all years of a project statement. The second is that the same discount rate is applied to all resources in a project statement, whether those resources are benefits or costs, and whether those costs are investment or operating costs. These assumptions can be varied, but the process of applying different discount rates in different years or to different resource effects needs careful justification and calculation.[11]

The effect of discounting can be illustrated by the following example involving a simple statement of project costs and benefits (Table 2.8).

At a discount rate of 12 per cent, the sum of the discounted benefits exceeds the sum of the discounted costs. The same result applies if the net benefits are discounted and summed directly. In addition, although the annual benefit and cost streams do not change between years, their discounted values do; discounted net benefits decline over time, due to the lower value placed on resources in later years.

Table 2.8 Discounted resource statement

Year	*0*	*1*	*2*	*3*	*4*	*5*	*6*
Costs	100	20	15	15	15	15	15
Benefits	0	50	50	50	50	50	50
Net benefits	(100)	30	35	35	35	35	35
Discount factor (12%)	1.0	.893	.797	.712	.636	.567	.507
Discounted costs	100	17.9	12.0	10.7	9.5	8.5	7.6
Discounted benefits	0	44.7	39.9	35.6	31.8	28.4	25.4
Discounted net benefits	(100)	26.8	27.9	24.9	22.3	19.8	17.7

Note: Figures in brackets are negative.

Discounting brings out the importance of timing in resource flows, which is emphasised also by the two further illustrations below (Table 2.9). In the first, two alternative projects have the same undiscounted net benefits but the time profile is different. The sum of the discounted net benefits is higher when net benefits occur more quickly. In the second, reference is made to different types of project as illustrated in the project statements above; the principal difference here is between a project with a short gestation period and one with a long gestation period. With discounting the net benefits of the latter need to be considerably higher than the former to compensate for the delay in their arrival; otherwise, discounting will favour projects with shorter gestation periods.

Two basic rationales for the process of discounting can be given. The first refers to the opportunity cost of resources.[12] The resources committed to the productive process in one project could alternatively be committed in another. For the first alternative to be preferable, the return on resources should be greater than the return on resources in the other project. More generally, for a project to be worthwhile it must generate a return on resources greater than in easily available alternative uses. The discount rate should be set equal to the return in alternative uses, to reflect the opportunity foregone when resources are committed to the project.

Table 2.9 Discounting and time profiles

Illustration I *Equal net benefits, different time profiles*

Discount rate 0.08	*Present Value*	0	1	2	3	4	5
Net benefits A:	85.38	–100	20	40	60	60	60
Net benefits B:	91.65	–100	48	48	48	48	48

Illustration II *Short and long gestation periods*

Discount rate 0.08	*Present Value*	0	1	2	3	4	5	6	7	8	9	10	11	12	13	14	15	16
Net benefits A:	54.82	–200	20	30	30	30	30	30	30	30	30	30	30	30	30	30	30	40
Net Benefits B:	41.82	–100	–100	10	20	34	34	34	34	34	34	34	34	34	34	34	34	44

The second rationale is based on subjective reasoning. It is presumed that resources will be committed to uses that generate an additional net income in the future. However, most people prefer additional income sooner rather than later. They have a positive rate of time preference implying that the same additional net income in year 2 is worth more than in year 3, which is worth more than in year 4, and so on. This may be because future incomes are seen as uncertain or because people may expect their incomes to be higher in the future and so income now is more valuable, or simply because most people have a very short time horizon. By this interpretation, the discount rate could be seen as representing the rate at which people's valuation of each successive year's income declines. This rate may differ for different people. A single rate of discount for participants in all projects, referred to as the rate of time preference, can be set by the government, to represent some average for all groups.[13]

ESTIMATING AN APPROPRIATE DISCOUNT RATE

The rate at which a resource statement or financial statement should be discounted depends upon the interpretation given to the discount rate and the point of view from which a project is being analyzed. However, any discount rate will have to be expressed in real terms to be applied to a resource or financial statement drawn up using constant prices. This means adjusting actual borrowing or lending rates, for example, for price increases using a recent or forecast rate of increase of prices. The real rate of discount can be calculated as

$$\text{Real rate of discount} = (1 + i)/(1 + p) \qquad (2.3)$$

where i is the nominal rate and p is the annual average rate of increase of prices.

For application to project resource statements, a real discount rate is required that reflects the opportunity cost of the project resources in the economy as a whole, and a discussion of this rate is given in Chapter 4.

In applications to project financial statements, the point of view is that of the project owner, and the project financial statement will include the costs of borrowed funds. A minimum condition for a project owner is that the project should generate resources in the future at a rate that will allow repayment of all borrowed funds. The cost of these borrowed funds needs to be expressed in real terms where the project financial statement is at constant prices; where there is more than one source of borrowed funds a weighted real cost of borrowing can be calculated.

Application of such a discount rate to a financial statement assumes that the project owner will be satisfied if the return on the equity proportion of financing is the same as the real weighted cost of borrowing. However, the equity funds can usually be invested in alternative projects whose return to equity is independent of the rate at which funds are borrowed or lent, because capital markets do not necessarily reflect these opportunities. In the case of both project resource statements and financial statements, a method of estimating a return to resources in alternative uses is required, and this relates to the measures of project worth explained in the next chapter.

CONCLUSION

A project involves the commitment of resources now to obtain extra resources in the future. The resources produced and used up by a project need to be recorded in a project statement. For decision-making purposes these resources are valued at constant prices. A project financial statement will also be recorded at constant prices, but will indicate the effects of a project from the owners point of view, allowing for financial and tax transactions.

There are several types of investment project. Comparison is made easier where clear assumptions and conventions are used in relation to the project life, replacement investments, operating costs, working capital, and other items included in project statements.

Project resource statements, and the corresponding financial statements from the owners viewpoint, will have a common characteristic; initial net outflows during the investment period will be followed by net inflows in most operating periods. For decision-making purposes, it is necessary that the annual net flows be added together in some way. The technique of discounting provides a means of assigning relative weights to the net flows in different years before they are added together.

APPENDIX 2.1 DISCOUNT FACTORS, ANNUITY FACTORS AND CAPITAL RECOVERY FACTORS

Project analysis is commonly applied with the use of microcomputers, especially spreadsheet packages. The process of discounting then simply requires the specification of a discount rate, *r*, and the specification of a range of values from the project statement that are to be discounted. Discounting will be applied according to the

$$\text{General Discount Factor} = 1(1 + r)^t \tag{2A.1}$$

as explained in the text, with the value of resources in successive years falling by a factor of *r*.

It is sometimes useful to apply other factors derived from the General Discount Factor. In circumstances where there is an equal annual amount of resources to be discounted, use can be made of the

$$\text{Annuity Factor} = \frac{(1 + r)^t - 1}{r(1 + r)^t} \tag{2A.2}$$

For example, suppose that a small project will generate annual net benefits of 100 per year from years 1 to 10 inclusive, where the discount rate is specified as 0.12 or 12 per cent. The General Discount Factor can be evaluated 10 times for the ten different years and applied to the net benefits in the corresponding years, the results being added to give the present value of total net benefits (Table 2A.1, columns 1–3).

Table 2A.1 Discounting a constant annual amount

Year	*1* *Net benefits*	*2* *Discount factor (12%)*	*3* *Discounted net benefits*
1	100	.893	89.3
2	100	.797	79.7
3	100	.712	71.2
4	100	.635	63.5
5	100	.567	56.7
6	100	.507	50.7
7	100	.452	45.2
8	100	.404	40.4
9	100	.361	36.1
10	100	.322	32.2
Totals		5.650	565.0

Alternatively the Annuity Factor can be evaluated once, for $r = 0.12$ and $t = 10$, and applied to the annual amount of net benefits. In this case the Annuity Factor is evaluated as 5.650. Applying this factor to the annual net benefits gives the total value of discounted net benefits as:

$$100 \times 5.650 = 565.0$$

the same result as at the bottom of column 2 in Table 2A.1. Evidently, the Annuity Factor is the sum of the Discount Factors for all ten years, as confirmed at the bottom of column 3 (Table 2A.1).

Of more use, especially in the construction of financial statements, is the Capital Recovery Factor. The Annuity Factor (AF) converts an equal annual amount into an equivalent present value. The Capital Recovery Factor (CRF) performs the reverse operation: it converts a present amount into an equivalent equal annual amount over a period of years.

Suppose a loan of 565.0 were taken now, to be repaid at 12 per cent per annum interest in equal annual instalments over ten years. Above we had:

$$100 \times AF = 565.0$$

Rearranging, this can be written as:

$$100 = 565.0 \times 1/AF$$

The equal annual amount 100 can be derived by multiplying the loan amount 565.0 by $1/AF$. The expression $1/AF$ is the Capital Recovery Factor, explicitly

$$\text{Capital Recovery Factor} = \frac{r\,(1 + r)^t}{(1+r)^t - 1} \qquad (2A.3)$$

This use of the Capital Recovery Factor can be illustrated by another example. Suppose a loan of 1000 taken now is to be repaid in equal annual amounts over eight years at an interest rate of 8 per cent. The equal annual amount (x) to be paid can be calculated by:

$$x = 1000 \times \text{CRF}$$

Here the Capital Recovery Factor is evaluated as 0.174, and the equal annual amount at 174. This amount has to be paid each year for eight years to repay fully the loan and the associated interest.

The General Discount Factor, Annuity Factor, and Capital Recovery Factor can be evaluated for different values of r and t. Tables of such factors can be found in most textbooks, and the most extensive exposition in World Bank (1973).

Further Reading

The conventions used in drawing up project resource statements have received little attention. In the context of agricultural projects, an outline is given in Gittinger (1982) chapters 3 and 4. ODA (1988) at part II,A illustrates the forecast data required to draw up an 'annual statement of financial costs and benefits at constant prices'. Detailed accounting data requirements for industrial projects are given in UNIDO (1978a). The construction of project financial statements has received much wider treatment: see UNIDO (1978a), annex I; Irvin (1978), chapter II; and Bromwich (1976) chapter 3. For a discussion specifically on working capital, see Sell (1989). The technique of discounting is covered in texts such as Gittinger (1982) and Irvin (1978). A modified discounting method is given in Kula (1988); for critical comments on this method, see Thomson (1988) and Price (1989).

3 Project Criteria

The construction of resource statements and the application of discounting are the basic tools of project analysis. However, the purpose of project analysis is to facilitate decision-taking on proposed projects, which requires a comparison of estimated benefits and costs. The purpose of this chapter is to outline the different ways in which this comparison can be made. It restricts itself to comparisons using discounted values of benefits and costs.[1]

The use of project criteria for decision-taking will be illustrated in two contexts. The first instance occurs when a decision is required about a single project proposal. A resource statement is constructed to represent the effects of the project. Using an appropriate discount rate, a decision is then required whether to proceed with the proposal or not.

The second context involves choice between project alternatives. In this case, more than one project statement is constructed to represent a proposed investment under different conditions, for example, at different locations or using different technologies. Two decisions are required; whether to proceed with the project at all, and if so, which alternative to select.

However, decision-taking can be carried out from different stand points. The principal one adopted here is that of total capital, the whole of the investment in the project. This allows a comparison of the project or the project alternatives, with other investments in the economy as a whole. However, reference will also be made to the point of view of the owner of the project.

PROJECT CRITERIA FOR SINGLE PROJECTS

To decide whether a single project proposal is acceptable or not, different project criteria can be used. The three criteria in frequent use for this purpose are the benefit–cost ratio(BCR), the net present value(NPV), and the internal rate of return(IRR). Each has its advantages and disadvantages and needs to be used in a different way for decision-making. However, where resource statements are drawn up using the same information and assumptions, these three criteria yield the same decision for single projects.

Benefit–Cost Ratio (BCR)

For a project to be acceptable, the discounted value of its benefits should exceed the discounted value of its costs. Discounted benefits can be expressed in a ratio to discounted costs.

Formally,

$$BCR = \frac{\sum_t (B(t))/(1 + d)^t}{\sum_t (C(t))/(1 + d)^t} \tag{3.1}$$

where

d is a rate of discount,
t is the number of years from the base year,
$B(t)$ and $C(t)$ are total benefits and total costs in year t.

The calculation of the benefit–cost ratio is illustrated in Table 3.1 for two different project resource statements using the same discount rate. For Example A, the BCR exceeds one; for example B, the BCR is less than one. Where d represents the opportunity cost of resources, then the BCR can be used for decision-making as follows:

At the discount rate d,
If BCR $>$ 1.0, accept the project proposal.
If BCR $<$ 1.0, reject the project proposal.
If BCR $=$ 1.0, there will be no net effect whether the project proposal is accepted or not.

The BCR for a project will depend not just upon the estimated future project effects but also upon the rate at which they are discounted. For the two examples from Table 3.1, this is illustrated in Figure 3.1. For a range of discount rates, the BCR will be greater than 1.0, and the proposal acceptable. For a higher range of discount rates, the BCR will be less than one, and the proposal should be rejected. The decision whether to accept the proposal or not therefore depends on the value of the discount rate d at which

Table 3.1 Resource statement (Rs.000): project criteria (discount rate 0.08)

Example A	*Years* Present Values @ 8%	*0*	*1*	*2–6*	*7*	*Example B*	*Years* Present Values @ 8%	*0*	*1*	*2–6*	*7*
Investment cost		1000				Investment cost		400			
Working capital		200			(200)	Working capital		40			(40)
Materials			400	500	500	Fertilizer		30	30	30	30
Energy			80	100	100	Seeds		20	20	20	20
Labour			90	100	100	Labour		200	200	200	200
Total costs	4607	1200	570	700	500	Total costs	1968	690	250	250	210
Revenue	5021		800	1000	1000	Revenue	1955	315	315	315	315
BCR	1.090					BCR	0.993				
Net revenue (NPV)	414	(1200)	230	300	500	Net revenue (NPV)	(13)	(375)	65	65	105
IRR (%)	16.6					IRR (%)	7.0				

Note
Figures in brackets are negative.

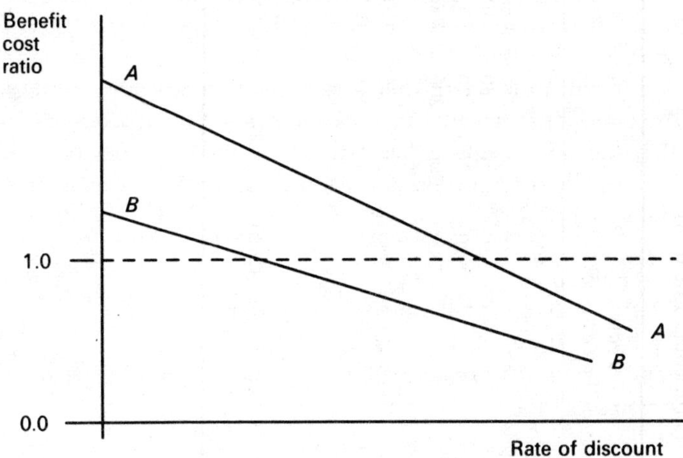

Figure 3.1 Benefit–cost ratio lines

decisions are made. The BCR lines slope downwards to the right as the rate of discount is increased, the key feature being where the BCR line crosses the horizontal line defining the value BCR = 1.0. This occurs at a much lower value for Example B than Example A.

Net Present Value (NPV)

Instead of forming the ratio of discounted benefits to discounted costs, the latter can simply be subtracted from the former. The result is called the net present value, and can be written formally as:

$$NPV = \sum_t B(t)/(1 + d)^t - \sum_t C(t)/(1 + d)^t \tag{3.2}$$

This value is also indicated on Table 3.1 for the two examples.

The NPV can be calculated in a different way, also illustrated in Table 3.1. For each year costs can be subtracted from benefits. These net resource values can then be discounted directly. Formally, this alternative procedure can be expressed as:

$$\text{NPV} = \sum_t [B(t) - C(t)]/(1 + d)^t \tag{3.3}$$

This alternative will give the same result as expression (3.2), although it only requires the discounting of one rather than two streams of values.

An investment is worthwhile at a given discount rate *d* if the sum of the discounted benefits exceeds the sum of the discounted costs so that the NPV using either expression above should be greater than zero. The decision criterion using the NPV can be expressed formally as follows;

At the discount rate *d*,
If NPV > 0, accept the project proposal.
If NPV < 0, reject the project proposal.
If NPV = 0, the project will have no net effect whether it is accepted or not.

Like the BCR, the NPV will vary with the rate of discount. This is illustrated for Examples A and B in Figure 3.2. The NPV for a project resource statement also slopes down to the right as the discount rate is increased. The function is not linear, and the different values are represented by a NPV curve.[2]

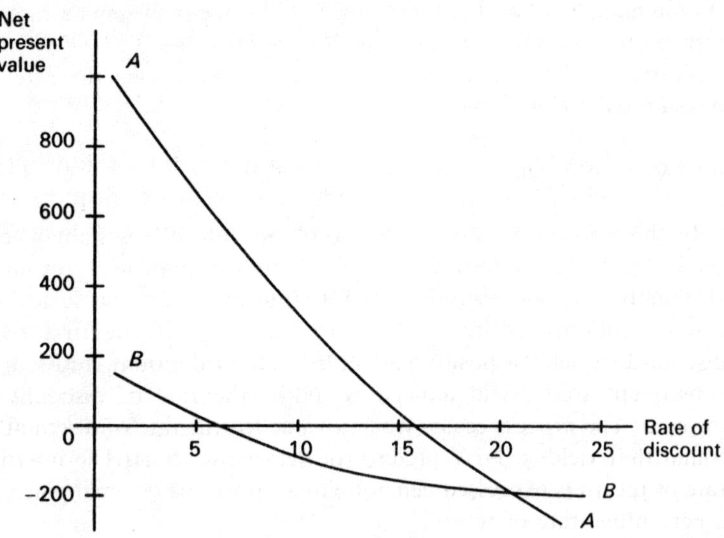

Figure 3.2 Net present value curves

The key feature of the NPV curves is the value they take at the discount rate *d*. For illustration, the NPV for Example A is positive at the discount rate of 8 per cent, whilst the NPV of Example B is negative. This value for the discount rate would give different decisions for the two examples, with A being accepted and B rejected. However, another key feature of the NPV curves are the points at which they cross the horizontal axis. For Example A, the NPV curve crosses the axis at a rate of discount of nearly 17 per cent; this is the rate at which the discounted value of benefits is equal to the discounted value of costs. For Example B, the NPV curve crosses the horizontal axis at a much lower rate of discount around 7 per cent.[3]

Internal Rate of Return (IRR)

The rate of discount at which the NPV curve crosses the horizontal axis for a particular project resource statement is called the internal rate of return. At this rate the discounted benefits equal the discounted costs and the NPV is zero. Normally, below this rate of discount the NPV is positive whilst above it the NPV is negative. As the name implies, the internal rate of return represents a rate of return on all the resources committed in a project.

Formally, the internal rate of return is defined as the rate of discount where;

$$NPV = \sum_t [B(t) - C(t)]/(1 + r)^t = 0 \qquad (3.4)$$

In this expression, *r* is the value of the rate of discount where NPV = 0. The internal rate of return for a project resource statement can be found by trial and error and a series of discounting procedures is used to locate it. If the first trial discounting yields a positive NPV, the rate of discount is raised; if subsequent trials yield a negative NPV, the rate of discount is lowered. The process ceases when a value for the rate of discount is found that yields a NPV of zero (or very close to it). The internal rate of return is expressed generally to at most one decimal place of a percentage rate of return.[4]

The discount rate *d* represents the opportunity cost of resources. For a project to be acceptable, it should generate an internal rate of return at least as great as that in alternative investments. The decision-making criterion using the internal rate of return is

At the discount rate *d*,
If IRR > *d*, accept the project proposal.
If IRR < *d*, reject the project proposal.
If IRR = *d*, the project will have no net effect whether it is accepted or not.

The internal rate of return has been calculated by trial and error for Examples A and B, and indicated in Table 3.1. Diagrammatically, these internal rates of return are shown for the two examples, in Figure 3.1, where the BCR lines cross the horizontal line (BCR = 1.0), and in Figure 3.2, where the NPV curves cross the horizontal axis (NPV = 0). They illustrate the key features referred to above; for a discount rate below these points the project is acceptable whilst for a discount rate above these points, the project should be rejected. In Example A, the discount rate of 8 per cent is below the internal rate of return, the point at which the NPV curve crosses the horizontal axis. So the project is acceptable. In Example B, the discount rate is above the corresponding point so the project should be rejected.

The internal rate of return has some features which require it to be used with caution in decision-making. First, the internal rate of return can be negative. In these circumstances, the undiscounted project benefits are not as large as project costs, let alone any additional return on costs. Evidently such projects should be rejected, as they will be for any positive discount rate.

Secondly, there are circumstances in which the internal rate of return is not unique, so there may be more than one internal rate of return for a project resource statement. In other words, the NPV curve may be irregular and cross the rate of discount axis at more than one point. The circumstances in which this may occur are when there is a substantial reinvestment in the middle of a project or substantial decommissioning costs at the end, giving a negative net resource flow in later years. An illustration is given in Appendix 3.2. This particular feature of the IRR limits its use for decision-making. In the case of multiple IRRs for a resource statement, it is better to use one of the other measures to decide whether the project should be implemented or not.

Equivalence of Project Criteria

The three criteria defined above will give the same project decision. Where the BCR is greater than 1.0 at the given discount rate, the NPV will be greater than zero; the IRR will also be greater than the discount rate (Example A). Where the BCR is less than 1.0 at the given discount rate, the NPV will be less than zero; the IRR will also be less than the discount rate (Example B). Formally;

For a given discount rate *d*,
If BCR $>$ 1.0, then NPV $>$ 0, and IRR $>$ *d*; accept the project.
If BCR $<$ 1,0, then NPV $<$ 0, and IRR $<$ *d*; reject the project.
If BCR = 1.0, then NPV = 0,and IRR = *d*; the project will have no net effect whether it is accepted or rejected.

In these circumstances, it does not matter in most cases which of the criteria is used for decision-making, and only one need be used. However, each of the criteria has different features.

The BCR does not indicate the absolute value of the net surplus generated by a project. The BCR can be high for large or small projects. Any project with a BCR greater than 1.0 at the discount rate is acceptable, and the ratio indicates the proportion by which discounted benefits exceed discounted costs.

The IRR is similar in that it also indicates the extent to which proportionately benefits exceed costs. Here the excess is expressed as a return on the project costs. Again, this return can be large for small or large projects. The IRR can be more useful in considering the way in which projects are financed; it can be compared with the rate of interest that would have to be paid by the project if all resource costs were financed through borrowing. However, although a high rate of return is desirable, whether a particular project is acceptable depends on the rate of return obtainable in other projects.

The NPV measure has the obvious advantage that it gives an indication of the absolute amount by which the economy or project owners will be better off if the project is accepted. The NPV indicates the extent to which a project can repay all resources committed to it at the given discount rate and still generate an additional surplus. It measures how the surplus will expand by choosing a particular project rather than the alternative projects available.

As stated above, in examining single projects, and using the same information and assumptions, each of the criteria should give the same project decision. The key element in this decision-making, however, is not only the project statement but the discount rate at which decisions are made. The important question is not which criterion should be used in project decisions, but what is the standard of acceptability being applied, represented by the alternative opportunities foregone if a particular project is accepted. This key parameter, the discount rate – discussed further in Chapter 4 – is not always easy to estimate.

Different Points of View: Total Capital and the Project Owner

The project criteria discussed above can be adapted to the different viewpoints discussed in the previous chapter. Table 3.2 illustrates a resource statement augmented to include the owner's point of view. In this illustration the difference stems from a supplier's credit, a loan, and tax on profits. The supplier's credit is given for two years at an interest rate of 5 per cent; the loan is given for five years at an interest rate of 8 per cent; and a profits tax of 25 per cent is levied on annual taxable profits after a tax holiday of five years. The main features of the project effects are captured in Figure 3.3 (on page 54) at different rates of discount. Both NPV curves, for total capital and for the owner, slope downwards to the right. However, they have different values and cross the horizontal axis at different points.

For this illustration, the discount rate is set at 9 per cent with regard to total capital and 8 per cent from the point of view of the owner. (These discount rates differ because of the tax on owner's profits.) At this level, the project should be accepted as the net resource benefits are greater than zero. However, it remains unacceptable to the owner because of the tax on profit (despite a supplier's credit available at only 5 per cent rate of interest). This point is also illustrated by the two IRRs. The IRR for total capital is above 9 per cent while the IRR for the owner, the return to equity, is below 8 per cent. There is a likelihood that the owner will not proceed with a project that is acceptable from the economic point of view. In these circumstances, what is important is the aspect from which the project decision is taken. If owners can decide on the basis of their perspective alone, the project will not proceed.

Table 3.2 Textile plant: different points of view (million shillings/sh.m.)

	0	*1*	*2*	*3*	*4*	*5*	*6*	*7–15*	*16*
Investment costs									
Construction materials	0.80	0.80							
Construction labour	0.20	0.20							
Machinery		3.00							
Working Capital			0.42						(0.42)
Operating costs									
Cotton			0.50	0.50	0.50	0.50	0.50	0.50	0.50
Imported fibres			0.50	0.50	0.50	0.50	0.50	0.50	0.50
Skilled labour			0.25	0.25	0.25	0.25	0.25	0.25	0.25
Unskilled labour			0.25	0.25	0.25	0.25	0.25	0.25	0.25
Electricity			0.10	0.10	0.10	0.10	0.10	0.10	0.10
Revenue			2.30	2.30	2.30	2.30	2.30	2.30	2.30
Net resource flow	(1.00)	(4.00)	0.28	0.70	0.70	0.70	0.70	0.70	1.12
Suppliers credit[a]		3.00	(1.61)	(1.61)					
Loan[b]		1.00	(0.25)	(0.25)	(0.25)	(0.25)	(0.25)		
Profits tax			0.00	0.00	0.00	0.00	0.00	0.175	0.175
Net financial flow	0.00	(1.25)	(1.58)	(1.16)	0.45	0.45	0.70	0.525	0.945
Discount rate	0.09	0.08							
NPV resource flow (Sh.m.)	0.259	0.607							
NPV financial flow (Sh.m.)	(0.236)	(0.020)							

[a] Suppliers' credit is repaid in two equal instalments commencing in year 2.
[b] Loan is repaid in five equal instalments commencing in year 2.

If the use of total capital is decisive, the project would be accepted, and a means of financing it would have to be found.

PROJECT ALTERNATIVES

Decision-taking about single project proposals is only one of the uses of project criteria. Equally common is their use in deciding between project alternatives, which can arise in different contexts.

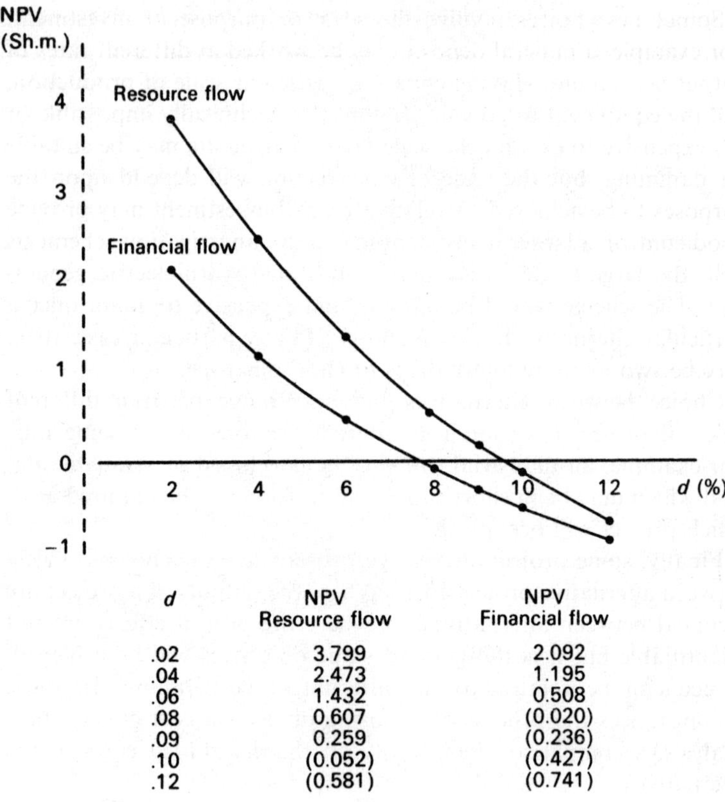

d	NPV Resource flow	NPV Financial flow
.02	3.799	2.092
.04	2.473	1.195
.06	1.432	0.508
.08	0.607	(0.020)
.09	0.259	(0.236)
.10	(0.052)	(0.427)
.12	(0.581)	(0.741)

Figure 3.3 NPV curves: different points of view

For example, a textile plant may be located at two sites, or may use a different mixture of process technology at a single site. In these circumstances, the project costs will be different; frequently there will be variations in project benefits as well, with outputs changing in small ways between the alternatives.

The essential feature in such situations is that the alternatives are mutually exclusive; the choice of one precludes the choice of others. Additional reasons for mutually exclusive choices in the same project might be alternative timing of the project investments, or phasing the investment in a number of stages, to correspond to growth in demand or needs.

Sometimes choices involve the scale or purpose of investment. For example, a mineral deposit may be worked at different rates of output per annum. Having chosen a particular scale of production, and the equipment to go with it, it may be technically impossible or too expensive to expand the scale later. A river site may be suitable for damming, but the scale of construction will depend upon the purposes to be achieved. A relatively small investment may provide flood control; a larger investment may serve an irrigation scheme as well; the largest alternative may also allow hydro-electric generation. The scheme would be difficult and expensive to adapt once a particular alternative has been chosen. In any particular case, there may be two or more alternatives to choose between.[5]

Choice between alternatives can also range between different types of project and not just different versions of the same one. For example, an industrial site may be developed on available flat land which may be in short supply. A decision will be required as to which project will occupy the site.

Finally, some project alternatives arise where the choice is solely between alternative project costs. Where the outputs of a project are identical between alternatives, or where the project effects are not quantifiable but it is thought the same objectives will be achieved, choice can be related to the alternative costs alone. In these circumstances the process of choosing involves a cost effectiveness analysis, a comparison based only on the discounted costs of the alternatives.

Use of the Project Criteria

Project criteria using discounted values of costs and benefits can be adapted to decisions between project alternatives. For illustration, Table 3.3 shows the resource statements for two project alternatives. Here a difference in technology shows up in the resource costs. Alternative 1 involves a larger expenditure on operating labour but less on investment in machinery; alternative 2 shows a larger expenditure on machinery and less on operating labour. For these two alternatives the essential questions are; which is the better alternative, and is it acceptable?

Figure 3.4 traces the NPV curves for these technological alternatives and identifies the main features of the choice between them.

Table 3.3 Resource statements ('000): project alternatives

Discount rate 0.05	*Present values*	*0*	*1–9*	*10*
Alternative 1				
Investment cost		1000		
Working capital		100		(100)
Materials			200	200
Power			100	100
Labour			300	300
Total costs	5672	1100	600	500
Revenue	5791		750	750
Net revenue	119	(1100)	150	250
BCR 1.021				
Alternative 2				
Investment cost		1900		
Working capital		100		(100)
Materials			200	200
Power			100	100
Labour			180	180
Total costs	5645	2000	480	380
Revenue	5791		750	750
Net revenue	146	(2000)	270	370
BCR 1.026				

The figure can be divided into four sections corresponding to different ranges of the rate of discount.

In section I the NPV curve for alternative 2 lies above that for alternative 1, and both are positive; in section II the NPV curve for alternative 1 is above that for alternative 2, but both are still positive; in section III the NPV for alternative 2 continues to be lower but has now turned negative; in section IV the NPV curve for alternative 1 is still higher than for alternative 2 but is now negative also. Clearly, the answer to both questions above depends upon the discount rate. Briefly, if the discount rate is in the range covered in section I, alternative 2 should be accepted; if it is in section II

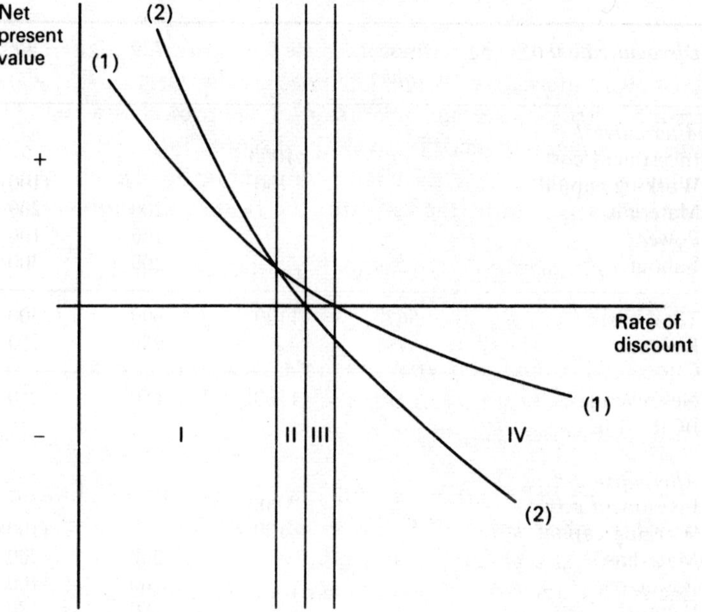

Figure 3.4 Net present value curves: project alternatives

alternative 1 should be accepted; if it is in section III only alternative 1 can be accepted; whilst if it is in section IV both alternatives, and therefore the project as a whole, should be rejected.

The use of the NPV criterion is an appropriate means of choosing between project alternatives, when the discount rate is known by the project analyst. Suppose here the discount rate has been estimated at 5 per cent. At this value:

$$NPV(2) > NPV(1) \text{ and } NPV(2) > 0$$

Alternative 2 should be accepted since it generates a positive return to the economy, over and above the rates of return available in other projects.

However, suppose that the discount rate is 8 per cent. At this value:

NPV(1) > NPV(2) but NPV(1) < 0

Alternative 2 should be rejected because it is worse than alternative 1. However, alternative 1 should be rejected also because it is worse than other projects so that no version of the project is acceptable. Here, two things happened between the discount rate values of 5 per cent and 8 per cent. First, the choice between the project alternatives changed, and secondly, the NPV for the better alternative became negative.

The conditions for accepting an alternative at the discount rate *d* are as follows:

Choose Maximum [NPV(*i*)] as long as Maximum NPV(*i*) > 0
where *i* refers to a project alternative.
Otherwise reject the project.

Use of the NPV criterion will always give an unambiguous conclusion since there will always be one alternative with the highest NPV at a given discount rate.

The NPV is the best criterion to use for choosing between project alternatives. Use of the other two criteria that have been discussed may result in false choices. Use of the benefit–cost ratio will satisfy one of the conditions indicated above since whenever the NPV is positive the BCR is greater than 1.0 and whenever the NPV is negative the BCR is less than 1.0. Hence the BCR can be used to check if the better alternative is acceptable, but it cannot be used to select the better alternative. Table 3.4 shows why. With discounted benefits greater than discounted costs for both alternatives, both are acceptable. However, the two alternatives involve different magnitudes for costs and benefits.

Table 3.4 Comparison of NPV and BCR criteria

	PV benefits	*PV costs*	*NPV*	*BCR*
Alternative A	1000	900	100	1.111
Alternative B	2000	1850	150	1.081

(Discounted values are at the same rate of discount.)

Basically, we are concerned with maximizing absolute additional benefits to the economy, and not with maximizing percentage returns. Because of the greater magnitudes for Alternative B, it has a higher NPV. However, the ratio of benefits per unit of costs is lower despite the larger absolute benefits that are generated so that it has a lower BCR. At the given discount rate the alternative which generates the greater absolute surplus in the economy, Alternative B, should be accepted, and not the alternative with the higher BCR.

The technological alternatives in Table 3.3 illustrate why the internal rate of return cannot be used to choose between project alternatives. If the discount rate is 5 per cent then both alternatives are acceptable. Alternative 1 has a higher IRR at 7 per cent than alternative 2 at 6 per cent, but this does not mean necessarily that it should be chosen. As can be seen from Figure 3.4 the alternative with the higher IRR does not have the higher NPV at a 5 per cent rate of discount. The situation is summarised in Table 3.5.

Table 3.5 Inconsistent results NPV and IRR

	NPV @ 5%	*IRR*
Alternative 1	120	7.1%
Alternative 2	146	6.4%

The two project criteria appear to reach different conclusions. However, what matters is the discount rate, which should reflect the opportunity foregone by not investing in other projects. If this rate is 5 per cent, Alternative 2 will yield the greatest surplus to the economy over and above the return achievable in other projects, as indicated by the NPV, and should therefore be chosen.

It should be noted that this conclusion applies regardless of the fact that Alternative 1 yields a greater return on project costs than Alternative 2, as indicated by the respective IRRs. Again, the implicit objective in project choice is to maximize net resources as a whole. This will be done by choosing the alternative with the larger NPV at a given discount rate, so that the NPV criterion is superior to both the BCR and the IRR for choosing between project alternatives.

Use of Project Criteria in Cost Effectiveness Analysis

The example of technological choice above involves the comparison of benefits and costs for different alternatives. Cost effectiveness analysis considers only the costs of two or more alternatives, treating the benefits as identical. Table 3.6 and Figure 3.5 present another example of project alternatives relating to a water supply project. Here the same quantity and quality of water per annum can be delivered using pipes of different diameters. The smaller pipe will involve greater pumping costs and last for a shorter time.

Table 3.6 Cost effectiveness: pipeline alternatives cost statements ('000)

Discount rate 0.10	*Alternative A*			*Alternative B*		
	0	*1–24*	*25*	*0*	*1–24*	*25*
Installation costs	90,000		(15,000)	70,000		
Operating and maintenance costs		20,000	20,000		22,500	22,500
Total costs	90,000	20,000	5,000	70,000	22,500	22,500
PV Total costs	270,156			274,233		

In order to make the alternatives equivalent, a salvage value has been entered in Alternative A since it has a working life beyond the 25 years of alternative B. The smaller pipeline Alternative B, costs less to install but more to operate. The question in this case is whether the extra investment costs of the larger pipeline A are worthwhile, given the associated savings in annual operating and maintenance costs.

Figure 3.5 shows that for some rates of discount the present value of costs for Alternative B is higher, and for higher rates of discount the present value of costs for Alternative A is higher. Which alternative to choose again depends upon the discount rate.

If the discount rate is set at 10 per cent, Alternative A will be chosen. Formally, this would correspond to:

At the discount rate d, Minimize [PVC(i)]

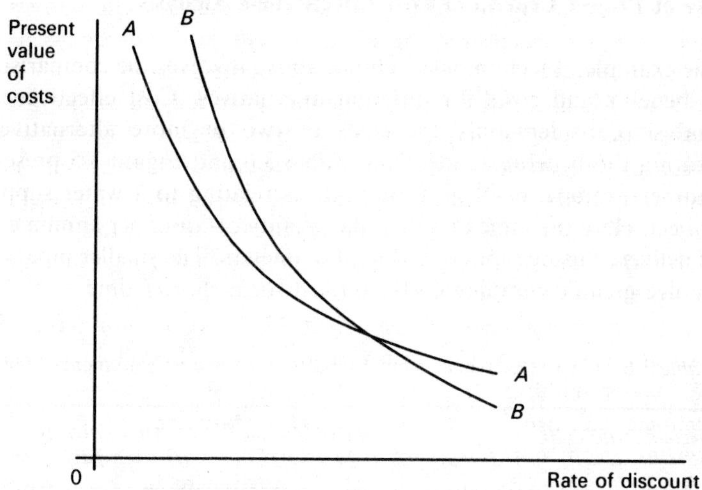

Figure 3.5 Project cost alternatives

where PVC is present value of project costs and *i* refers to a project alternative.

For rates of discount below 10 per cent, Alternative A will still be chosen. Alternative B has the lower present value of costs only at discount rates above 12.3 per cent.

As the name implies, cost effectiveness analysis only addresses the question of how to minimize costs for undertaking a particular activity. There is no further question of whether the project is acceptable as a whole.

A Further Approach to Choosing between Project Alternatives

The clearest criterion to use in choosing between project alternatives is the NPV, or in the context of cost effectiveness analysis, the present value of costs (PVC). However, another approach for choosing between project alternatives is available. Rather than simply comparing project criteria for two alternatives, the difference between the two alternatives can be calculated and project criteria applied to this difference. The resource statement that results from taking the difference between the two alternatives is called the incremental resource statement and can be used in conjunction with the NPV, BCR or IRR criterion.

Table 3.7 illustrates an incremental resource statement for a project that can be implemented in two locations. In the first, closer to the market area for the output, the investment and operating costs are larger, because of an additional transport element. On the other hand, the revenue (net of transport and distribution costs) is higher also. In the alternative location, costs are lower but so is the net revenue.

The incremental resource statement, obtained by subtracting the costs and revenues of Location B from those of Location A, shows the greater initial costs of the first alternative and the additional revenues that would be obtained. This statement addresses the question: is it worth bearing the greater costs of Location A in order to achieve greater revenues? The answer again depends upon the discount rate. At a discount rate of 10 per cent the incremental resource flow is positive, so the additional costs are acceptable. Formally, the criterion for deciding between the alternatives is:

Where the resource flow at B has been subtracted from the resource flow at A, and discounted at the rate d,

If IncrNPV > 0, accept Alternative A, as long as NPV(A) > 0
If IncrNPV < 0, accept Alternative B, as long as NPV(B) > 0
If IncrNPV $= 0$, either Alternative can be accepted, as long as their NPV is positive.
(where Incr refers to incremental)

However, at different rates of discount the decision might be different (Figure 3.6). At a discount rate higher than 10 per cent the additional revenues may not prove adequate compensation. It is worthwhile calculating the internal rate of return of the incremental resource statement, termed the incremental internal rate of return, to compare it with the discount rate. The incremental internal rate of return from Table 3.7 is 12 per cent. At this rate of discount the NPVs for both alternatives are the same. This incremental internal rate of return is greater than the discount rate of 10 per cent, and confirms the adoption of Alternative A. Formally the choice using the incremental internal rate of return method can be formulated as follows:

Table 3.7 Incremental resource statement (Rs.000)

Discount rate 0.1	*Location A Present Values*	*0*	*1*	*2–9*	*10*	*Location B Present Values*	*0*	*1*	*2–9*	*10*
Investment cost		500	550				475	525		
Working capital			100		(100)			100		(100)
Materials				350	350				320	320
Power				95	95				95	95
Other inputs				150	150				125	125
Total costs	4167	500	650	595	405	3832	475	625	540	440
Revenue	4188			800	800	3848			735	735
Net revenue	21	(500)	(650)	205	305	16	(475)	(625)	195	295
Location A – Location B										
Incr. investment cost		25	25							
Incr. working capital			0							
Incr. materials cost				30	30					
Incr. power cost				0	0					
Incr. other inputs cost				25	25					
Incr. total costs	335	25	25	55	55					
Incr. revenue	340			65	65					
Incr. net revenue	5	(25)	(25)	10	10					
Incr. BCR 1.014										
Incr. IRR 12%										

Note
Incr = Incremental

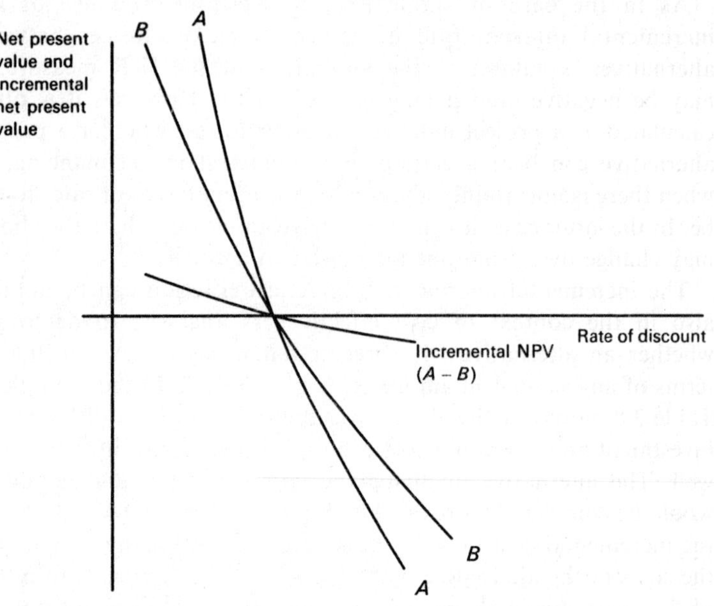

Figure 3.6 Incremental resource flow

If IncrIRR > *d*, accept Alternative A, as long as NPV(A) > 0 at *d*
If IncrIRR < *d*, accept Alternative B, as long as NPV(B) > 0 at *d*
If IncrIRR = *d*, either alternative can be accepted as long as NPV > 0 at *d*.

The incremental internal rate of return can be looked at in a different way. Up to this rate of return, Alternative A is preferable to Alternative B, shown by both a direct comparison of their NPVs and by the NPV of the incremental resource statement; but beyond this rate of return, Alternative B becomes preferable. The choice between Alternative A and B changes at the rate of discount given by the incremental internal rate of return. For this reason it is also called the cross-over discount rate, the rate at which the choice crosses over from one alternative to the other. For rates of discount above the incremental internal rate of return, the second alternative B should be preferred to the first, A.

As in the case of single project decisions, the use of the incremental internal rate of return to make choices between alternatives is subject to the limitations of the IRR measure; it may be negative, and it may not be unique. However, it is often calculated as a project indicator in order to test whether a project alternative can bear a certain rate of interest in its financing, or when there is uncertainty about what the exact discount rate should be. In the latter case, it is useful to have an idea of where the choice may change over from one alternative to another.

The incremental internal rate of return criterion can be applied also in the context of cost effectiveness analysis, to determine whether an alternative with greater initial costs is worthwhile in terms of any savings in annual costs it may yield. In the example of Table 3.8 moreover the alternatives not only involve a difference in investment and operating costs, but in the phasing of investment as well. The alternative involving the larger investment (Method 2) would be completed more quickly. Figure 3.7 (on page 67) illustrates the incremental cost flow for these alternatives, obtained by taking the costs of the alternative with larger, earlier investment from that of the alternative with smaller, later investment, at different rates of discount. The incremental cost flow involves negative values at the beginning, corresponding to the higher investment costs, followed by positive values, corresponding to the saving in operating costs. The question asked through the incremental cost flow is whether the larger investment costs of Method 2 are adequately repaid by later saving in operational costs.

Again the answer depends upon the discount rate. At a discount rate of 10 per cent the incremental cost flow has a positive present value; the additional investment costs of Method 2 are worthwhile. Put another way, at a 10 per cent discount rate the present value of costs for Method 1 are larger than for Method 2. This comparison can be restated formally as follows:

Where the costs of Method 2 have been subtracted from the costs of Method 1,

If Incr IRR $>$ d, accept Alternative 2
If Incr IRR $<$ d, accept Alternative 1
If Incr IRR $=$ d, either Alternative can be accepted

This incremental approach to the choice between two alternatives has the advantage that discounting can be reduced to one process. It

Table 3.8 Incremental resource cost statement (Rs.000)

Discount rate 0.10	*Method 1 Present Values*	*0*	*1*	2	*3–19*	*20*	*Method 2 Present Values*	*0*	*1*	2	*3–19*	*20*
Investment cost		300	300	300				500	500			
Working capital		30	30	30		(90)		42	42			(84)
Labour			100	200	300	300			135	270	270	270
Materials			150	300	450	450			210	420	420	420
Total costs	6613	330	580	830	750	660	6583	542	887	690	690	606
Incr.total costs	30	(212)	(307)	140	60	54						
CDR	11.0%											

Note
Incr. = incremental
CDR = cross-over discount rate

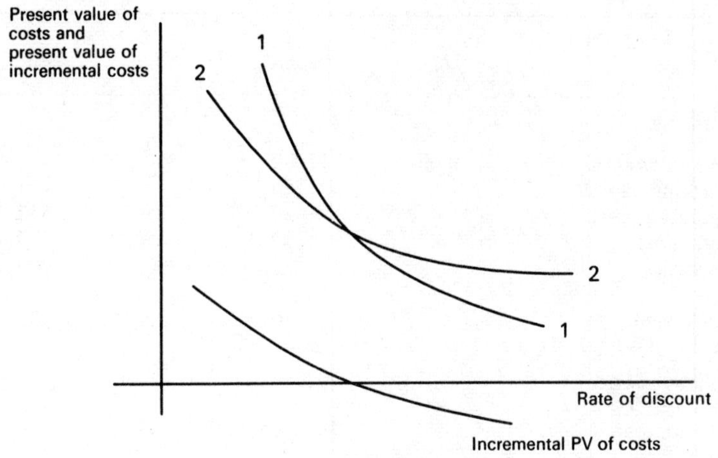

Figure 3.7 Incremental resource cost flow

also has the advantage that the differences between two alternatives are laid out clearly in the incremental resource or cost statement. For these reasons, an incremental analysis can supplement the direct comparison of NPVs or PVCs illustrated earlier.

Project Criteria and a Shortage of Investment Funds

It has been argued above that the NPV or PVC criteria are the most straightforward to use in choosing between project alternatives. These criteria are calculated at a given discount rate representing the alternative opportunities foregone by not investing in other projects. However, this assumes that there are adequate investment funds available to implement all acceptable projects. Where there is a shortage of investment funds choices will have to be made between projects with different investment requirements, to fit within the funding constraint. Here a choice based simply on the NPV or PVC may no longer be appropriate.

Table 3.9 shows the resource statements for three different projects which have different investment requirements. The discount rate has been set initially at 8 per cent and at this discount

Table 3.9 Resource statements (Sh.000) and investment constraint

Discount rate 0.08	*Present Values*	*Years 0*	*2–9*	*10*
Project 1				
Investment costs	1000	1000		
Working capital		150		(150)
Operating cost			650	650
Total costs	5442	1150	650	500
Revenue	6039		900	900
Net revenue	597	(1150)	250	400
PV/K 1.60				
BCR 1.11				
IRR 18.0%				
Project 2				
Investment cost	450	450		
Working capital		30		(30)
Operating cost			500	500
Total costs	3821	480	500	470
Revenue	4194		625	625
Net revenue	373	(480)	125	155
PV/K 1.83				
BCR 1.10				
IRR 23.0%				
Project 3				
Investment cost	2200	2200		
Working capital		200		(200)
Operating cost			1500	1500
Total costs	12373	2400	1500	1300
Revenue	13085		1950	1950
Net revenue	712	(2400)	450	650
PV/K 1.32				
BCR 1.06				
IRR 14.0%				

Note
PV/K = present value of net benefits divided by present value of investment costs.

rate all three projects are acceptable. However, in the period when financial arrangements for the projects are being made it becomes apparent that insufficient funds are available to finance them all. Total investment in all three is 3650 (excluding working capital). Total funds available are only 2300.[6] If the NPV criterion is adopted, Project 3 with the highest NPV will be chosen. However, this would not leave sufficient investment funds to undertake either of the other two projects. The issue is whether the choice of Project 3 would maximize the surplus in the economy within the constraint of the available investment funds.

One indicator that can answer this question is an adjusted form of the benefit–cost ratio, similar to a net output to capital ratio. Distinguishing between investment and operating costs, the discounted net benefits of a project can be compared with its discounted investment cost. Formally this indicator can be written as:

$$PV/K = \sum_t \left\{[B(t) - OC(t)]/(1 + d)^t\right\} / \sum_t [K(t)/(1 + d)^t] \quad (3.5)$$

where
$B(t)$ are benefits in year t as before,
$OC(t)$ are operating costs in year t, and
$K(t)$ are investment costs in year t.

It gives an indication of the net operating benefits achieved per unit of investment. The results of applying this and the other indicators to the three projects of Table 3.9 are summarised in Table 3.10. These calculations show that Project 3, the largest project with the largest NPV, has the lowest value for this indicator; it generates net benefits at a lower rate per unit of investment than the other projects. Project 3 also has the lowest return on the resources as given by the internal rate of return for each Project.

From these results, it is clear that the limited investment funds could be reallocated. If they were allocated first to Project 2 and then to Project 1 there would be a total NPV generated of 597 + 373 = 970, exceeding the 712 of Project 3. Also, from the available funds of 2300 there would be a residual of 850 which could be invested in other projects at an 8 per cent rate of return, which is the return assumed obtainable on additional investment. The absolute

Table 3.10 Project criteria: investment fund constraint

	Initial investment costs	*NPV @ 8%*	*PV/K @ 8%*	*IRR*
Project 1	1000	597	1.60	18
Project 2	450	373	1.83	23
Project 3	2200	712	1.32	14

returns on the investment of 850 will clearly exceed those on the residual of 100 investment units if Project 3 is chosen. This combination of Project 2 and Project 1 would not be selected if the NPV is used as the decision criterion where there is a shortage of investment funds.

Both the PV/K indicator and the IRR for these projects suggest a different ranking from the NPV. Moreover, the IRRs indicate what will be given up if the limited investment resources are allocated to Project 3; that is two alternative projects with IRRs of 18 per cent and 23 per cent. This suggests that the discount rate of 8 per cent will not be appropriate where there is a shortage of investment funds. If the discount rate is raised to reflect the higher opportunity cost of investment funds, then some previously acceptable projects are going to be rejected. This is what happens to Project 3 here. The discount rate should be above 14 per cent, which is the return on Project 3 that will be given up if the combination of Project 2 and Project 1 is chosen.[7]

If the discount rate is adjusted accurately – so the discount rate is re-estimated with a knowledge of the overall investment funds available and the types of project ready for decision – then the NPV criterion can again be applied. For example, if the new discount rate is 15 per cent, the three Projects discussed above give the following results (Table 3.11). Now Project 3 is excluded on the NPV criterion; and at this appropriate discount rate, the PV/K indicator for Project 3 is less than 1.0, meaning the present value of operating net benefits do not cover the present value of investment costs.

Hence, by adjusting the discount rate to allow for a shortage of investment funds, the NPV criterion can continue to be used. The

Table 3.11 Project criteria: adjusted rediscount rate

	NPV @ 15%	*PV/K @ 15%*
Project 1	142	1.14
Project 2	155	1.34
Project 3	(92)	0.96

PV/K criterion can then be seen as a useful indicator where an investment fund shortage is expected to be temporary. In the longer term, its use should be replaced by an adjustment to the discount rate.

CONCLUSION

Various project criteria can be applied both to decisions on single project proposals and to choices between project alternatives. The three most common discounted project criteria – the BCR, the NPV and the IRR – will yield equivalent decisions for single projects at the same discount rate (with the possible exception of those unusual cases where the IRR is not unique). However, a project can be analysed from different points of view, and the same project criterion may yield different decisions from that of total capital and that of the project owner.

The project criteria may need adapting to the choice between project alternatives. The NPV is the most straightforward criterion in these circumstances, and can simply be replaced by the PVC criterion in the case of cost effectiveness analysis. However, an alternative approach is to calculate the incremental internal rate of return for the incremental project statement between pairs of alternatives. Also the NPV approach may have to be amended to the PV/K criterion where there is a temporary shortage of investment funds.

In any application of these project criteria the role of the discount rate is crucial. Apart from determining whether project proposals should be accepted or not, the discount rate determines the choice between project alternatives. This crucial role underlines the importance of having an estimate of the discount rate that is as accurate and up to date as possible.

APPENDIX 3.1 ESTIMATION OF INTERNAL RATE OF RETURN

The iterative process of locating the internal rate of return of a project resource flow depends on finding that point at which the NPV curve crosses the rate of discount axis. This point can be estimated if two trials yield NPV values close to zero.

Suppose the following results have been found:

Rate of discount .10 .12
NPV 306 (192)

The internal rate of return lies between 10 per cent and 12 per cent; where it lies in this range depends upon the distance between the two NPV values. The absolute distance here is 306 + 192 = 498, and this corresponded to a change in the rate of discount of 12 − 10 = 2 per cent.

The internal rate of return can be estimated by noting that the rate of discount has to be raised from 10 per cent sufficiently for the NPV to fall by 306 to zero; within the 2 per cent range given by these values, it has to fall in the proportion 306 to 498.

The internal rate of return can thus be estimated as:

$$10\% + (2\% \times 306/498) = 10\% + 1.2\% = 11.2\%$$

It should be noted that this estimate assumes the NPV curve is linear between the 10 and 12 per cent values. This assumption yields a small over-valuation of the IRR. It should be rounded down to 11 per cent; using this approach IRR estimates should not be made over more than a 2 per cent range for the rate of discount.

APPENDIX 3.2

Table 3A.1 Illustration of a resource flow with more than one internal rate of return

	Year	*0*		*1*		*2*
Net benefits		(300)		800		(520)
Rate of discount	0.1	0.2	0.3	0.4	0.5	0.6
Present value	(2.5)	5.6	7.7	6.1	2.2	(3.1)

This resource flow is unusual. It involves an initial investment that allows a rapid increase in net benefits. However, the raw material base is quickly exhausted (in one year) and the project area has to be reconstituted in the second year, at a cost exceeding the initial investment.

The present values recorded at different rates of discount indicate that the NPV = 0 at a rate between 10 and 20 per cent, and also between 50 and 60 per cent. These two internal rates of return are approximately 12 and 55 per cent.

This illustration is a specific example of the more general possibility that there may be more than one IRR at positive rates of discount when there is a change of sign in the net benefit values; that is, after the initial investment, there are other years in which the net benefits are negative not positive.

Further Reading

Several texts provide a basic introduction to project criteria and their application both to single projects and to project alternatives: see Fitzgerald (1978), chapter 2, and Irvin (1978), chapter 1. Gittinger (1982), chapters 9 and 10 provides a more extensive treatment with several project criteria. UNIDO (1978a), chapter IV includes a brief discussion of the difference between financial and real resource statements.

There are many other statements of the principles behind the use of project criteria, for example, in Marglin (1967) and Abouchar (1985). The principles are restated from a Soviet viewpoint in Novozhilov (1970).

Microcomputer spreadsheet applications have become routine in project analysis calculations. Introductions to the use of spreadsheets for this purpose can be found in Remenyi and Nugus (1988), part one, and Yaffey (1988).

4 National Economic Returns and the Use of Shadow Prices

So far the project statements that have been considered, either from the owner's point of view or that of the economy as a whole, have been drawn up using market prices, that is, those at which transactions will actually take place, to value project inputs and outputs. It is assumed that these prices can be sufficiently accurately predicted over the operating life of the project. Estimates of the investment costs, operating costs, working capital and benefits are put together into the project statements at constant market prices.

However, if projects are to be analysed from the national point of view, as referred to at the beginning of Chapter 2, adjustments may need to be made both to the items included as inputs and outputs of a project, and to the prices at which these are valued. The purpose of this chapter is to outline and illustrate the main features of analysis from the national point of view. For ease of reference, the term economic analysis will be used to refer to project analyses from the national viewpoint.

The first section of this chapter elaborates on those items in a project statement that refer to transfers within the national economy, and can therefore be omitted from economic analyses of projects. The second section traces the origin and introduces the basic principles of the use of shadow prices in project analysis, whilst the third section illustrates the application of shadow prices to the inputs and outputs of a project. The fourth section discusses the meaning of the net project benefits resulting from such an application, while the fifth section considers the implications for project decision-taking.

TRANSFERS AND OTHER ADJUSTMENTS

In a project statement, items that do not refer to the use of a resource but which merely transfer purchasing power from one group within the national economy to another are termed transfers, and should be omitted from economic calculations. For example, the cost of machinery or construction, of material inputs or labour, and the value of physical outputs, all refer to resources that are committed to or produced by a project and that would have been used or produced in alternative projects. However, payment of a sales tax on the output or the receipt of a cash subsidy by an enterprise do not refer to resource effects but rather transfers of purchasing power, in this case between the project operators and the government. This distinction has already been used to distinguish the viewpoints of total capital and of the project owners, but the nature of transfers needs to be elaborated further.

Several types of transfer may be included in project statements from the owner's point of view. Some will be recorded explicitly as direct transfers, others will be implicit in the market prices of inputs and outputs. The most common form of direct transfers is the payment of taxes or the receipt of subsidies. Normally, all can be omitted from a project statement for economic calculations. However, application of this principle is sometimes difficult because of the problem of identifying the appropriate taxes and subsidies. Occasionally, what are recorded as taxes may be charges for the use of resources, in the sense that they are identified with a particular service; for example, a land tax that is spent on the provision of infrastructure and landscaping, or a water tax that covers the cost of a water system. Where such special taxes refer to the use of resources in this way they should be retained as an estimate of the resource costs involved.

Subsidies can also be given to producers or projects indirectly through controls on the price of inputs or outputs. For example, where agricultural inputs such as seed or fertilizer are made available at controlled prices, a subsidy may be implicit if the controlled price is below the full cost of the inputs. Such inputs should be valued at the full cost of increasing the supply of the seed or fertilizer, not at their subsidised price.[1]

A further item that may involve simply a transfer of purchasing power is rent payments. Rent may appear as a project cost. However, from the national point of view a rent payment simply transfers purchasing power from the project to the owner of the asset being rented. In this case, the rent payment should not be included as a cost. The exception is again where the rent payment implicitly refers to certain services provided by the asset owner, for instance, the maintenance and cleaning of office accommodation, in which case it can be retained as representing the resource cost involved.

The omission of transfers, or their replacement by the true resource cost, is fairly straightforward for direct transfers that appear in the project statement. However, a project will also involve hidden transfers in the prices at which it purchases inputs. Project inputs may be subject to all the types of transfer noted above, to taxes and subsidies, and to rent payments divorced from services, at different levels in the chain of production. A comprehensive and consistent method needs to be applied to adjust input values for all these items. The technique of shadow pricing outlined below achieves these adjustments by replacing market prices with an alternative set of prices.

As discussed in Chapter 2, financing items also need to be removed from project statements for economic analysis. The receipt of a loan, the payment of interest, or repayment of a loan, transfers purchasing power but does not represent directly the use of resources.

The removal of direct and indirect transfers from a project statement is not the only adjustment that has to be made from a national point of view. The indirect effects of a project may have to be considered as well and a value introduced for the land which a project occupies. These indirect effects may refer to either costs or benefits. An indirect cost may be caused by the disposal of industrial waste, for example, where this waste, discharged into a river, affects the fishing catch of those lower downstream. From the national point of view, such indirect costs should be attributed to the project and added to the statement of costs.

Indirect benefits may also accrue from a project. For instance, where a project increases the supply of a good substantially, this may affect the price of the good for existing producers as well as the project. In this case, all sales will be at a lower price, raising the real incomes of purchasers. This indirect benefit – the goods affected multiplied by the difference in price to existing purchasers – should also be included in the project statement. For economic analysis, the project statement should therefore be broadened to include any major indirect costs and benefits.[2]

Land is often omitted as a financial cost from a project statement, either because it may already be owned by the project and is therefore regarded as a cost met in the past, or, in some countries, because land cannot be purchased there only being a right to use it. Moreover, where a financial cost for land is included it may be affected by speculative activities and give no clear indication of its worth from a national point of view. The cost of land may appear as a rent payment; as before, if this relates to services rendered by the owner it can be retained as a project cost. More likely, where it does appear, the cost of land is given by a purchase value at the outset of a project. It is this financial cost that needs to be adjusted to remove any excess profit to the land-seller. The way in which the value of land can be estimated from a national viewpoint is to consider the alternative use of it in the absence of the project. How much would it generate in terms of net benefits each year and what is an approximate present value for this stream of net benefits in the alternative use? In other words, any financial cost of the land should be replaced by its opportunity cost, and an opportunity cost value explicitly introduced where no financial cost exists.

Shadow Prices: The Use of Trade Opportunity Cost Values

The economic analysis of a project also requires that inputs and outputs be valued at their contribution to the national economy, through shadow prices, and it is the notion of opportunity cost that underlies the application of shadow prices in project analysis. From the national point of view, it is the alternative production foregone or the cost of alternative supplies that should be used to value project inputs and outputs. There is no reason to suppose that market prices represent these opportunity cost values; generally, they do not.

The idea that market prices fail to represent national opportunity costs, and that an alternative basis of valuation needs to be established, grew out of several debates over development in the 1950s and 1960s. The first debate related to the character of so-called labour surplus economies. Where land was in relatively short supply and the population growing, the marginal contribution of extra labour to rural production was thought to be very small. As investment in industry and government services attracted more labour away to urban areas, the lost production in rural areas was small, perhaps close to zero. However, the industrial sector in particular could pay wages above the levels of rural income because of the greater productivity of labour in new industrial production. These wage levels would be entered as the cost of labour at market prices. However, for the national economy the cost of labour was the value of rural production lost as labour migrated to take up new wage employment, and this was in general much lower than the wage. If labour were valued at its opportunity cost and not its wage, more projects would appear viable, and the economy as a whole would benefit from a greater movement of labour into higher productivity occupations. The difference between the opportunity cost and the wage of labour could partly be made up by a subsidy to wage employment.

Arguments of this sort were related also to debates about the appropriate choice of technology. Here the market price of machinery, particularly imported machinery, was questioned as well as that of labour. It was argued, as above, that an appropriate economic cost of labour was given by its opportunity cost in rural areas. If this value were used in analysing new investments rather than the market wage, more projects of a labour-using nature would be chosen. At the same time, some argued that investment goods, particularly imported machinery, were valued at market prices lower than their opportunity cost. Investors were therefore encouraged to use inappropriate production techniques. The basis of this argument was the exchange rate regime of the 1950s and 1960s. Most countries held their currency at a fixed rate relative to the US dollar or some other international currency, which did not necessarily reflect the value of extra foreign currency to the economy. Import-intensive production was encouraged and exports discouraged. The project analyst's response to this situation could be to use an alternative exchange rate to value foreign currency items in a project statement. A substitute exchange rate, closer to the opportunity cost of foreign currency earnings or savings, would influence the choice of technology in new investments as much as using an opportunity cost for labour.

The initial focus on labour and equipment in the application of opportunity cost values was subsequently extended to all project inputs and outputs. The main contexts in which this grew up related to import substitution policies on the one hand, and government pricing policies on the other. Import substitution policies had been implemented to encourage domestic investment. These policies involved protecting domestic markets with import duties or quotas to shelter new industries from foreign competition. The consequence was a large number of commercially profitable industries that produced goods at a higher price than alternatives available on the world market. More important, these new industries, even after some years, remained high cost so that the economy was devoting more resources to new industrial investments than were embodied in alternative sources of supply on the world market. However, such investments were often profitable for the owners because of the protection they enjoyed.

The realization that industrial projects were using up a disproportionate share of resources led to the belief that profitability to owners, under protection, could be a misleading criterion for investment. The comparison was made with the world market for similar products. Setting up new industries under protection involved a considerable cost which in some cases might be too high. Removing the protection again would simply lead to the collapse of the newly established industries, but a means had to be found of ensuring that high resource-using investments were not repeated in the future. One solution was to test the international competitiveness of new investments by conducting project analyses at international or world prices. If a project was analysed at world prices, this would give an indication, first, of whether it could survive in the long term, and second, of whether its output could be obtained more cheaply from international sources.

Following these arguments, the alternative source of supply for many inputs and outputs was through international trade. The price at which to value a project input was its import price if it had to be imported, or its export price if greater domestic use led to a reduction in exports. Similarly, the price at which to value a project output was its export price if it added to exports, or its import price if local production led to a saving in imports. For such goods, since international trade forms the alternative source of supply, the use of world prices to value project inputs and outputs amounts to applying the principle of trade opportunity cost.[3]

However, this principle could not immediately be applied to all project inputs and outputs since not all actually enter into foreign trade. Indirect methods had to be devised to value inputs that were not traded, like local transport services. Also, ways had to be found to measure land and labour inputs in comparable terms (see the next chapter). Moreover, there were some non-traded project outputs to which a different principle had to be applied (see Chapter 7). Nevertheless, an alternative set of shadow prices can be obtained largely through this principle, and where appropriate trade opportunity cost values are substituted for market prices in economic analysis of projects.

AN ILLUSTRATION USING CONVERSION FACTORS

The substitution of shadow for market prices involves considerable information. World prices have to be put in operational terms. For each country, an internationally traded good will have a border price, that is simply a price at its border. For imports, the border price will correspond to the amount of foreign currency needed to pay for the good at the border, the import cif price. For exports, the border price will correspond to the amount of foreign currency received at the border, the export fob price. However, shadow prices are required at the project location rather than the border itself, and hence it is necessary to calculate border parity prices, which include adjustments for the handling, transport and transfer payments between the project location and the border.

For non-traded goods used as project inputs, breakdowns relating to production costs are needed for the indirect application of the trade opportunity cost principle, since although the items themselves have no world price most of their inputs can be measured at world prices. Direct measures are required of the opportunity costs for labour and land. Not least, an estimate is required of the opportunity cost of investment funds, the discount rate. This additional information can either be assembled on a project-by-project basis, or some of it can be collected at the national level and applied in all projects, through the estimation of what are termed national economic parameters (see Chapter 11).

Where the appropriate information has been collected, the mechanics of revaluing a project resource flow is quite simple. For each output and input a conversion factor can be calculated where the conversion factor is the ratio between shadow and market prices for the project item, so that

$$\text{conversion factor} = \frac{\text{shadow price}}{\text{market price}} \qquad (4.1)$$

Such a conversion factor (CF) can be used to revalue resources from their market to their shadow values.[4] Hence:

$$\text{Shadow price value} = \text{CF} \times \text{market price value}$$

For example, if radio components are to be imported at a cif price of 1000 per unit, but, after a tariff, will be bought by a factory for 1250 per unit, then, ignoring handling and other costs, the conversion factor for radio components will be:

$$\text{CF} = \frac{1000}{1250} = 0.8$$

and the value of the annual throughput of 65 000 radio units will be:

Value at market prices	Value at shadow prices
65 000 × 1000 = 65 000 000	0.8 × 65 000 000 = 52 000 000

Similar conversion factors can be calculated for all project outputs and inputs, including labour and land where the conversion factor is calculated respectively as:[5]

$$\text{for labour, CF} = \frac{\text{opportunity cost at shadow prices}}{\text{wage rate}} \qquad (4.2)$$

$$\text{for land,} \quad \text{CF} = \frac{\text{opportunity cost at shadow prices}}{\text{land cost}} \qquad (4.3)$$

Table 4.1 illustrates the use of conversion factors for revaluing project items from market to shadow prices, for a simple resource flow. The first section of Table 4.1 shows the market price resource statement. This is followed by a column of conversion factors, defined according to the principle above. The final section shows the resource statement converted to shadow price values. Each resource statement has been discounted to give a net present value. The market price resource flow is discounted using a discount rate representing the opportunity cost of investment funds at market prices; for the resource flow at shadow prices, a discount rate should be used representing the opportunity cost of investment funds at shadow prices. The net present values differ both because of the use of conversion factors and of different discount rates.

Table 4.1 Application of conversion factors

	Market prices					Conversion	Shadow prices				
Years	*0*	*1*	*2*	*3–9*	*10*	*factors*	*0*	*1*	*2*	*3–9*	*10*
Costs											
Investment: construction	1000				(500)	0.87	870.0				(435.0)
machinery	1000					0.93	930.0				0
Working capital	200				(200)	0.83	166.0				(166.0)
Materials		450	675	900	900	0.83		373.5	560.3	747.0	747.0
Power		50	75	100	100	0.84		42.0	63.0	84.0	84.0
Transport		25	38	50	50	0.67		16.8	25.5	33.5	33.5
Skilled labour		150	150	150	150	0.92		138.0	138.0	138.0	138.0
Unskilled labour		100	150	200	200	0.50		50.0	75.0	100.0	100.0
Revenue		900	1350	1800	1800	0.78		702.0	1053.0	1404.0	1404.0
Net resource flow	(2200)	125	262	400	1100		(1966.0)	81.7	191.2	301.5	902.5
Discount rate	0.10						0.09				
Net present value	163.7						(71.6)				

SHADOW PRICING AND THE NUMERAIRE

Conversion factors are based on the comparison of the national opportunity cost of a project item with its market price. For many project items, the opportunity cost will be given directly by its border price with minor modifications discussed in Chapter 5. The implicit objective of project analysis when project items are valued at opportunity cost is to maximize the net resources available to the economy. If the resources used in a project can generate a greater rate of return in other ways, this will be reflected in their opportunity costs, and the project under analysis will be rejected since the redeployment of resources to other uses will raise the total net resources available.[6]

However, shadow prices can be expressed in two ways. Either they can all be expressed directly in foreign exchange units, valuing all project effects at world prices – termed using a world price numeraire – or they can be expressed in domestic price units – termed using a domestic price numeraire. In general, where domestic market prices differ from border prices for similar goods, the average difference defines the relation between the world price and domestic price numeraires. The use of a different numeraire to express opportunity costs will not affect the relative value of project outputs and inputs.

An illustration will be used to explain the difference between the numeraires. Suppose there are two forms of output, both having the same foreign exchange effect; an export product worth £100 at the fob border price and an import substitute product worth £100 at the cif border price. At shadow prices given by their price at the border, these two products will be worth the same to the economy. If the official exchange rate between pounds and domestic currency is Sh.15 = £1, the foreign exchange effect of the export or the import substitute product in local currency is Sh.1500. However, suppose in addition that the price of the import substitute product is raised by an import duty on competing imports of 40 per cent; and that on average for all traded goods domestic prices are 40 per cent higher than border prices.[7] There is no tax or subsidy on the export product, which sells in the domestic market at Sh.1500, whereas the import substitute product sells in the domestic market at Sh.1500 plus 40 per cent, or Sh.2100. In domestic market prices, the import substitute has a higher price, although the value to the national economy at world prices is equal to that of the export product.

How can the domestic market prices for these two products be adjusted to reflect the fact that they are worth the same from the national point of view? The adjustment can take place in two ways. If a world price numeraire is adopted, then the domestic market price of the import substitute needs to be adjusted downwards to its world price by the ratio Sh.1500/Sh.2100 (or 0.714 approximately); it can then again be directly compared with the export product. Conversely, if a domestic price numeraire is adopted, the border price of the export product needs to be adjusted upwards by the factor 1.4, to convert its border price value of Sh.1500 into the equivalent domestic price value of Sh.2100. In general, the adjustment can be either to adjust one price downwards or to adjust the other price upwards providing the factors used are the inverse of each other. In either case, the adjusted values for the export and import substitute goods will be equivalent.

This illustration can be extended by considering the inputs required to produce the export and import substitute good. Suppose that both require the same mixture of inputs, an imported product that costs £50 at border prices, and a domestically produced good that is not available on the world market and costs Sh.600. If both of these inputs are subject to the average difference between border price and domestic market prices, then the imported input will have a value of £50 × Sh.15 = Sh.750 in the world price numeraire and £50 × Sh.15 × 1.4 = Sh.1050 in the domestic price numeraire. The domestic input will have a value of Sh.600 × 0.714 = Sh.428.4 in the world price numeraire, and Sh.600 in the domestic price numeraire. These values can be put together in Table 4.2 which summarises the value of each output and input when expressed in the different numeraires.

The net revenue in the world price numeraire is Sh.321.4 and Sh.450 in the domestic price numeraire. This does not mean that production is more profitable if it is measured through one numeraire rather than another. There is a clear relationship between these two values – Sh.450/Sh.321.4 = 1.4, the extent to which domestic market prices in general exceed border prices. As long as a particular numeraire is chosen and used consistently to value all outputs and inputs, it does not matter which is used; the values in one can be readily translated into the other. If production

Table 4.2 Alternative numeraires for shadow price values

Market prices		*Export product/Import substitute product* *World price numeraire*	*Domestic price numeraire*
Revenue	£100	£100 × Sh.15 = Sh.1500	Sh.1500 × 1.4 = Sh.2100
Imported input	£50	£50 × Sh.15 = Sh. 750	Sh.750 × 1.4 = Sh.1050
Domestic input	Sh.600	Sh.600 × 0.714 = Sh.428.6	Sh.600
Net revenue		Sh.321.4	Sh.450

is profitable as measured through one numeraire, it will also be profitable if measured through the other. The details of shadow pricing using the two numeraires are discussed in Chapters 5 and 6.

DECISION-MAKING WITH ALTERNATIVE SETS OF PRICES

Where a project resource statement is constructed at both market and shadow prices, there will be a different internal rate of return in each case. In principle, there will be a different discount rate with which to compare the IRRs. The situation can be depicted as in Figure 4.1 where the market price and shadow price NPV curves cross the discount rate axis at different points and where the appropriate discount rates for decision-taking indicate different values for the NPV.

For the project in Figure 4.1 there is a different decision for the market price and shadow price cases. At the appropriate discount rates, the project is acceptable from the national point of view but not at market prices. However, in principle, there are four possibilities as depicted in Table 4.3. First, the market and shadow price calculations can both indicate acceptance; secondly, the market price calculations can indicate acceptance but the shadow price calculations indicate rejection; thirdly, the opposite can occur, where a nationally acceptable project does not show an adequate result at market prices; finally, both calculations can indicate the

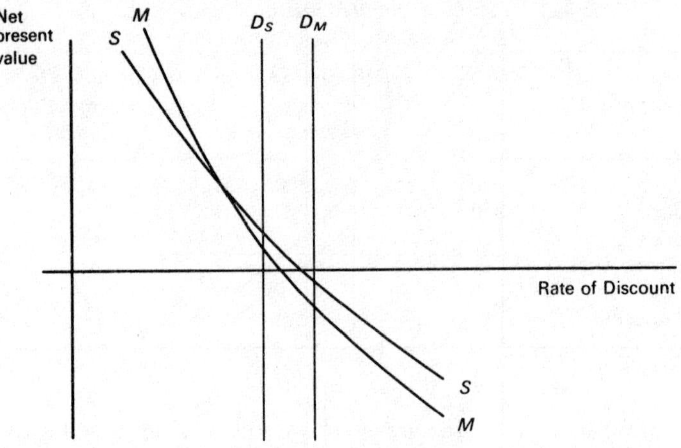

Figure 4.1 Conflicting decisions: market and shadow price calculations (case 3)

project is unacceptable. The other three situations are indicated in Figure 4.2 for different pairs of discount rates.

Table 4.3 Decision combinations at market and shadow prices

Case	*Market price NPV*	*Shadow price NPV*	*Decision*
1	Positive	Positive	Accept
2	Positive	Negative	?
3	Negative	Positive	?
4	Negative	Negative	Reject

Where the decision criteria at market and shadow prices agree, as in Cases 1 and 4, the project decision is unambiguous; where both are positive the project should be accepted; where both are negative the project should be rejected. However, the instances where the

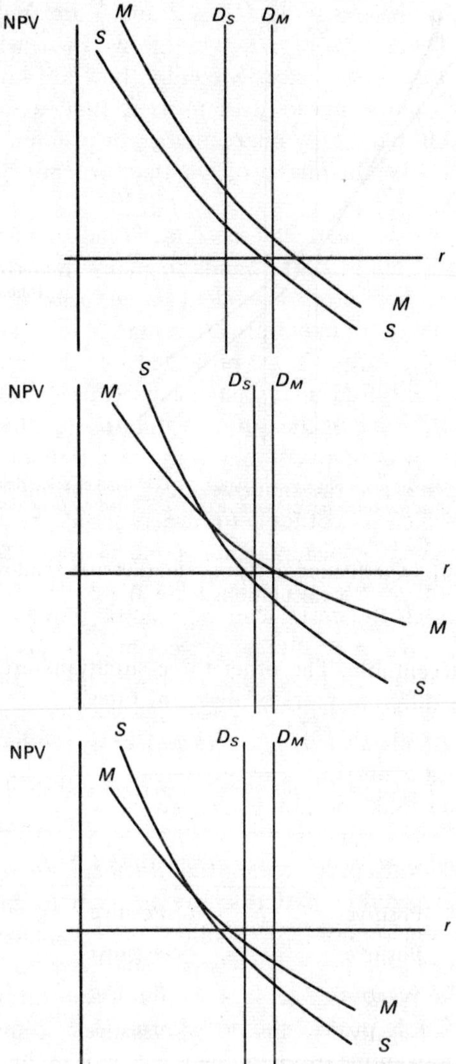

Notes *M–M* Market price net present value. *DM* Market price discount rate
S–S Shadow price net present value. *DS* Shadow price discount rate

Figure 4.2 Alternative results: market and shadow price calculations

decision criteria disagree as in Cases 2 and 3 are frequent and of most interest. These cases raise two questions. First, which decision criterion is to take precedence? Secondly, how are investors to be prevented from going ahead with projects that are profitable at market prices but nationally unacceptable, or prompted to proceed with nationally worthwhile projects that are not profitable at market prices?

The issues involved can best be understood in relation to two examples. Case 2 above corresponds to many import substitution projects that are themselves dependent on imported inputs, of both investment goods and materials. Acceptability at market prices would result if the output were protected by quotas or tariffs, or if finance was subsidized or tax payments reduced by concessional terms. The world price of the output would be less than its market price, and the project unacceptable from the national point of view. In these circumstances, the shadow price calculations would tell us that a project which is profitable to owners should be stopped. It is difficult to convince Ministers, lenders and investors that a profitable project should be stopped. However, if such projects are repeated too often the result can be macroeconomic imbalances. Taken on their own, a profitable project may be accepted despite the shadow price calculation; but if this is done too often, the foreign trade balance in aggregate will deteriorate.

Case 3 can be illustrated by an export crop production project that the government wants to go ahead as the output would generate substantial foreign exchange earnings. However, the structure of prices domestically, with farmgate prices set below world market levels, may mean that farmers are unwilling to change their production patterns. In these circumstances, which again are not uncommon, the shadow price calculations would indicate an acceptable project whilst the market price calculations confirm it not to be profitable. It is again not easy intuitively to see why an unprofitable project should be promoted. Some means has to be found, for example by changing the cost of inputs and finance or raising the direct revenue of the producers by increasing farmgate prices, to ensure that farmers benefit sufficiently to pursue the project.

These examples of import substitute and export projects illustrate the consequence of undertaking both shadow price and market price calculations. Although the project decision-making criteria are unambiguous, an adequate return to the producers has to be ensured as well as to the national economy as a whole. In principle, projects that are acceptable at shadow prices by definition generate additional net resources for the economy; the problem is how those net resources are distributed. In turn, this is not just a question of how the project is designed but also of the existing structure of prices and incentives. The appropriate circumstances to achieve viability from both the national and owner's point of view may be achieved either through some general changes in economic policy, or through project specific incentives and disincentives.

General changes in economic policy can affect the profitability of new investments. For example, if tariffs are reduced and standardized for the economy as a whole, some import substitution projects would no longer appear profitable. The existence of several project proposals showing similar characteristics may persuade the government to reduce the level of financial and tax concessions. Subsidies implicit in the pricing of infrastructure services may also be reduced. In short, the price and incentive system could be adjusted to become closer to shadow price values. However, since they affect the profitability of existing production as well as new investment, general policy changes imply a shift in economic strategy, not simply in the process of project selection.

Project-specific measures can be adopted to ensure that nationally acceptable projects are made sufficiently attractive to producers, even when the general price and incentive structure operate against the project. Conversely, for economically unacceptable projects, credit and tax concessions may be withdrawn, or effective tariffs reduced by a reallocation of quotas or foreign exchange; price controls or special profits taxes may be introduced to counteract the monopolisation of markets.

Compensations for inadequate profitability, or moves to bring profitability closer to shadow price results through generalised policy changes or project specific actions, take place in an uncertain environment. This uncertainty attaches not just to the project forecasts of quantities and prices but also to the future scope and character of government policy itself. To some extent, this uncertainty blurs the distinction between Cases 1–4 above. Nevertheless, where shadow price calculations are made there is always the possibility that the results will differ from those at market prices. In these circumstances, the decision process must deal not just with the issue of whether the project should be accepted or not but with the issue of the conditions under which it will be undertaken. Projects which show an adequate generation of resources to the national economy are for that reason inherently acceptable; it should be possible to distribute the resources in a way acceptable to all project participants to ensure that they will go ahead.

CONCLUSION

To analyse a project from the national point of view, a resource statement has to be drawn up excluding items which are transfers from the owner's viewpoint, and including any indirect costs or benefits attributable to the project but which do not accrue to the project owners. In addition, resources have to be valued at their national opportunity cost. In operational terms, shadow prices for project inputs and outputs are based on the principle of trade opportunity cost.

For traded goods a border price can be estimated directly; for non-traded goods a border price equivalent value can be estimated indirectly through revaluing their marginal production costs. For each project item a conversion factor can be calculated which reflects the ratio of shadow prices to market prices for each item; and these conversion factors can be applied to the project resource statement with an appropriate discount rate to analyse the project worth from the national point of view.

The application of both market and shadow prices to a project resource flow may result in conflicting decisions from different points of view. Projects which are acceptable from a national aspect will generate more resources nationally than alternative projects; it is thus necessary for there to be an adequate return to the project owners and producers as well.

Further Reading

The principles of removing transfer payments, incorporating indirect effects and applying shadow prices are dealt with in several texts. See, for example,

Gittinger (1982), chapter 7; Irvin (1978), chapter IV; and Little and Mirrlees (1974), part one and chapter IX. Implications of the use of world prices is discussed in McKean (1968) and Sen (1972) both in Layard (1972). A brief discussion of the choice of numeraire and the valuation of project resources can be found in UNIDO (1978) chapters III and IV and in ODA (1988), chapters 2 and 3. A recent reflection on the principal ideas behind the use of shadow prices is in Scott (1990).

5 World Price System of Economic Analysis

The previous chapter discussed the need to assess projects from a national position and introduced the use of different numeraire. However, the concept of opportunity cost used in the economic analysis of projects is more complex than that discussion implied. Benefits created or foregone by the activities of projects can only be defined in terms of specific objectives. Project analysis has generally taken government rather than individuals' objectives as the basis for the definition of opportunity costs, with most attention given to three main objectives:

(1) the efficient utilization of the existing resources of the economy;
(2) the growth of those resources over time;
(3) greater equity in the distribution of consumption between different social classes and income groups.

Potentially these objectives may be in conflict. The first implies maximizing incomes in the short run, whilst the second focuses on their growth over time. The third is concerned with the distribution of the gains from growth, in relation to the standard of living of different groups. Theoretically, conflicts or trade-offs between these objectives can be reconciled by a set of weights, and the procedure for identifying such weights is discussed in Chapter 10. At this point it is important simply to stress that projects will have a variety of effects and that opportunity costs can only be quantified if the objectives projects are to meet are agreed clearly.

In practice most project analyses now focus on the first of the three objectives noted above, so that opportunity costs are defined in terms of the benefits foregone from the use of existing resources in one project rather than in their most likely alternative use. This will be termed an efficiency analysis, reflecting its focus on resource utilization. Chapters 5, 6 and 7 discuss economic analysis from this perspective, before wider objectives are considered in Chapters 9 and 10.

The present chapter extends the earlier discussion of a numeraire to show in detail how a project can be assessed using a world price numeraire – what we term a world price system. Throughout the chapter the focus is on projects that produce traded goods – those bought and sold on the world market – and whose main direct benefits are in foreign exchange. Economic analysis shows whether such projects are acceptable by the criteria of trade efficiency by assessing whether, allowing for the resources they require, they are an efficient means of generating foreign exchange.

The chapter first distinguishes between traded and non-traded commodities or goods, produced or used by projects. It then turns to the factors of production – labour, land and capital – used by projects. The chapter concludes with a case-study illustration of a project analysis using the world price system.

TRADED AND NON-TRADED COMMODITIES

Traded goods are those whose production or use by a project has an effect on the country's balance of payments, because either the goods themselves are exported or imported, or because they are close substitutes for goods which are exported or imported. The extent to which the production or use of these goods affects the foreign exchange position of the economy is determined by their price on the world market. Non-traded goods, on the other hand, do not enter into international trade, so that their production and use can only affect the supply available to the economy.[1]

For an individual project classification of some commodities as traded or non-traded may be straightforward. Where output is exported and inputs imported it is clear that trade will be affected. Slightly less obvious examples of traded goods occur where project output substitutes for imports, and where project purchase of inputs diverts goods away from the export market. However, what is required is an assessment of whether goods will remain traded over the life of a project. Just because trade takes place currently does not mean that it will always do so, if cost conditions or policy towards trading partner countries change. It is necessary to assess both market conditions and future trade policy, and base the classification of commodities on what is judged likely to hold over the life of a project. In principle this may mean that a commodity shifts from one category to the other at a certain year of a project's life.

The role of government trade policy in determining the classification of commodities is very significant, and led to a distinction between traded and tradeable goods, with the latter defined as potential imports or exports that would be traded in the absence of government trade restrictions. For example, a project may produce an output similar to imports; if quota controls prevent imports of this type, it is not possible to class the project output as traded since its production has not actually saved foreign exchange. However, the output is tradeable if there is a demand for imports that is blocked by trade policy. The suggestion was made in the early literature that goods should be classed as traded and valued at world prices, if they are potentially tradeable.[2] This approach, which assumes away all government trade restrictions, can be misleading since what is required is to assess the impact of projects in the light of actual policies and resource use. If projects are to operate within a particular policy environment this cannot be ignored in assessing their viability.

It is clear that the more open trade becomes between countries, the larger the number of commodities that can be classed as traded. Where developing countries employ relatively few quantitative restrictions on trade – in the form of import and foreign exchange quotas – much of the directly productive activity of the economy, for example in agriculture and industry, will be traded. In most economies, though, a significant part of national income will be non-traded.

Commodities may be non-traded for various reasons. First, the characteristics of physical immobility, and high transport cost mean that some activities can only be carried out domestically. This covers a range of services, such as transport, distribution, education and health, public utilities, such as power and water, and construction. This does not mean that such sectors do not have a significant element of traded goods in their costs, but rather that there is normally no possibility of these activities taking place outside the economy, so that each sector's output is not exportable or importable. Second, goods may be non-traded because of quality differences between them and the broadly similar goods sold on the world market. One can include here simple manufactures aimed at local, low-income markets, which cannot be exported because of their poor quality by world market standards, and which are not considered as substitutes for imports by better-off local consumers; similarly, bulky low-quality subsistence foodstuffs may also fall into this category. Third, there can be some goods which may be non-traded because of government restrictions on their import or export – either by import or export quotas or prohibitively high import tariffs. Many of the policies associated with import-substitution industrialization in the 1960s and 1970s had the effect in many countries of making much of the industrial sector non-traded for project analysis. However, the trend in many countries for trade controls to be relaxed will allow more potentially tradeable goods to be treated as traded.

VALUATION OF TRADED GOODS

The importance of this classification of commodities is that for traded goods shadow prices are based on prices on the world market, with no reference to value in domestic use or supply. World prices reflect conditions in a range of international markets some of which will be manifestly uncompetitive, dominated by small producer groups or cartels. They are used not because they are seen as competitive prices but because they represent the terms on which a country can participate in world trade and are therefore the opportunity costs of using or producing traded goods. Planning of resource allocation in non-autarkic policy environments must assess the alternatives of allocating resources to non-traded or traded sectors, and within the latter to import-substitute and export activities. World prices may have a long-run trend unfavourable to developing country exports, and may be subject to short-run fluctuations caused by dumping or speculative purchases. However, with suitable adjustments they provide a norm against which to assess the costs of domestic production of traded goods.

In practice identification of appropriate world prices is not always straightforward. For all but homogeneous primary goods, there will be no unique world price but a range of prices varying with product specifications and source of supply. For goods actually to be exported and imported by a project, as output and inputs respectively, estimates and price quotations can be obtained from marketing agencies and overseas suppliers. However, where the traded output is an import substitute, and the traded inputs are potential exports, finding the appropriate world price will be more difficult, since it requires an assumption about where imports would have come from or exports gone to. Faced with a range of world prices for a good, one approach is to be optimistic and take the lowest import price and the highest export price. This assumes that additional foreign exchange for imports will be untied, so that the economy can import from any source, whilst additional exports can be sold in the most lucrative of the possible markets. An alternative, more cautious and probably more appropriate procedure is to recognize the difficulty of assessing precise alternative world prices, and take an average of the range available.

It is conventional for analyses to be conducted on the assumption that the demand or supply of an individual project will have no impact on the world prices facing the economy; so that additional demand for imports does not push up their prices, nor additional supply of exports depress their prices. This is normally a fairly safe assumption for all but large primary export projects, where the economy concerned is a major world producer and the project is a major addition to production capacity. Where world prices are changed by a project the relevant concept is a marginal one, so that the benefit per unit of export is marginal revenue, allowing for the fact that projects of other exporters in the same country will receive lower revenue from their existing sales as a result of the fall in price brought about by the supply of the new project. Therefore, the output of the new project is not valued at the actual price received for the exports, but at the new price minus the loss of revenue to existing exporters per unit of output from the new project.[3]

Further adjustments to world prices are required where current prices are judged to be temporary, either because of speculative purchases or because of dumping, where goods are sold at prices that do not cover long-run costs of production. It is long-run prices, in terms of a particular base year, that should be applied in an appraisal.

BORDER PARITY PRICING

World prices are normally measured as border prices, reflecting the value of a traded good at the border or port of entry of a country.

However, values in project financial statements will normally be at prices received by the project (ex-factory or farm-gate prices) or paid by the project for inputs. To move from market to shadow price analysis, therefore, shadow prices must be in terms of prices to the project. This means that for traded goods domestic margins, relating to transport and distribution (including port handling), will have to be added to prices at the border to obtain values at the project level. The incorporation of these margins is referred to as border parity pricing.

The economic principle involved is that production or use of a traded good has a dual effect, both in terms of direct foreign exchange given by the border price of the good, and also in terms of the resources that go into its transport and distribution between the project location and the border. To assess the full economic value of a traded good in a world price system requires both its foreign exchange worth at the border, plus the value at world prices of the non-traded activities of transport and distribution required per unit of output.

The procedure is clear for goods that are traded directly by a project. For example, where a project exports its output the border parity price to the project is the fob price minus the value of transport and distribution. These latter costs must be deducted since real resources are required before the good can be exported. Similarly, where a project imports an input its border parity price is the cif price plus transport and distribution costs.

The analysis is less straightforward whenever a project does not actually import or export the goods concerned, but produces goods that save imports (import substitutes) and uses domestic goods that could have been exported (exportables) or could have been imported (importables). The complication here is that what are relevant are the net transport and distribution costs; these are the difference between actual costs and those that would have been incurred if the good in question had been imported or exported. For example, domestic production of an import substitute saves foreign exchange given by the border price; if per unit transport and distribution costs between the project and the consumption centre, say the capital city, is less than the transport and distribution costs between the border and the capital city, this saving in real resources per unit of output is also a benefit to be added to the cif price to give the border parity price. Where domestic production involves higher transport and distribution costs there will be a net cost to be subtracted from the cif price. Similar arguments apply in the case of a project that uses traded inputs. If an input is exportable the fob price must be adjusted for the difference between transport and distribution costs in moving the input to the project and to the port for export. Where it is more expensive to move the input to the project this is an additional cost that must be added to the fob price, since more resources go into transport and distribution than if the input had been exported (similarly net cost savings must be deducted from the export price). Figure 5.1 illustrates some of the possibilities.

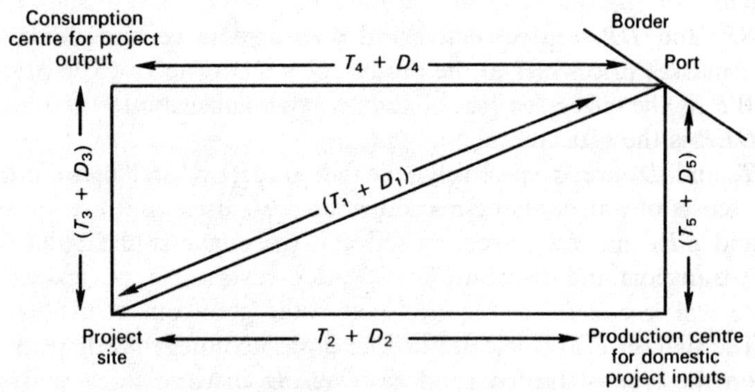

Figure 5.1 Transport and distribution element in border parity pricing

where
T and D are transport and distribution costs respectively,
T_1 and D_1 refer to costs between the project and the port,
T_2 and D_2 to costs between the project and producers who supply domestic inputs,
T_3 and D_3 to costs between the project and the domestic consumption centre for project output,
T_4 and D_4 to costs between the domestic consumption centre and the port.
T_5 and D_5 to costs between the port and producers who supply domestic inputs.

For an import substitute project
cost saving on output $= (T_4 + D_4) - (T_3 + D_3)$
cost saving on domestically produced importable inputs $= (T_1 + D_1) - (T_2 + D_2)$
cost saving on domestically produced exportable inputs $= (T_5 + D_5) - (T_2 + D_2)$
cost incurred on imported inputs $= (T_1 + D_1)$

The quantitative significance of the additional adjustments for transport and distribution will vary, with the adjustments likely to be more important in large economies with projects located far from borders, and for heavy items that are difficult to transport.

In a world price system it is conventional to convert world prices into local currency at the official exchange rate; so that the shadow price of a traded good i can be expressed as:

$$SP_i = (WP_i \times OER) + (T_i.CF_T + D_iCF_D) \quad (5.1)$$

and its conversion factor as $CF_i = \dfrac{SP_i}{DP_i}$

where

SP_i and DP_i are respectively the shadow price and domestic market prices of i to the project;

WP_i is the cif or fob price of i in foreign currency;

OER is the official exchange rate;

T_i and D_i are, respectively, the net transport and distribution costs of i at domestic market prices;

and CF_T and CF_D are, respectively, the conversion factors for transport and distribution.

The sign on T_i and D_i can be either positive or negative depending upon the type of traded good involved. In a world price analysis where all costs and benefits must be expressed at world prices, conversion factors are required to convert T_i and D_i to costs at world prices.

The approach can be illustrated with a simple numerical illustration. An import substitute project produces an output with a cif price in local currency of 100 per unit and a domestic ex-factory price of 120. Transport and distribution costs from the port to consumers are 15 per unit at domestic market prices. However, the project is located closer to the consumption centre and from the project to consumers these costs are only 5 per unit. The shadow price of the output of the project is therefore the cif price plus the net saving in transport and distribution cost of 10. The net cost saving of 10 is at domestic market prices and must be converted to a world price equivalent. If the CF for transport and distribution is 0.8, the shadow price of the good is 108, and its CF is 0.90.

$$SP = 100 + (15 - 5) \times 0.8 = 108$$

$$\text{and } CF = \frac{108}{120} = 0.90$$

VALUATION OF NON-TRADED GOODS

By definition production or use of non-traded goods by a project will generate no direct gains or losses in foreign exchange. Their valuation requires an estimate of their foreign exchange equivalent value, which takes account of their indirect foreign exchange effect. Depending upon how such goods relate to a project, their valuation requires either detailed information on their cost of supply or estimates of their worth to domestic users or consumers. Both alternatives can pose demanding problems for accurate valuation. In this chapter non-traded goods are considered only as project inputs. The particular problems that arise when they are project outputs are discussed in Chapter 7.

Non-traded inputs to a project may be either in variable or fixed supply. In the first case, demand from a project generates a supply response, so that production increases to meet the needs of the project. In the second, there is a supply constraint, so that additional demand from a project forces other users to forego their requirements, and if the market is not controlled, will create a price rise.

NON-TRADED INPUTS IN VARIABLE SUPPLY

In practice it is common that the first case is assumed on the grounds that scarcity due to fixed capacity in supplying sectors can be taken as a short-run phenomenon, and that over the life of a project new investment in the supplier activities will take place to meet project demand. The shadow price of a non-traded input under this scenario is given by the long-run marginal cost of additional supply. In a world price analysis this supply cost must be at world prices with all inputs into the production of the non-traded good valued at an equivalent world price.

In algebraic terms, for non-traded good j which is produced by traded inputs, other non-traded inputs and labour, this can be expressed as

$$SP_j = \sum_i a_{ij}\, P_i.CF_i + \sum_n a_{jn}\, P_n.CF_n + \sum_L a_{Lj}.W_L.CF_L \qquad (5.2)$$

where

SP_j is the shadow price of j;
i is a traded input into j;
a_{ij} is the number of units of i used per unit of j;
P_i is the domestic market price of i and CF_i converts this to world prices;
n is a non-traded input into j, and a_{nj} is the number of units of input n used per unit of output j;
P_n is the domestic market price of n and CF_n converts this to world prices;
L refers to categories of workers;
a_{Lj} is the number of workers of category L used per unit of output j;
W_L is the market wage for category L and CF_L converts this to world prices.

All items in (5.2) refer to marginal not average costs.

It should be clear that the cost at world prices of a non-traded activity, like electricity or road transport, is not necessarily the same as cost per KWH or ton-mile in another country. Even if both countries face the same world prices, due to productivity and technical differences one would expect unit costs to differ. The procedure involved can be illustrated with a numerical example for electricity.

Table 5.1 gives a simplified cost breakdown in Rs. per KWH at domestic market prices. Unit costs have been separated into Operating and Capital costs. Operating costs are fuel, local materials and labour. Both fuel and local materials are traded. Whilst fuel is imported directly, locally supplied materials are importable, so that additional demand from the electricity sector leads other users to import their requirements. Both fuel and local materials are expressed at world prices using conversion factors derived following the principle of border parity pricing discussed above. Fuel is imported with a very low import tariff, whilst the local materials have considerably higher import protection. This means that the world price of fuels is much closer to its domestic price than is the case for the domestic materials, resulting in a much higher conversion factor for fuel.

Table 5.1 Illustration of conversion factor for non-traded activity – electricity

	Cost at domestic market prices (Rs/KWH)	*CF*	*Cost at shadow prices (Rs/KWH)*
Operating costs			
Fuel	30.00	0.961	28.83
Local materials	60.00	0.670	40.20
Labour			
Skilled	80.00	0.900	72.00
Unskilled	10.00	0.500	5.00
Capital costs			
Equipment	60.00	0.950	57.00
Buildings	60.00	0.737	44.22
	300.00		247.25

Note

$$\text{CF for Electricity} = \frac{247.25}{300.00} = 0.824$$

The labour employed in the electricity sector is disaggregated into skilled and unskilled, and both wage costs per KWH are converted to world prices using labour conversion factors. The derivation of conversion factors for labour is discussed separately below. What is required is to estimate labour's opportunity cost at world prices. For skilled labour an economy-wide average conversion factor of 0.90 is applied, whilst for unskilled a labour conversion factor of 0.50 is estimated.

The unit capital costs of a non-traded activity can be found by applying a capital recovery factor, based on the economic discount rate and the length of life of the assets, to total investment costs. This will give an annual capital charge over the life of the supplying activity, which can be converted to a per unit basis by dividing by the total units to be supplied per year. In this example the estimated capital charge of Rs.120/KWH is divided equally between equipment and buildings. Equipment covers imported items used in electricity generation and its CF of 0.95 is derived from a comparison between border parity and project prices. Buildings must be adjusted by a CF for construction, taken to be 0.75. As a non-traded activity a construction conversion factor must be derived also by revaluing costs of production. (Appendix 5.1 illustrates how a CF for construction can be estimated.)

Any annual profits generated in supplying a non-traded input that are above the estimated annual capital charge will be surplus profits; that is, owners of capital in the non-traded sector will be earning profits above the opportunity cost rate of return on capital. Surplus profits arise from a monopolistic or protected market position, and are another form of transfer payment. They have an economic value of zero. In this example no surplus profits are involved.

In Table 5.1 the revalued cost of electricity at shadow prices is Rs248 per KWh, in comparison with the actual electricity tariff of Rs300. This means that when electricity costs are broken down into different components and valued at world prices, they come to approximately 83 per cent of the tariff. Therefore, although electricity itself is not traded internationally by the economy, it can be given a world price equivalent value derived from its unit cost of production at world prices.

This simplified example ignores a couple of theoretical complications that should be noted briefly. First, all non-traded sectors will use as inputs some goods produced by other non-traded sectors. In this example the construction sector will provide inputs to electricity as part of the buildings element of capital costs, and these construction items must be valued at shadow prices. However, electricity will in turn be an input into construction, so that the shadow price of electricity will be one of the factors determining the shadow price of construction. This interdependence implies that a consistent solution must be based on a simultaneous valuation of all non-traded goods and labour, since workers' output foregone will have some non-traded component. The computational procedure that allows for this interdependence is discussed in Chapter 11. Nevertheless, there are short-cut procedures that are used in practice, and where non-traded inputs are not a major cost item an approximate treatment will be all that is required. Secondly, cost data on non-traded sectors should be marginal not average costs and refer to the likely source of additional supply. Therefore, if a project uses electricity supplied through thermal capacity, cost data should refer to this type of system not an average of costs for thermal and other sources like hydro.

NON-TRADED INPUTS IN FIXED SUPPLY

It will be recalled that some non-traded inputs may face a supply constraint, so that rather than generating an expansion of production, demand from a new project diverts such goods away from other users. How this category of non-traded input is valued depends on whether demand from the project is sufficiently large to push up the input's market price. If there is no price rise the market price can be taken as a measure of the value of the input to other users. In other words, if other users are willing to pay this price for the input it is taken to reflect its worth, since if its contribution to their additional production were below the market price it would not be purchased.[4] Where project demand raises the price of a non-traded input the situation is more complex. Now the old market price will understate the value of the input, since users are willing to pay more for it. Strictly, a measure of user willingness to pay is required. This is discussed in Chapter 7 in the context of the valuation of non-traded outputs.

In an analysis at world prices there is a further complication in the treatment of non-traded inputs in fixed supply. If an estimate of value to users is available, based either on the current market price or on willingness to pay, to be consistent with other costs and benefits this must be converted to world prices. This requires a conversion factor for goods that are likely to be broad substitutes for the inputs involved. In the absence of more detailed information an average or aggregate conversion factor for the whole economy might be used.

For example, if willingness to pay for such a good is Rs20 at domestic prices, this has to be converted to an equivalent figure at world prices. If an aggregate conversion factor of 0.80 is used, then this willingness to pay is equivalent to Rs16 of foreign exchange at the official exchange rate. In this example the consequence of using the input concerned on a new project is that the expenditure that would have been made on this input by other users is now diverted to other goods at a cost in foreign exchange of Rs16. This is the equivalent foreign exchange cost of the input concerned.

STANDARD OR AVERAGE CONVERSION FACTOR (ACF)

Normally, in any economy there will be some divergence between world and domestic market prices for similar goods. A weighted average ratio of world to domestic prices for the main sectors of the economy is termed the average or standard conversion factor. It is often useful to have such an aggregate conversion factor to revalue relatively minor items for which detailed information is not available. For example, in the case of a non-traded input like electricity, if its share in total project costs is small, there may be little loss of accuracy in converting the tariff of Rs300 per KWh to world prices by the ACF, rather than calculating a specific conversion factor as illustrated in Table 5.1. Use of the ACF implies that the average ratio of world to domestic prices for the economy is a reasonable approximation to the ratio relevant for a particular good or type of expenditure.

There are two main ways of estimating the ACF. One is to use a simple formula based on the assumption that for traded goods (ignoring transport and distribution margins) the difference between world and domestic prices is determined by taxes and subsidies on trade.

$$ACF = \frac{M + X}{(M + T_m - S_m) + (X - T_x + S_x)} \tag{5.3}$$

where

M and X are the total value of imports and exports in a given year, converted into local currency at the official exchange rate;

T_m and T_x are total trade taxes on imports and exports respectively;

and

S_m and S_x are total trade subsidies on imports and exports respectively.

All values in (5.3) should either refer to the same year or be averages over the same period. The logic of the formula is that a tax on an import raises its domestic price above the cif price, whilst a subsidy reduces it. Hence the total value of imports at domestic prices will be their cif value (M) plus import taxes (T_m) minus import subsidies (S_m). Similarly, an export tax will reduce the domestic price of an export below its fob price, whilst an export subsidy will increase it. The total value of exports at domestic prices will thus be fob value (X) minus export taxes (T_x) plus export subsidies (S_x).

This expression for the ACF has the advantage of using data that is generally readily available, apart from the difficulty in identifying values for trade subsidies. However, the formula is extremely crude. Its main limitations are that

(a) it uses the existing average shares of goods in the foreign trade of the economy as weights; strictly it is marginal shares in additional expenditure that will be relevant;
(b) it includes only traded goods in the comparison, although in practice the ACF is applied to convert non-traded items to world prices;
(c) it omits the effect of trade controls, such as import quotas and licences, which where they are operative will add an additional scarcity margin to the domestic price of traded items; for economies with tight controls on trade use of this expression for the ACF can be quite misleading.

The alternative and more satisfactory approach to the average conversion factor is to treat it as a genuine average. Where a set of CFs are available for different sectors of the economy the ACF will be given as a weighted average of the CFs for the main productive sectors, both traded and non-traded. Although still using existing shares in production or value added as weights, this approach overcomes the second and third objections to the other ACF formula. Both traded and non-traded sectors are covered, and if sectoral CFs for traded goods are derived from direct comparisons of world and domestic prices they will incorporate the price effects of trade restrictions. Most detailed studies now adopt this approach to the ACF, which is discussed further in Chapter 11.

LABOUR IN A WORLD PRICE SYSTEM

It is conventional to distinguish between the two broad categories of unskilled and skilled labour, with the former defined as workers who can undertake project work without any minimum formal training. In practice these categories are somewhat arbitrary, and it is perhaps more satisfactory to distinguish between workers in excess supply, where there is a shortage of jobs relative to workers, and those in excess demand with a shortage of workers relative to jobs. The conventional treatment classes unskilled workers in developing countries as being in excess supply facing unemployment or underemployment, with skilled workers in excess demand. However, it should be clear that this will vary between economies; the most obvious contrasts are the Middle Eastern oil states, where there has been a scarcity of unskilled labour, and the south Asian economies, like India, Pakistan and Bangladesh, with low land–labour ratios and large labour surpluses.

In a competitive national labour market there will be full mobility of labour between different regions and jobs, with one single wage for a particular category of work. Workers will be employed up to the point at which their contribution to output (marginal productivity) just equals the wage they are paid, and the latter in turn is equal to the income necessary to compensate workers for the effort and loss of leisure from their employment (supply price).

It is well known that many labour markets in developing countries do not function in this way. Markets are fragmented in that wages can differ for similar types of worker in different sectors or geographical locations. Some of these differences may reflect higher living costs or costs of transfer between locations. In other instances they may be due to institutional features of labour markets; for example, government minimum wage legislation or trade union bargaining may keep up wages of workers in activities covered by these arrangements relative to those of similar workers in the rest of the economy. In addition, other structural features of developing countries, such as social and geographical barriers to labour mobility, lack of information on job opportunities, and the existence of monopoly profits in certain sectors that allow the payment of higher wages, can also work to prevent wages adjusting competitively on a national level.

WORKERS IN EXCESS SUPPLY

The importance of this discussion is that where labour is in surplus supply the market wage paid by a new project may differ considerably from the opportunity cost to the economy of employing such workers. This opportunity cost is the economic value of the output workers would have produced in their alternative occupation, which may offer only part-time work or underemployment.

In a world price system labour, along with all other inputs, must be valued at world prices. This does not mean that international wage rates are used instead of domestic ones, but that the physical units of output foregone are valued at world rather than domestic prices. In this way the direct and indirect foreign exchange consequences of additional employment by a project are estimated.

The shadow wage rate can be expressed algebraically as

$$SWR = \sum_i a_i m_i . CF_i \tag{5.4}$$

where *SWR* is the shadow wage rate
ai is the proportion of new workers coming from activity *i*;
m_i is the output foregone at domestic market prices for workers drawn from activity *i*;
CF_i is the conversion factor for activity *i* to convert output foregone to world prices;

The *CF* for labour is therefore

$$CF_L = \frac{SWR}{MWR}$$

where *MWR* is the market wage rate;
and CF_L is the labour conversion factor.

Equation (5.4) allows for the fact that workers can come to a new project from different supplying sectors – perhaps a combination of agriculture and urban activities such as construction and services. However, the equation can be simplified so that only one supplying sector such as agriculture is assumed. In this case *i* will refer to different types of agricultural output, and the CFs to different agricultural goods.[5]

Underemployment shows up in a low value of output foregone. What is required is an estimate of the foreign exchange cost of employing a worker. Where that worker would have produced a traded output, the loss of foreign exchange is clear, since either more imports or less exports will result from a shift to a new job. Although where a worker would have produced non-traded output, it is assumed that expenditure that would have been made on this output is diverted directly or indirectly to traded goods. The normal procedure would be to convert the value of such expenditure at domestic prices to world prices using an average conversion factor for consumption (CCF).[6] If the latter is 0.80, this implies that for the goods bought by the average consumer, their prices on the world market will be 80 per cent of their cost to consumers at domestic prices. Therefore, any expenditure diverted from non-traded goods is assumed to have an indirect foreign exchange cost of 80 per cent of its value at domestic prices.

A numerical example may illustrate the procedure. A new project employs workers at an annual wage of Rs.10 000 for permanent employment and draws workers solely from rural areas. Rural workers have two distinct work patterns during the year. During the peak agricultural season – with planting, sowing and harvesting – they can find work as wage labourers on commercial farms producing export crops, with an estimated productivity of Rs.20 per day at domestic prices. The peak season lasts for 150 days per year. During the rest of the year they work on their own small family plots producing domestic crops which on average give an income of Rs. 5 per day at domestic prices. At domestic prices annual output foregone in the export sector will be Rs.3000 per worker (Rs20 × 150), and in the domestic sector Rs.1075 per worker (Rs5 × 215). Both these figures must be converted to world prices to obtain a cost in foreign exchange. For export crops prices paid to farmers are kept below the border parity price so that the export crop conversion factor (a weighted average of the CFs for a range of export crops) is 1.38. The average consumption conversion factor is 0.80.

With this information the annual shadow wage can be estimated, as

$$SWR = \underbrace{(\text{Rs}3000 \times 1.38)}_{\text{Output foregone in export crops}} + \underbrace{(\text{Rs}1075 \times 0.80)}_{\text{Output foregone in domestic crops}}$$

$$SWR = \text{Rs}5000$$
$$CF_L = \frac{SWR}{MWR} = \frac{5000}{10\,000} = 0.50$$

The interpretation of the result is that allowing for seasonal underemployment, and the divergences between domestic and world prices in the economy, the opportunity cost of employing a worker on the project concerned when measured at world prices is 50 per cent of the annual wage the worker receives. This opportunity cost is equivalent to a sum of foreign exchange.

WORKERS IN EXCESS DEMAND

Where there is a scarcity of labour, so workers are in excess demand, there are two possibilities:

(1) that additional demand from a new project attracts workers away from activities where they were previously employed full time;
(2) that additional demand generates further supply through labour training or immigration.

In the first case, the opportunity cost is the productivity of the workers in the full-time employment from which they are drawn, converted to world prices. In practice, a common treatment for this type of worker is to assume that the market wage on a new project is a reasonable proxy for their productivity elsewhere, at domestic prices. In terms of equation (5.4) for the SWR this assumes that

$$MWR = \sum_i a_i m_i$$

Output foregone must still be converted to world prices and a common procedure is to use the ACF for this conversion. This is on the assumption that labour in excess demand is mobile within the economy, and can be drawn from all sectors. Thus the average ratio of world to domestic prices for the economy can be used to convert its productivity to world prices. This procedure means that the conversion factor for this type of labour is the ACF.[7]

However, this is not necessarily the appropriate treatment for skilled labour. In some countries such workers may be in surplus supply if the skills they possess are not those required by new projects. Further, government wage controls or employer bargaining strength may prevent wages from moving in response to productivity changes. In both cases direct estimates of output foregone will be required, since the market wage will not be an adequate proxy. In the former case it is likely to be below the market wage and in the latter above it.

Where labour supplies expand to meet project demand, opportunity cost is determined by the resources that go into generating this additional supply. For national workers, who are unskilled but receive training, the opportunity cost per worker will be output foregone, calculated as explained above, plus the training cost per worker; the latter should also be at world prices.

If foreign workers are required the cost to the economy will be defined differently. If one assumes that the workers would not have immigrated in the absence of the project under appraisal, they will have no direct output foregone for the economy. Their economic cost will be the savings they send abroad as remittances, plus the foreign exchange cost of their consumption, when they spend locally what they do not remit.

Algebraically the shadow wage of foreign workers can be expressed as

$$SWR_F = \underset{\text{(wage remitted)}}{r.MWR_F} + \underset{\text{(cost of local consumption)}}{(1 - r)\, MWR_F \times CCF} \quad (5.5)$$

where SWR_F is the shadow wage of a foreign worker;
and MWR_F is the market wage;
r is the proportion of this wage remitted abroad;
$(1 - r)$ is the proportion spent locally;
and CCF is the consumption conversion factor for foreign labour.

If foreign workers earn Rs. 1000 per month, and send back Rs.500, this is a direct drain of foreign exchange. As such it is already valued at world prices. The remaining Rs.500 they spend domestically will generate indirect foreign exchange costs, leading to more imports or less exports. A specific CCF for foreign workers should be used since their consumption patterns are likely to differ from that of consumers in general. However, in the absence of other data the average CCF could be applied. Where it is the assumption is that if on average every Rs.1 of consumption expenditure leads to a cost in foreign exchange of Rs.0.80, then the Rs. 500 spent by foreign workers will cost the economy Rs.400 of foreign exchange. The total cost of foreign workers will thus be Rs.500 remitted directly plus Rs.400 to give Rs.900. The CF for foreign labour is therefore Rs 900/Rs1000 = 0.90.

Shadow wage estimates can be made at different levels – nationally for broad categories of worker, such as skilled and unskilled, regionally for similar broad categories differentiated by region or economic zone, and finally at the project-level for more specific types of worker. National and regional estimates are important for calculations of macro level economic parameters (see Chapter 11) and as initial approximate estimates for individual projects. However, within a country labour markets can vary substantially and estimates of output foregone will require careful assessment of the type of workers required and where they are likely to be drawn from. For this reason where labour is an important input into a project, detailed estimates of the shadow wage should be made so that local employment conditions and migration trends can be allowed for. Where labour is only a minor input, national or regional estimates may be sufficient.

LAND IN A WORLD PRICE SYSTEM

Land is often a relatively minor item in industrial projects, but in agriculture and some infrastructure investments it can be far more significant. In a competitive land market prices would equal the expected future gain from the purchase or rental of an additional unit of land. However, it is not obvious that existing land markets are sufficiently competitive for price to be an adequate guide to productivity. In urban areas land markets may be dominated by speculative purchases by buyers whose intention is to hold the land to influence the price, and in rural areas land use may follow from custom rather than economic calculation.

The shadow price of land is given by its opportunity cost – the net income at world prices that could be obtained from the land in its most likely alternative non-speculative use. Where land for a factory site was previously unused its direct opportunity cost will be zero, since no output would be lost by building the factory on the land, and only land-clearing costs can be properly attributed to the project. If land is a major project cost, it is best treated as a project-specific item whose value is estimated taking account of the situation in the project area and the most likely uses of the land. Where the analysis is at world prices, land like all other inputs must be valued at world prices. A numerical example can illustrate the procedure.

A sugar mill is to be established that requires the expansion of sugar-cane farming. The aim is that small farmers previously growing cotton will shift to cane, a higher value crop. The cost of land that is considered here is not that for the factory site, but the much larger area that was previously used for cotton cultivation. This land cost must be included as part of the cost of sugar cane supplied to the mill. Here the opportunity cost of the land is the return per acre at world prices if farmers had continued to grow cotton. This return is the difference between the value of cotton output per acre minus all purchased inputs, such as fertilizer and pesticide, minus also an allowance for the costs of family labour, with all items converted from domestic to world prices. This is shown in Table 5.2.

Table 5.2 Estimated returns to land at world prices

	Domestic Market prices Rs. per acre	*CF*	*World Prices Rs. per acre*
Output			
Cotton	56.0	1.25	70.0
Inputs			
Family labour	20.0	1.25	25.0
Fertilizer	5.5	0.95	5.2
Pesticide	5.5	0.95	5.0
Bullocks	11.0	0.80	8.8
Water	5.5	0.80	4.4
Net Return	8.5		21.6

In this example cotton and the alternative export crops that farmers might grow have border parity prices 25 per cent above prices paid to farmers (CF = 1.25).[8] Fertilizer and pesticides are imported at low import duties with conversion factors of 0.95. Bullocks and water are non-traded items, which for lack of data are revalued to world prices by the ACF of 0.80. The opportunity cost to the economy per acre of land used for cotton cultivation is Rs.22 at world prices. This must be included in the cost of cane cultivation, since only if the benefits from the sugar mill are sufficient to cover all costs to the economy, including those generated by the diversion of the land to cane cultivation, will the project be justified. The opportunity cost of the land calculated in this way need bear no direct relation to its market purchase or rental value.

THE DISCOUNT RATE – ALTERNATIVE APPROACHES

Capital has several meanings – as physical assets, as a social relationship between workers and employers, and as investment funds. Here capital is discussed in this latter sense, so that the market for capital is one for funds and the market price is the interest rate. In a perfectly competitive capital market, the interest rate will equal both the rate of return on an additional project (the marginal return on capital) and the income savers require to compensate them for foregoing immediate consumption (savers' time preference). At this equilibrium the level of savings and investment is optimal in that no further saving is justified, and all projects that are viable can attract finance.

It is well known that capital markets do not function in this way. They are often fragmented with different borrowers facing different rates of interest and access to credit, only partially explained by levels of risk. In some countries government intervention to control interest rates has been significant, aimed particularly at keeping down the cost of borrowing to priority sectors. Furthermore, decisions of private savers have often generated savings levels that are clearly inadequate in relation to planned government targets. Even where capital markets have been decontrolled and rates of interest allowed to rise in line with the demand for funds, this does not guarantee that the resulting rates will equal the marginal return on capital, since demand for funds is based on expectations of financial not economic returns.

The conventional discount rate for economic analysis focuses on the use of investment funds by projects and measures their decline in value over time. Apart from practical problems of estimation there are also confusions as to what should constitute the basis for the discount rate. In principle, the discount rate reflects the opportunity cost of committing investment funds to a new project, however, there can be different opportunity costs depending on the sources of the funds and how their use on a new project affects other activities. Assuming that one is considering the discount rate for the public sector one can identify three main scenarios.

(a) Where the public investment budget is fixed over a given time period. This requires that the discount rate be a rationing device to screen government projects competing for limited funds. The opportunity cost of funds will be the return on the marginal project – that is the least attractive project for which funds are available. Any new investment must earn a return at least as great as this to justify its selection over that of the marginal project. This means that the discount rate will be given by the marginal rate of return in the public sector from the range of available government projects; in a world price analysis this return must be at world prices.

(b) Where the total investment of the economy is fixed over a given time period, but the government investment budget can be expanded by taxation or borrowing from the private sector. Here an additional government project will displace a marginal private, not public sector investment, and the opportunity cost of the funds will be the return that could have been obtained in the private sector, again at world prices.

(c) Where the supply of funds for investment is flexible, so that the investment budget can be expanded by drawing on additional domestic or foreign savings. Here the opportunity cost will be the cost of the supply of funds, normally interpreted as a real rate of interest, the nominal rate adjusted for inflation. Where both foreign and domestic savings are involved in the finance of additional projects, the discount rate will be a weighted average of two real interest rates, relating to these different sources.

Further complications are possible; for example, governments may be able to finance additional investment through a combination of reducing private investment and raising domestic savings. Alternatively, a few developing countries may have sufficient funds to contemplate overseas investment, so that external returns on this may define opportunity cost. However cases (a), (b) and (c) represent the main possible alternatives, each providing a different basis for the estimation of the discount rate. The rates calculated under each approach need not be equal.

More formally where case (a) is involved *r*, the discount rate is

$$r = q.CF_q \tag{5.6}$$

where q is the return on the marginal public sector project at domestic prices, and CF_q is the conversion factor required to express this return at world prices.[9]

For case (b) the expression for *r* remains the same except that *q* now refers to marginal private sector investment.

For case (c) *r* is given as a real rate of interest so that

$$r = a_1 i_1 + a_2 i_2 \tag{5.7}$$

where *i* refers to a real interest rate and 1 and 2 are foreign and domestic rates respectively, and a_1 and a_2 are the shares of foreign and domestic savings in the finance of additional investment.[10]

CONCLUSION

This discussion has focused on how all project outputs and inputs can be valued at world prices: where non-traded inputs, domestic labour and land are involved there will be no direct world price, but an equivalent world market value can be derived by valuing all costs of production, in the case of non-traded inputs, and output foregone, in the case of labour and land, at world prices. These adjustment allow estimates of the full -direct plus indirect -- foreign exchange effects of projects. Table 5.3 summarises the adjustments noted in this chapter.

Table 5.3 Use of world prices

Project item	Treatment
Traded goods	Valued at border parity prices – border price plus or minus adjustment for costs of transport and distribution, where the latter are also valued at world prices.
Non-traded inputs	Where these can be increased to meet the needs of new projects valued at unit costs of additional production with all cost items expressed at world prices. Where these are in fixed supply priced at their value to users converted to world prices by an aggregate conversion factor for consumption or the ACF.
Labour	Where workers in excess supply valued at output foregone elsewhere as a result of their new employment on a project, with this output valued at world prices. Where workers in excess demand valued at their market wage adjusted to world prices by an aggregate conversion factor like the ACF. Where foreign workers are involved remittances are a direct foreign exchange cost, and local expenditure converted to world prices by a consumption conversion factor.
Land	Opportunity cost defined as net returns from land in alternative use with returns measured at world prices.
Discount rate	Specified as opportunity cost of investment funds reflecting either returns available on alternative investment, where returns measured at world prices, or cost of additional borrowing from domestic or foreign sources.

The project NPV will show the impact of these effects on the balance of payments, so that any project with a positive NPV will make a positive contribution to foreign exchange earning. To illustrate the procedure in more detail the appendix to this chapter gives a project case study analysed in the world price system.

APPENDIX 5.1 CASE STUDY POLYESTER STAPLE FIBRE PLANT

The Project

A textile producing country decides to establish a polyester staple fibre (PSF) plant in order to produce PSF for blending with raw cotton. Previously, all PSF used in the country had to be imported. The project will therefore save the foreign exchange which would otherwise have to be spent on imports of PSF. The project will also use up considerable foreign exchange, since all the machinery and the main raw materials, the chemical products ethylene glycol (EG) and terephtalic acid (TPA) will be imported.

Most imports into the country are subject to import duties. PSF imports have a 60 per cent duty, whilst EG and TPA have duties of 25 per cent and 20 per cent, respectively. All machinery imports are allowed duty-free as a concession for this project. The domestic producers of PSF plan to charge a price of Rs.7.5 per lb, since although this is above the current cif price of PSF, it is less than the landed price (cif plus import duty), and will make domestic production price competitive with imported supplies. Since the new project is nearer to the textile factories that buy PSF than is the port, there is a small cost saving in moving local supplies of PSF to the market as compared with moving PSF imports (see Table 5A.1).

Table 5A.1 Market prices of key traded goods

	PSF Rs/lb	
Import price (at OER)	5.0	
Transport cost		
– from project to users of domestic PSF	0.15	
– from port to users of imported PSF	0.22	
Distribution cost		
– from project to users of domestic PSF	0.05	
– from port to users of imported PSF	0.10	
Project selling price of PSF	7.50	
	TPA Rs/lb	*EG Rs/lb*
Import price (at OER)	2.40	2.70
Import duty	0.40	0.68

(Table 5A.1 continued)	*TPA* *Rs/lb*	*EG* *Rs/lb*
Transport Cost		
– from port to project	0.10	0.10
Distribution cost		
– from port to project	0.10	0.10
Price to project	3.08	3.58

The main local resources involved with the project will be in the construction element of capital costs and the electricity element in operating costs. There is a number of other relatively minor items in operating costs which involve local resources; these are transport and distribution costs and packing materials. Labour in operations is all skilled and a small part of total costs.

The project will take four years to construct and will commence production in Year 4. The working life of the project is expected to be twelve years with a residual value at the end of this period, which includes both the resale value of plant and buildings and inventories left at the end of production and sold in the final year.

Table 5A.2 sets out the resource statement for the project at market prices. The first column gives the present value of all costs and benefits at 10 per cent, which is taken as the discount rate for shadow price analysis. At domestic market prices the IRR is approximately 19 per cent.

Shadow Price Adjustments

In estimating CFs for items specific to this project, the convention used is that the results are given to three decimal places to minimize rounding errors. However, estimates from national average data, such as the ACF and CFs for transport, distribution, electricity and labour, are given only as approximate rounded figures.

ACF

In the economy import controls in the form of quotas and licences are important, and these keep domestic prices above world prices for similar goods. A research study estimates the ACF as a weighted average of the main sectoral CFs (see Table 5A.3).

The ACF is used for the minor non-traded items other capital costs, packing materials and other minor inputs, for which more details are not available.

Table 5A.2 Resource statement for PSF project (market prices)

Rs million	*Present Value at 10%*	*Year*	*0*	*1*	*2*	*3*	*4*	*5*	*6*	*7*	*8*	*9*	*10*	*11*	*12*	*13*	*14*	*15*
Benefits																		
1. Sales revenue	1404.38							232.9	266.1	299.4	299.4	299.4	299.4	299.4	299.4	299.4	299.4	299.4
PSF							199.5											
Costs																		
1. Investment																		
Equipment	201.96		38.7	116.2	87.1													(60.0)
Construction	43.53		4.9	14.7	11.0	33.0												(36.0)
Others	13.95		2.5	7.6	5.5													
2. Working capital																		
PSF	24.27						39.9	6.7	6.7	6.7								(60.0)
TPA	10.88						17.9	3.0	3.0	3.0								(26.9)
EG	4.78						7.9	1.3	1.3	1.3								(11.8)
3. Operating costs																		
TPA	503.41						71.6	83.5	95.4	107.3	107.3	107.3	107.3	107.3	107.3	107.3	107.3	107.3
EG	220.43						31.3	36.5	41.8	47.0	47.0	47.0	47.0	47.0	47.0	47.0	47.0	47.0
Electricity	80.10						12.5	13.9	15.3	16.7	16.7	16.7	16.7	16.7	16.7	16.7	16.7	16.7
Skilled labour	18.29						2.6	3.0	3.5	3.9	3.9	3.9	3.9	3.9	3.9	3.9	3.9	3.9
Packing materials and others	31.47						4.5	5.2	6.0	6.7	6.7	6.7	6.7	6.7	6.7	6.7	6.7	6.7
Net resource flow	251.31		(46.1)	(138.5)	(103.6)	(33.0)	11.3	79.8	93.1	106.8	117.8	117.8	117.8	117.8	117.8	117.8	117.8	312.5

Note
Figures in brackets are negative; negative costs under Investment and Working capital are terminal values.

Table 5A.3 Estimated ACF

Sector	*CF*	*Share in GDP*	*Weighted average*
Manufacturing	0.86	0.150	0.129
Domestic Agriculture	0.95	0.300	0.285
Export Agriculture	1.20	0.150	0.180
Transport	0.80	0.046	0.037
Distribution	0.68	0.154	0.105
Construction	0.74	0.104	0.077
Electricity	0.82	0.051	0.042
Other Activities	1.00	0.045	0.045
		1.000	0.900

Note
ACF = 0.900

Labour

There is considerable underemployment in the economy. All unskilled workers are drawn from rural areas, and a conversion factor for unskilled labour at world prices of 0.50 is used in the valuation of non-traded inputs. Chapter 5 gives an illustration of how a labour conversion factor of 0.50 might be calculated. In this project unskilled labour is employed in the non-traded inputs used by the project, such as construction and electricity. All the workers employed on the project itself are treated as skilled. Following the procedure discussed in Chapter 5 skilled labour is revalued by the ACF of 0.90.

Traded Items

The main traded goods associated with the project are PSF, and the raw materials TPA and EG. Their CFs are shown in Table 5A.4. The procedure to estimate these is to break down the domestic market price to the project of each commodity into different components and to revalue each of these separately at world prices. The final shadow price is the total at world prices of the different components, and the ratio of this shadow price to the domestic price is the CF for the commodity.

For the output PSF, the cif price is the main element of the shadow price. It is already at world prices so it has a CF of 1.0. The difference between the transport and distribution costs in moving imports of PSF to the market, and the costs involved in moving the new domestic supplies of PSF from the project to the market, is a net saving of Rs0.12 per lb. This must be

Table 5A.4 Conversion factors for main traded commodities

Output – PSF *Rs/lb*	*Domestic market price*	*CF*	*Shadow price (world price numeraire)*
cif price	5.00	1.0	5.000
Transport cost saving	0.07	0.80	0.056
Distribution cost saving	0.05	0.68	0.034
Profit margin[a]	2.38	0	0
Price to project	7.50		5.090
PSF conversion factor = $\frac{5.090}{7.500} = 0.679$			
Inputs (1) *TPA*			
cif price	2.40	1.00	2.400
Import duty	0.48	0	0
Transport cost port to project	0.10	0.80	0.080
Distribution cost port to project	0.10	0.68	0.068
Price to project	3.08		2.548
TPA conversion factor = $\frac{2.548}{3.080} = 0.827$			
(2) *EG*			
cif price	2.70	1.0	2.700
Import duty	0.68	0	0
Transport cost port to project	0.10	0.80	0.080
Distribution cost port to project	0.10	0.68	0.068
Price to project	3.58		2.848
EG conversion factor = $\frac{2.848}{3.580} = 0.796$			

Note
[a] treated as surplus profit

converted to world prices, and separate conversion factors of 0.80 and 0.68 are available for the non-traded activities of transport and distribution, respectively. The margin between the cif price plus these cost savings and the price to be charged by the project is treated as surplus profits going to the project owners; as transfer payments surplus profits have a CF of zero. For the two traded inputs TPA and EG the procedure is identical. The cif price has a CF of 1.0, since it is already at world prices. The import duty has a CF of zero as a transfer payment. The costs of transport and distribution from the port to the project are expressed at world prices by the respective conversion factors of 0.80 and 0.68.

The other significant traded item is the equipment part of the capital costs of the project. The CF for equipment is close to one, since it is all imported duty free. The cost of equipment to the project is 93 per cent foreign exchange cost plus 5 per cent transport and 2 per cent distribution from the port. The full CF for equipment is therefore 0.984 (0.93 × 1.0 + 0.05 × 0.8 + 0.02 × 0.68).

Non-Traded Items

Non-traded items can be discussed in two groups. First, there are those minor costs which are converted to world prices using the ACF. These are other capital costs, packing materials and other inputs (Table 5A.5).

Table 5A.5 Construction conversion factor

	Share of costs at domestic *market prices*	*CF*	*Weighted average CF*
Imported materials	0.16	0.791	0.127
Cement	0.06	0.870	0.052
Local materials	0.12	0.900	0.108
Labour			
Skilled	0.05	0.900	0.045
Unskilled	0.25	0.500	0.125
Capital costs			
Equipment	0.25	0.940	0.235
Others	0.05	0.900	0.045
Transfers			
Taxes	0.02	0.000	0.000
Surplus Profits	0.04	0.000	0.000
	1.00		0.737

Note
CF for Construction = 0.737

Second, there are the more important non-traded costs, the construction element of capital cost and the electricity input in operating cost, which are be examined in more detail. These can be interpreted as non-traded inputs where supply expands to meet the demand of the project, so their cost of production must be revalued at world prices.

For electricity the CF of 0.83, derived in the example in Table 5.1 is used. This can be seen as a national average CF for different sources of electricity supply. For construction the CF used here is based on the structure of construction cost of the PSF project (see Table 5A.5).

Imported materials used in construction have a CF of 0.791. Average import tariffs on construction materials are 20 per cent, and transport and distribution costs from port to construction sites are approximately 5.0 and 7.5 per cent respectively of the cost of these materials. Each unit cost of imported materials is therefore composed as shown in Table 5A.6, and using the appropriate conversion factors for each of these items gives a weighted average of 0.791.

Table 5A.6 Cost composition of imported materials

	Share of cost	*CF*	*Weighted average*
cif price	0.700	1.00	0.700
Import tariff	0.175	0.00	0.000
Transport cost	0.050	0.80	0.040
Distribution cost	0.075	0.68	0.051
	1.000		0.791

Cement, although locally supplied to the project, is also imported. Local production is protected by import tariffs of 20 per cent, but the full degree of protection is not used. On average domestic cement prices are 15 per cent above import prices, whilst the transport and distribution costs in moving imported cement to construction sites are approximately the same as those for moving local cement. The CF for cement is therefore 1.00/1.15 or 0.87.

Local materials and other capital costs in construction are treated as minor non-traded inputs and converted at the ACF of 0.90. Skilled labour is also converted at the ACF, whilst for unskilled labour a CF of 0.50 is used.

The equipment element of construction capital costs is imported at a low average import tariff of 5.3 per cent of the cif price. Transport and distribution costs are 3 per cent and 2 per cent respectively of the total cost of equipment to construction enterprises. Each unit cost of equipment is therefore composed as shown in Table 5A.7, and using the appropriate conversion factors the overall conversion factor for equipment is 0.940.

Table 5A.7 Cost composition of improved equipment

	Share of cost	*CF*	*Weighted average*
cif price	0.902	1.00	0.902
Import duty	0.048	0.00	0.000
Transport cost	0.030	0.80	0.024
Distribution cost	0.020	0.68	0.014
	1.000		0.940

Finally, all transfers have a zero economic value. The transfers in construction include both taxes and surplus profits that result from the monopoly position of construction firms.

The final result for construction is a CF of 0.737. Although this is a project specific CF, for simplicity it is assumed that it can also be used as national CF for construction cost in general. It is used to value construction in the ACF calculation (Table 5A.3) and the construction element of electricity costs (Table 5A.2).

Analysis of Project at World Prices

With this set of CFs the data on the project at domestic market prices from Table 5A.2 can be converted to world prices (Table 5A.8). The results are shown in Table 5A.8 for a 10 per cent discount rate. The NPV of the project is reduced and is now negative at 10 per cent. At a 10 per cent discount rate, at domestic market prices the BCR is 1.22 and at shadow prices it is 0.98. The IRR has fallen from 19 per cent at domestic market prices to 9 per cent at shadow prices. The project uses only a limited number of local non-traded inputs and has only a weak employment effect, chiefly in the construction sector. It saves foreign exchange on the output side, but uses foreign exchange through its import of raw materials and capital equipment. Profitability at market prices is achieved through protection of output at a rate higher than protection of the inputs used by the project. The economic analysis removes the effect of protection by valuing all traded items at world not protected domestic prices. The resulting CFs are lower for the PSF output than for any of the inputs, so that the benefits of the project are reduced by more than the costs. This means that the project is only attractive financially because of the protection granted by the tariff system. If 10 per cent is an adequate measure of investment returns available elsewhere the project should not be undertaken, since a higher return in foreign exchange could have been obtained by investing elsewhere.

Table 5A.8 Resource statement at shadow prices (world price system) Present values at 10% (Rs million))

	Domestic market prices	*CF*	*Shadow prices (World price numeraire)*
Benefits			
1. Sales Revenue	1404.38	0.679	953.57
Costs			
1. Investment			
Equipment	201.96	0.984	198.73
Construction	43.53	0.737	32.08
Others	13.95	0.900	12.56
2. Working capital			
PSF	24.27	0.679	16.48
TPA	10.88	0.827	9.00
EG	4.78	0.796	3.80
3. Operating			
TPA	503.41	0.827	416.32
EG	220.43	0.796	175.46
Electricity	80.09	0.824	65.99
Skilled labour	18.29	0.900	16.46
Packing materials and others	31.47	0.900	28.32
Net resource flow	251.31		-21.63
IRR	19.0%		9.0%

Further Reading

The seminal statements of the world price system are in Little and Mirrlees (1968) and (1974), with some minor modifications in Squire and van der Tak (1975). Irvin (1978) is a helpful general commentary, and Powers (1981), chapter 1 is another useful introduction. Brent (1990) considers the objectives that can be used to define opportunity costs and adds a fourth objective to the three referred to in this chapter. Linn (1977) and Bruce (1976) illustrate the approach to some of the more important parameters discussed here. Weiss (1978) discusses the role of the ACF in simplified approaches. Schohl (1979) illustrates the calculation of the two versions of the ACF discussed in the text. ODA (1988), chapter 3 introduces the world price system whilst Ray (1984) considers at an advanced level many of the issues raised in this chapter.

6 Domestic Price System of Economic Analysis

The previous chapter discussed how all project outputs and inputs can be valued at world prices to assess their trade opportunity costs. Economic analyses can be carried out using different units of account or numeraire. As with distance, which can be measured in miles or kilometres, the choice of different units makes the same calculation appear different, but provided equal accuracy is used, the results will be directly equivalent. This chapter considers how domestic prices can be used to measure trade opportunity costs, in what we will term a domestic price system. It commences by discussing the conditions under which world and domestic price systems give equivalent results. It then considers the shadow exchange rate, a key parameter in the domestic price system. The detail of how conversion factors for traded and non-traded goods and labour are derived in a domestic price system is discussed, before land and the discount rate are considered briefly. The appendix reworks the PSF case study in a domestic price system.

CHOICE OF PRICE UNITS

The choice of price units in which to express the value of project benefits and costs does not in itself determine the opportunity cost of an item. For example, the production or use of traded goods by a project creates foreign exchange effects that must be valued at world prices. This is common to both systems, however, when domestic prices are the numeraire the world price of these traded goods must be expressed as equivalent to a value in units of domestic prices. This is analogous to the procedure in the world price sytem of converting non-traded goods to an equivalent world price value. Similarly, use of domestic prices as the numeraire does not mean that inevitably domestic market prices define the opportunity cost of non-traded goods. Where such market prices are used it is because they are taken to be a reasonable proxy for the economic value of the good in units of domestic prices.

The difference between a world and domestic price numeraire arises because in most economies the domestic prices at which traded goods are sold differ from their prices on the world market (converted at the official exchange rate) by more than the margin for domestic transport and distribution costs. Taxes, subsidies, quota or licensing controls on foreign trade and monopolisation of markets, all create a divergence between domestic and world prices net of adjustments for transport and distribution. The average divergence provides a simple link between domestic and world price units.

SHADOW EXCHANGE RATE

Generally, the net effect of these measures is to raise domestic prices for traded goods above border parity levels.[1] For example, an import good is priced at US $10, and at the official exchange rate of Rs10 per US $ its price converts to Rs100. However, if domestic prices are the numeraire, allowance must be made for any general divergence between domestic and world prices in the economy. If the average divergence is 40 per cent, and this is applied to the import, Rs100 is raised to Rs140. This adjustment implies that trade taxes and controls will increase the domestic price of the import by the average increase for all traded goods. Addition of the 40 per cent margin is equivalent to valuing the good at an alternative exchange rate of Rs14 per US $. This alternative rate is generally referred to as the shadow exchange rate (SER). When compared with the official rate (OER), the ratio SER/OER gives the conversion factor for foreign exchange. In a domestic price system a SER will be required if the OER does not reflect the full value of additional foreign exchange to the economy.

The average ratio of domestic to world prices has a direct parallel with the ACF in a world price system. The latter is a ratio of world to domestic prices for a basket of goods. Where the same goods are included in the comparison and the same weights are used, the ACF will be the inverse of the CF for foreign exchange, so that

$$\frac{1}{ACF} = \frac{SER}{OER}$$

Foreign exchange is valuable not in itself, but because of the goods that it makes available to the economy. Theoretically, therefore, additional foreign exchange generated by projects should be valued on the basis of the marginal bundle of goods that are made available. However, in practice tracing these additional goods will be highly complex. Foreign exchange generated by a project can lead to more consumption of tradeables, more imports or more domestic use of potential exports. Less foreign exchange as a result of a project's imports may lead to greater exports, where other producers expand production to cover the shortfall, or to lower imports by others. Also a project's impact on supply and demand in the foreign exchange market may be sufficient to alter the exchange rate, causing price effects that change both imports and exports.

In attempting to identify the goods affected by the availability of additional foreign exchange, a common simplification is to assume that a good's existing share in foreign trade can be used to indicate its future share. This combined with the assumption that the difference between domestic and world prices for traded goods is determined solely by taxes and subsidies on foreign trade, allows equation (5.3) for the ACF to be used for the CF for foreign exchange.

Now the CF for foreign exchange is

$$\frac{SER}{OER} = \frac{(M + T_m - S_m) + (X + S_x - T_x)}{(M + X)} \tag{6.1}$$

where $SER/OER = \dfrac{1}{ACF}$

Theoretically, this is an approximation for the reasons given in Chapter 5. A more rigorous treatment allows for the effect of quantitative trade controls on domestic prices and uses marginal not average shares in trade as weights. Where a direct comparison between domestic and world prices is used the conversion factor for foreign exchange becomes

$$\frac{SER}{OER} = \sum_i a_i.\frac{DP_i}{WP_i} + \sum_j a_j.\frac{DP_j}{WP_j} \tag{6.2}$$

where
i and j are import and export goods, respectively,
a_i is the share of import i and a_j is the share of export j in additional use of foreign exchange,
DP_i and DP_j are the domestic market prices of i and j at the border,
and WP_i and WP_j are the border prices of i and j converted into local currency at the *OER*.

Here the effect of quotas and other direct controls will be included in the domestic prices of i and j, and if project demand leads to a change in the exchange rate trade elasticities can be used to estimate how this will affect the composition of additional trade.[2]

The procedure can be illustrated with a numerical example. Trade for an economy is composed of only three goods, machines and wheat which are imported, and rice which is exported. The share of these goods in additional foreign trade is determined by their trade elasticities.[3] A price survey has been carried out to identify domestic prices for these goods and these are compared with their world prices in Table 6.1. The CF for foreign exchange is derived as the weighted average price ratio of 1.24.

The interpretation of this example is that where a project's additional demand for foreign exchange causes a rise in the rupee/US dollar exchange rate (a devaluation of the rupee), this will lead

Table 6.1 Illustration of CF for foreign exchange

Commodities	*Total value US $ million*	*Weights*	*Domestic price Rs*	*World price Rs*	*Price ratio*
Rice	20	0.33	1200	1000	1.10
Wheat	16	0.12	1440	1200	1.20
Machines	14	0.55	2000	1500	1.33
SER/OER				weighted average	1.24

Note
OER = Rs 10/US $

to less imports and more exports. Domestic users and consumers will forego imports of wheat and machines because they are now more expensive, and also forego consumption of rice since more is now shifted to the export market where sales are more profitable with the exchange rate change. For the weights given in Table 6.1 the weighted average ratio of domestic to world prices for this bundle of goods is 1.24. If domestic market prices are used as a measure of the worth of these goods, this implies that on average foreign exchange is 24 per cent more valuable than the official exchange rate. In this case, with the OER Rs10 per US dollar, the SER is Rs12.4.

The shadow exchange rate is often used with a measure of economic efficiency that compares the net foreign exchange effect of a project with the domestic resources in terms of labour and non-traded goods, required to generate this foreign exchange. This indicator, termed the Domestic Resource Cost ratio is discussed in Appendix 6.2.

EQUIVALENCE OF WORLD AND DOMESTIC PRICE SYSTEMS

In a domestic price system the role of the shadow price of foreign exchange is to raise the value of traded relative to non-traded goods, since the world price of all traded items is converted into local currency at the SER. Whenever on average domestic prices exceed world prices, the SER will be above the OER, and there will be a positive premium on foreign exchange given as (SER/OER – 1.0) per cent. The equivalent adjustment in the world price system is to reduce the value of non-traded relative to traded goods by converting non-traded goods from domestic prices into world price equivalents by a CF of below 1.0.

Provided identical assumptions are adopted both systems give equivalent results. In the simplest case, a world price analysis converts all domestic prices for non-traded goods into world price equivalents, assuming that the economy-wide ratio of world to domestic prices (ACF) holds for each non-traded item. This is directly comparable with the procedure in a domestic price system of valuing these goods at their domestic market prices, but converting all world prices for traded goods into local currency at the SER, derived as an economy-wide ratio of domestic to world prices.

Chapter 4 illustrates this procedure for the simplified example involving traded output produced by two inputs, one traded and the other non-traded. The average ratio of domestic to world prices is 1.40 implying a premium on foreign exchange of 40 per cent, and an ACF of 0.714 (1 / 1.4). In the domestic price system the non-traded input is valued at Sh.600, whilst in the world price analysis this is converted by 0.714 to obtain its world price equivalent of Sh.428.6. This treatment is equivalent in both systems, and the net revenues are directly comparable since Sh.321 × 1.40 = Sh.450. Equivalence between the two systems does not rest on this simple case, however. Whenever the same level of detail and the same assumptions are adopted, the results will be comparable.

A more rigorous approach is to estimate a specific CF for each non-traded item as is illustrated for electricity in Chapter 5. This can be applied in both systems, by breaking down each non-traded activity into its costs of production, and valuing these at shadow prices in either world or domestic price units. Equivalence between the two systems requires that the specific CF in the domestic price system is greater than that in a world price system by the margin given by SER/OER.

The more detailed application of both approaches can be illustrated by modifying the example from Chapter 4. Now in the world price system the non-traded input priced at Sh.600 is converted using a specific CF of 0.80. This CF implies that opportunity costs of production for this input measured in world price units are 80 per cent of its domestic price. The equivalent treatment in a domestic price system is to use a CF for this input of 1.12 (0.8 × 1.40), which implies that opportunity costs of production in domestic price units are 12 per cent above the domestic market price. Table 6.2 gives the revised calculation for the example with this new treatment for the non-traded input.

Now the net benefits differ from those in the example in Chapter 4. Again, they are directly equivalent in both systems since the net benefits in domestic price units exceed those in world price units by a 40 per cent margin given by the ratio SER/OER (Sh.378 = Sh.270 × 1.40). Since different price units are involved the absolute size of the NPV will differ between the systems. However, the IRR, as a

Table 6.2 Numerical example in world and domestic price systems

	World price system	*Domestic price system*
Output		
Traded good	US$100 × 15 = Sh.1500	US$100 × 15 × 1.40 = Sh.2100
Inputs		
Traded good	US$50 × 15 = Sh.750	US$50 × 15 × 1.40 = Sh.1050
Non-traded goods	Sh.600 × 0.80 = Sh.480	Sh.600 × 1.12 = Sh.672
Net benefit	Sh.270	Sh.378

Note
OER = Sh.15 per US $
SER = Sh.21 per US $
SER/OER = 1.40

ratio of benefits to costs, is the same for both price units and project ranking by NPVs will also be the same in both systems.

Formally, when identical assumptions are made in both systems the project decision will be the same since

$$NPV_{DP} > 0, \text{ when } NPV_{WP} > 0$$

and $NPV_{DP} = NPV_{WP} \times CF_F$

where
NPV_{DP} is net present value at domestic prices
NPV_{WP} is net present value at world prices
and
CF_F is the conversion factor for foreign exchange given by

$$\frac{SER}{OER}$$

This can be illustrated in Figure 6.1 using *NPV* curves. Here at discount rate *r*, $NPV_{DP} = NPV_{WP} = 0$. The NPV curve at domestic prices always exceeds the curve at world prices by the same proportion given by CF_F. Although logically there is no reason why one system should be used with more rigour than the other, in practice it is the domestic price system that tends to be associated with more approximations. A key short cut is in the treatment of some non-traded goods where their domestic market price is used as their shadow price. Use or production of such goods implicitly is taken as having a zero foreign exchange effect. The more aproximate is the analysis the greater the number of non-traded items treated in this way. Justification for a simpler treatment is that it may be difficult to estimate an accurate foreign exchange equivalent for many non-traded items, and that a more detailed analysis will only be required for those that are significant in their impact on project benefits and costs. Simplification in the treatment of non-traded goods is discussed further in the next section, and the appendix illustrates two alternative cases in relation to the PSF case study.

On the other hand, where a full analysis is applied in both systems, so that all project effects are converted into foreign exchange equivalents, the domestic price system involves an extra step of applying the CF for foreign exchange. In other words, if all

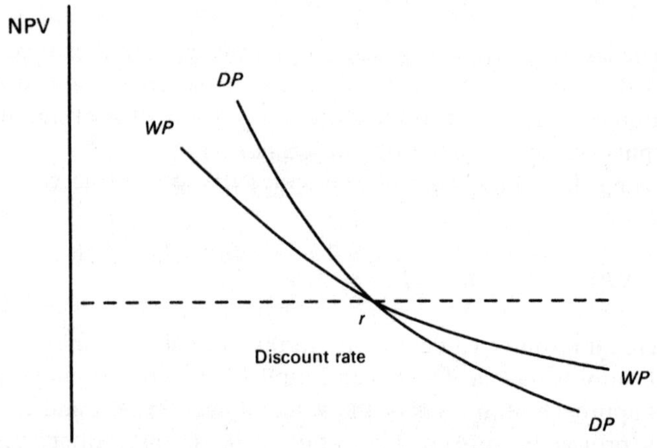

Figure 6.1 Equivalence of world and domestic price systems

project benefits and costs are expressed at world prices it does not matter what exchange rate is used to convert these to local currency, since the choice of exchange rate will affect the absolute, but not the relative size of benefits and costs. Project ranking will be unaffected by the exchange rate, so that application of the SER rather than the OER adds no further information to that contained in a world price calculation.

APPROXIMATIONS IN BOTH SYSTEMS

Approximations can be illustrated more formally by looking at project resource statements from a different point of view. Up to now the focus has been on deriving conversion factors for specific items, such as a traded output (like PSF), or a non-traded input (like electricity). However, one can also break down project statements into different resource categories. A classification used commonly is

(a) Foreign exchange (F)
(b) Domestic resources (N)
(c) Unskilled labour (LU)
(d) Skilled labour (LS)
(e) Transfer payments (T)

The last three are self-explanatory, whilst foreign exchange covers traded goods (valued at world prices at the OER), and domestic resources covers non-traded goods as both project inputs and outputs (valued at domestic market prices).

Using the symbols given above the NPV of a project at market prices can be expressed as

$$NPV = F + N + LU + LS + T$$

where all resource categories are in present values at market prices, and outputs have a positive and inputs a negative sign. To pursue this approach requires that the value of each benefit and cost item of a project be broken down into these resource categories. The appendix to this chapter illustrates the procedure, and here a simple example only is given.

A project input is imported and its domestic price paid by the project is 100, comprised as follows

cif price	60
import tariff	30
transport and distribution	10
	100

Therefore if the total cost of the input at market prices is Rs10 000 (discounted as a present value), 60 per cent of this cost will be entered under F as a foreign exchange cost, 30 per cent under T as a tax, and 10 per cent under D as a non-traded domestic cost covering transport and distribution.

Under both price systems the economic net present value (ENPV) of a project can be found by applying conversion factors to the different resource categories. Therefore

$$ENPV = F.CF_F + N.CF_N + LU.CF_{LU} + LS.CF_{LS} \qquad (6.3)$$

CF_F, CF_N, CF_{LU} and CF_{LS} are conversion factors for foreign exchange, non-traded goods, unskilled and skilled labour respectively. Since transfers have a CF of zero, T is not included in ENPV.

In a world price system, since world prices are converted at the official exchange rate and foreign exchange is the numeraire, $CF_F =$ 1.0. All non-traded items must be expressed as a foreign exchange value at world prices. Ideally, this should involve specific conversion factors for individual non-traded items, so that in equation (6.3) CF_N can be thought of as a set of different conversion factors.

If conversion factors are available for all non-traded goods, this has the important result that each non-traded item associated with a project can be broken down into its F, N, LU, LS, and T components. In turn the N items can themselves be decomposed until the market price of each non-traded good is totally decomposed into F, LU, LS, T; that is foreign exchange, labour and transfers. These can be added to the direct foreign exchange and labour costs of the project so that ENPV can be rewritten as

$$ENPV = F^1.CF_F + LU^1.CF_{LU} + LS^1.CF_{LS} \qquad (6.4)$$

Now the terms F^1, LU^1, and LS^1 differ from their values in (6.3) since N has been fully decomposed, and its F, LU, and LS

components added (or subtracted where N is negative) to their original values. Where N refers to outputs, the F, LU and LS elements of N must be added to the original values as benefits. For non-traded inputs the F, LU and LS elements of N must be subtracted from the original values as costs.

In practice this level of detail is rarely applied to individual projects. There will be some non-traded items for which specific information is not available. For consistency these must still be expressed at world prices and the simplest way to do this is by the ACF. In this modified version of the world price system

$$ENPV = F^{11}.CF_F + LU^{11}.CF_{LU} + LS^{11}.CF_{LS} + N^1.ACF \quad (6.5)$$

where N^1 covers non-traded goods for which it is not possible to do a further cost decomposition. These are termed N^1 to indicate that they are normally less than the total non-traded goods (N) involved with a project. The larger is the total value of N^1 the more approximate will be the analysis. Goods under N^1 can cover inputs used directly by a project (for example packing materials and other costs in the PSF case study), or indirectly as inputs into non-traded inputs used by a project (for example local materials used in construction for the PSF project). Non-traded project outputs will not normally be included in N^1, since at the least they can be decomposed using an aggregate conversion factor for consumption.

In equation (6.5) the F, LU and LS components are written as F^{11}, LU^{11} and LS^{11} to denote that where N is not fully decomposed these will differ from where it is fully decomposed (as in equation 6.4).

Precisely analogous steps can be followed in a domestic price system using the letters DP to refer to a domestic price analysis.

$$DPENPV = F.CF_F + N.DPCF_N + LU.DPCF_{LU} + LS.DPCF_{LS} \quad (6.6)$$

Here $CF_F = SER/OER$

and $DPENPV$, $DPCF_N$, $DPCF_{LU}$ and $DPCF_{LS}$ are domestic price economic net present value, and domestic price conversion factors for non-traded goods, unskilled labour and skilled labour, respectively.

Again, in a full analysis where all non-traded items have individual conversion factors, the non-traded items N can be fully decomposed into their F, LU, LS and T components, so that $ENPV^1$ becomes

$$DPENPV = F^1.CF_F + LU^1.DPCF_{LU} + LS^1.DPCF_{LS} \quad (6.7)$$

where now F^1, LU^1 and LS^1 differ from their value in (6.6) due to the decomposition of N.

However, where N cannot be fully decomposed there will be a residual term N^1. As domestic prices are the unit, and N^1 is already at domestic market prices, there is no need for further adjustment provided the assumption can be made that these prices are a proxy for value in domestic price units. The conversion factor for N^1 is therefore 1.0, ($DPCF_N = 1.0$) and $DPENPV$ becomes

$$DPENPV = F^{11}.CF_F + LU^{11}.DPCF_{LU} + LS^{11}.DPCF_{LS} + N^1.DPCF_N \quad (6.8)$$

where F^{11}, LU^{11} and LS^{11} are as in equation (6.5), and $DPCF_N = 1.0$.

Again, where in both systems N^1 covers exactly the same goods and

$$\frac{SER}{OER} = \frac{1}{ACF}$$

then the direct equivalence, $ENPV \times SER/OER = DPENPV$ holds.

However, differences will arise where the residual category N^1 is not the same in both systems. The PSF case study in the appendix to this chapter examines two alternatives where N^1 covers different shares of non-traded costs. In a domestic price system inclusion of non-traded items under N^1 implicitly gives them a zero foreign exchange content. None the less, where non-traded items are minor their classification under N^1 will not reduce the accuracy of the results significantly.

TRADED GOODS IN A DOMESTIC PRICE SYSTEM

Having noted the formal equivalence of the world and domestic price systems the following two sections discuss the derivation of CFs for traded and non-traded goods in a domestic price system.

For traded good i, using the letters DP to refer to a domestic price system

$$DPSP_i = (WP_i \times OER) \times CF_F + (T_i.DPCF_T + D_i.DPCF_D) \quad (6.9)$$

where

$DPSP_i$ is the shadow price of i to a project, in a domestic price system,
WP_i is its border price,
OER is the official exchange rate,
CF_F is the conversion factor for foreign exchange (SER/OER)
T_i and D_i are the transport and distribution costs per unit of i from port to project at domestic prices
$DPCF_T$ and $DPCF_D$ are CFs for transport and distribution in a domestic price system.

Since CF_F = SER/OER, (6.9) can be expressed as

$$DPSP_i = (WP_i \times SER) + (T_i.DPCF_T + D_i.DPCF_D) \quad (6.10)$$

This means that for i, the shadow price is the world price converted at the shadow exchange rate, plus or minus transport and distribution costs per unit at shadow prices in domestic price units. The derivation of CFs for transport and distribution in a domestic price system is discussed below under non-traded inputs.

The relevant CF for i is

$$DPCF_i = \frac{DPSP_i}{DP_i} \quad (6.11)$$

where DP_i is the domestic market price of i to the project and $DPCF_i$ is the conversion factor in a domestic price system.

NON-TRADED GOODS IN A DOMESTIC PRICE SYSTEM

Theoretically, as in a world price system non-traded inputs in variable supply are again valued at long-run marginal costs of production, except that now costs are in domestic not world price units. The same equation (5.2) from the world price analysis holds so that for a non-traded project input j

$$DPSP_j = \sum_i a_{ij}.P_i.DPCF_i + \sum_n a_{nj}.P_n\ DPCF_n + \sum_L a_{Lj}.W_L\ .DPCF_L \quad (6.12)$$

where all terms are as in equation (5.2), except that $DPCF_i$ and $DPCF_N$ and $DPCF_L$ now refer to CFs in a domestic price system. The new conversion factor for j is

$$DPCF_j = \frac{DPSP_j}{DP_j} \quad (6.13)$$

In the most approximate approach domestic market prices of non-traded activities are used as proxies for their shadow prices ($DPCF_j = 1.0$). In a world price system this is equivalent to using the ACF to convert such items to world prices. Alternatively, in a more detailed approach shadow prices will be used to revalue some or all inputs in the non-traded activity.

Differing levels of detail can be illustrated for the electricity example discussed in Chapter 5. Two CFs for electricity in a domestic price system are shown in Table 6.3. Case (1) is the simpler approach and here only the direct imports, fuels and equipment are treated as foreign exchange costs. No foreign exchange element is identified in local materials and buildings, even though the former are importable and their use in electricity will force others to import, and the latter have some foreign exchange element in their construction. Some foreign exchange is incorporated in unskilled labour's output foregone for workers employed directly in the electricity sector, but the unskilled labour content in building costs is not allowed for. The SER used to convert all world prices to local currency is approximately 11 per cent above the OER, and the CF for foreign exchange (SER/OER) is 1.111.[4]

CFs for the traded items fuel and equipment are derived by disaggregating their domestic market prices into cif price, domestic transport and distribution, and import tariffs. The cif component is multiplied by the CF for foreign exchange of 1.111. Domestic transport and distribution costs have their own CFs of 0.888, and 0.755 respectively.

In Case (1) local materials and buildings are not decomposed into traded and labour costs, but are treated as non-traded inputs whose shadow and domestic market prices are equal. Also for skilled

Table 6.3 Electricity conversion factor-domestic price system

	Domestic market prices *Rs/KWH*	*CF*	*Case (1) Shadow Prices Domestic price Numeraire Rs/KWH*	*CF*	*Case (2) Shadow Prices Domestic price Numeraire Rs/KWH*
Operating costs					
Fuel	30.00	1.068[a]	32.04	1.068	32.04
Local materials	60.00	1.000	60.00	0.744[b]	44.64
Labour					
Skilled	80.00	1.000	80.00	1.000	80.00
Unskilled	10.00	0.555[c]	5.55	0.555[c]	5.55
Capital costs					
Equipment	60.00	1.055[d]	63.30	1.055[d]	63.30
Buildings	60.00	1.000	60.00	0.819[e]	49.14
	300.00		300.89		274.67

CF for Electricity, Case (1)

$$= \frac{300.89}{300.00} = 1.003$$

CF for Electricity, Case (2)

$$= \frac{274.67}{300.00} = 0.915$$

Notes

	Cost breakdown at domestic market prices	*CF*	*Weighted average CF*
a. Fuel			
cif price	0.916	1.111	1.018
transport	0.030	0.888	0.027
distribution	0.030	0.755	0.023
import tariff	0.024	0.000	0.000
domestic price	1.000		1.068
b. Local materials			
cif price	0.611	1.111	0.679
transport	0.040	0.888	0.035
distribution	0.040	0.755	0.030
import tariff	0.309	0.000	0.000
domestic price	1.000		0.744

c. See the following section on labour

Table 6.3 Electricity conversion factor-domestic price system (*cont.*)

	Cost breakdown at domestic market prices	*CF*	*Weighted average CF*
d. Equipment			
cif price	0.913	1.111	1.014
transport	0.025	0.888	0.022
distribution	0.025	0.755	0.019
import tariff	0.037	0.000	0.000
domestic price	1.000		1.055

e. See Appendix 6.1

labour market wages are taken as a proxy for output foregone at domestic prices. A more detailed treatment is given for unskilled labour, allowing for the fact that some of labour's output foregone will be in the form of traded goods (see following section).

The electricity CF in Case (1) is 1.003, implying that in domestic price units the shadow price of electricity almost exactly equals the market price charged for it. However, this case adopts the crude assumption that local materials and building costs have a zero foreign exchange element, which is abandoned in Case (2). Here the local material and building cost elements of electricity are decomposed to allow for their use of traded goods and labour. Local materials are treated as traded goods, and as with fuels and equipment are disaggregated into cif price, transport and distribution, and import tariffs. Buildings are converted by a CF for construction. The derivation of this CF, which follows the same detail as in the world price analysis, is given in the appendix to this chapter.

In Case (2) the CF for electricity is 0.915 implying that the shadow price of electricity at domestic prices is approximately 92 per cent of the electricity tariff actually charged. This second estimate, approximately 8 per cent below that of Case (1), is more accurate because it examines two of the inputs into electricity – local materials and buildings – in more detail. The new adjustment is particularly important for local materials, which have a direct foreign exchange cost as they substitute for imports, and whose world price is well below their protected domestic market price. One can interpret the result of Case (1) as an approximate, and of Case

(2) as a more detailed estimation of the shadow price of electricity. The result of Case (2) is equivalent to that of the world price analysis in Table 5.1, since 0.824 × 1.111 = 0.915.

UNSKILLED LABOUR IN A DOMESTIC PRICE SYSTEM

In principle the treatment of labour is directly comparable in a domestic and a world price system. Labour's shadow wage is again output foregone, but in a domestic system this must be measured in domestic not world price units. The general expression for the shadow wage (equation 5.4) will be relevant again except now there will be a new set of CFs for the different commodities foregone so that

$$DPSWR = \sum_i a_i.m_i.DPCF_i \tag{6.14}$$

where *DPSWR* is the shadow wage in domestic prices, and $DPCF_i$ is the domestic price conversion factor for good *i*.

The numerical example for labour from Chapter 5 can be used again for illustration. Recall that a project employs new workers for a permanent wage of Rs10 000 per annum. These workers would otherwise have been working in rural areas at two distinct activities, growing export crops for some of the year and non-traded domestic crops for the rest. In domestic prices output foregone per worker from export crops is Rs3000 and from subsistence crops Rs1075 per annum.

In the world price example both forms of output foregone are converted to world prices; export crops by a CF of 1.38 and domestic non-traded crops by a CCF of 0.80. Since following this approach all output foregone is in foreign exchange, the exactly equivalent treatment in a domestic price calculation requires that these foreign exchange effects be converted to local currency at the SER to allow for the premium on foreign exchange.

The shadow wage is therefore

$$DPSWR = (\text{Rs}3000 \times 1.38 \times 1.111) + (\text{Rs}1075 \times 0.80 \times 1.111)$$

	Output foregone from export production	Output foregone from domestic non-traded production

$$DPSWR = \text{Rs}5555$$

$$DPCF_L = \frac{\text{Rs}5555}{\text{Rs}10000} = 0.555$$

A slightly different result is obtained if one drops the assumption that the domestic non-traded crops foregone have a foreign exchange equivalent value. If one assumes they are consumed domestically with no indirect effects in terms of foreign exchange, one can use their domestic retail price as a measure of willingness to pay and thus of their domestic shadow price.[5] Their CF is now 1.00 and the new shadow wage is

$$DPSWR = (\text{Rs}3000 \times 1.38 \times 1.111) + (\text{Rs}1075 \text{ x } 1.00)$$

$$DPSWR = \text{Rs}5675$$

$$DPCF_L = \frac{\text{Rs}5675}{\text{Rs}10000} = 0.568$$

SKILLED LABOUR IN A DOMESTIC PRICE SYSTEM

Where skilled labour is in excess demand, as we have seen, a common procedure in the world price system is to use the ACF as its conversion factor. The equivalent approach in domestic price calculations is to use a conversion factor of 1.00; in other words, to assume that the market wages of these workers are sufficiently competitive to reflect their productivity. This is not inevitably the appropriate treatment, since direct output foregone estimates can also be made for skilled labour and expressed at shadow prices by the appropriate conversion factors for the commodities involved.

In the case of foreign labour equation (5.5) can be modified readily for domestic price calculations. If all the local consumption component can be identified as a foreign exchange cost the new expression becomes

$$DPSWR_F = [r\ MWR_F + (1-\text{r.})\ MWR_F \times CCF] \times CF_F \quad (6.15)$$

where $DPSWR_F$ is the shadow wage in a domestic price analysis and CF_F is SER/OER. This new shadow wage is simply the world price shadow wage adjusted for the premium on foreign exchange.

On the other hand, an alternative assumption is that foreign labour's local consumption has a zero foreign exchange content, and simply deprives other local consumers of the goods. In this case, it becomes a non-traded cost which may be approximated by the domestic market price of the goods purchased. Now the shadow wage for foreign labour in a domestic price system becomes

$$DPSWR_F = (r.MWR_F \times CF_F) + (1 - r).\ MWR_F \qquad (6.16)$$

In this latter form the proportion of the wage remitted is the only foreign exchange cost to be adjusted by the premium on foreign exchange. The local consumption element is now valued at domestic market prices, and has an implicit CF of 1.00.

The implication of these alternative treatments can be illustrated with the numerical example from Chapter 5. The wage for foreign workers is Rs1000 per month, of which Rs500 is remitted directly, whilst Rs500 is spent locally on consumer items. In the earlier example this latter component is assumed to cost the economy Rs400 in foreign exchange; this is the foreign exchange cost of the goods foreign workers buy. Total foreign exchange cost is therefore Rs900 and in a domestic price system this must be adjusted by the conversion factor for foreign exchange, which is again taken to be 1.111. The domestic price shadow wage is thus Rs1000 (Rs900 × 1.111), which gives a CF for foreign labour of 1.00.

If the alternative assumption is made, that local consumption by foreign workers has a zero foreign exchange content, the shadow wage becomes Rs1055 (Rs500 × 1.111 + Rs500); only the remitted portion of Rs 500 is raised by the premium of 11 per cent, whilst the local consumption element remains at Rs500. In this case the CF is 1.055. Which is the more accurate result depends on whether the CCF from the world price analysis is estimated more accurately than the conversion factor for foreign exchange of SER/OER.[6]

LAND AND THE DISCOUNT RATE IN A DOMESTIC PRICE SYSTEM

Briefly, for land the procedure discussed for the world price analysis remains valid, except that now conversion factors will be those for a domestic price system. In the example of Chapter 5, if all outputs and inputs are traded the net return to land in domestic price units will be Rs24 per acre (Rs21.6 × 1.111 where 1.111 is the CF for foreign exchange).

As far as the discount rate is concerned, the change of price unit in itself will have no impact. This can be seen most directly in equation (5.6) where

$$r = q.CF_q$$

Here the marginal return on investment is converted to world prices by a conversion factor CF_q. In a domestic price system world prices must be converted to local currency at the SER. However, since r is a ratio of net economic surplus to net capital stock, both sides of the ratio are at world prices and must be converted to domestic price units. For example, if $r = 0.10$, this implies

$$\frac{10 \times \text{SER/OER}}{100 \times \text{SER/OER}}$$

which reduces to 0.10. Therefore, a change in price units on its own will not alter the discount rate. This is consistent with the fact that a project's IRR will be the same in both systems, provided they are applied at the same level of detail.

FUTURE DEVALUATION OF THE DOMESTIC CURRENCY

So far nothing has been said about how anticipated devaluations of the currency are handled in project analysis. Any estimated overvaluation of the currency should be implicit in the set of CFs. This is most obvious in a domestic price system where the CF for foreign exchange is derived from a comparison of the shadow and official exchange rates. Any additional real devaluation above that implied by the initial estimate of the SER will be handled by the introduction of a revised SER, and a rise in the CF for foreign exchange.

In a world price system there is a similar adjustment although it is less intuitively obvious. A real devaluation means a rise in the price of traded outputs. The CCF converts willingness to pay for non-traded goods from domestic to world prices. However, after a devaluation any given domestic expenditure will buy less foreign goods. Whenever there is a real devaluation this implies a fall in the CCF, so that willingness to pay at domestic prices is worth less in terms of foreign exchange. Similarly, whenever labour is employed producing non-traded output its economic cost falls after a real devaluation. The initial estimate of the CCF will contain an allowance for exchange rate overvaluation but if a further real devaluation is anticipated in the future, the CCF must be adjusted downwards to reflect this.

In addition, in both systems the deflationary impact on aggregate demand associated with devaluation will lead to substitution between inputs in non-traded sectors, and thus a shift in input coefficients. Further, with a fall in demand for non-traded activities excess capacity may emerge, so that only variable costs of these activities should be included in their shadow price. In principle these effects should be incorporated in the CFs for non-traded inputs, since any change in input mix will alter the CF for an activity. However, in practice forecasting how a future real devaluation will effect the structure of production in non-traded sectors is extremely difficult. Most applied studies only work with the initial estimate of overvaluation implicit in the ACF and SER, and do not attempt either to forecast any further devaluation or to adjust CFs for non-traded inputs to allow for input substitution and the emergence of excess capacity.

CONCLUSION

The domestic price system can be made directly comparable with a world price system, provided equivalent assumptions are adopted. However, in practice the domestic price system is often associated with more approximate approaches, particularly towards non-traded goods. In some circumstances there is no doubt that small losses of accuracy can be compensated by savings in time and effort. Short cuts can also be used in a world price analysis, and what is most important is that one system be selected, understood and used consistently. The appendix to this chapter examines the PSF case study from the previous chapter in a domestic price system.

APPENDIX 6.1 PSF CASE STUDY IN A DOMESTIC PRICE ANALYSIS

The PSF project from Appendix 5 is examined here using a domestic price analysis. For comparability with the world price example the conversion factor for foreign exchange (SER / OER) is taken to be (1 / ACF). With the earlier ACF of 0.90, this gives a CF_F of 1.111.

All traded items are broken down into cif price, import tariffs or surplus profits, and transport and distribution costs. Each of these components is revalued in domestic shadow price units. CF_F is 1.111, and conversion factors for transport and distribution are 0.888 and 0.755, respectively (see Table 6A.1).

Table 6A.1 CFs for transport and distribution: domestic price system

	Cost composition	*CF*	*Weighted average CF*
Transport			
Labour[a]	0.30	0.555	0.166
Transfers	0.05	0.000	0.000
Foreign exchange	0.65	1.111	0.722
			0.888
Distribution			
Labour[a]	0.40	0.555	0.222
Transfers	0.12	0.000	0.000
Foreign Exchange	0.48	1.111	0.533
			0.755

Note:
[a] For simplicity only one kind of labour is identified and the single labour CF used elsewhere is applied here.

Table 6A.2 gives CFs for all traded goods involved with the project. These are the CFs from the world price example multiplied by 1.111.

For non-traded items two alternative treatments are used. In Case (1) all non-traded project costs, that is other capital costs, electricity, construction, packing materials and others, are each given CFs of 1.0; thus their domestic market prices are taken to equal their shadow prices. This crude approach is modified in Case (2), which is directly equivalent to the world price example. In Case 2 the two more significant non-traded costs, electricity

Table 6A.2 CFs for main traded commodities: domestic price system

Rs/lb	*Domestic market price*	*CF*	*Shadow price (domestic price numeraire)*
PSF			
cif price	5.00	1.111	5.555
Transport cost saving	0.07	0.888	0.062
Distribution cost saving	0.05	0.755	0.037
Profit margin	2.38	0.000	0.000
Price to project	7.50		5.654
CF for PSF = 5.654 / 7.500 = 0.754			
TPA			
cif price	2.40	1.111	2.666
Import duty	0.48	0.000	0.000
Transport cost port to project	0.10	0.888	0.088
Distribution cost port to project	0.10	0.755	0.075
	3.08		2.829
CF for TPA = 2.829 / 3.080 = 0.919			
EG			
cif price	2.70	1.111	3.000
Import duty	0.68	0.000	0.000
Transport cost port to project	0.10	0.888	0.088
Distribution cost port to project	0.10	0.755	0.075
Price to project	3.58		3.163
CF for EG = 3.163 / 3.580 = 0.884			

Table 6A.2 continued overleaf

Table 6A.2 Cont.

	Cost composition	CF	Weighted average CF
Equipment			
cif	0.93	1.111	1.0332
Transport cost	0.05	0.888	0.0444
Distribution cost	0.02	0.755	0.0151
	1.00		1.0927

CF for Equipment = 1.093

and construction, are examined in detail and adjustment is made for their indirect foreign exchange cost through their use of traded inputs, and their employment of labour. In both cases skilled labour is given a CF of 1.0, so that it is assumed that the market wage reflects output foregone at domestic prices. Unskilled labour is adjusted by the CF of 0.555 whose derivation is illustrated in the text. In Case (2) the detailed treatment of electricity is illustrated in this chapter, and the CF of 0.915 derived in Table 6.3 has been used. The construction CF is estimated to be 0.819 (see Table 6A.3).

Table 6A.3 Conversion factor for construction: domestic price system:

	% of costs at domestic market prices	CF	Weighted average CF
Imported materials[a]	0.16	0.879[a]	0.141
Cement[b]	0.06	0.967[b]	0.058
Local materials	0.12	1.000	0.120
Labour			
Skilled	0.05	1.000	0.050
Unskilled	0.25	0.555	0.139
Capital costs			
Equipment[c]	0.25	1.044[c]	0.261
Others	0.05	1.000	0.050
Transfers			
Taxes	0.02	0.000	0.000
Surplus Profits	0.04	0.000	0.000
	1.00		0.819

CF for construction = 0.819

Notes	*Share of cost*	*CF*	*Weighted average*
[a] Imported materials			
cif price	0.700	1.111	0.778
Import duty	0.175	0.000	0.000
Transport costs	0.050	0.888	0.044
Distribution costs	0.075	0.755	0.057
Price to construction firms	1.00		0.879

[b] Cement			
cif price	0.870	1.111	0.967
Surplus profit	0.130	0.000	0.000
Transport and distribution costs	0.000	0.000	0.000
Price to construction firms	1.000		0.967

In the case of cement the difference between the domestic and import price goes as surplus profit to producers. Transport and distribution costs are net costs covering the difference between costs from the domestic cement producer and costs from the port. These are zero.

[c] Equipment			
cif price	0.902	1.111	1.002
Import tariff	0.048	0.000	0.000
Transport costs	0.030	0.888	0.027
Distribution costs	0.020	0.755	0.015
Price to construction firms	1.000		1.044

In revaluing the costs of construction three costs cover foreign exchange items: these are direct imports into construction, locally purchased cement which substitutes for imports, and imported equipment. In determining a CF for each of these traded items, each is broken down into cif price, import tariffs or surplus profits, transport and distribution costs. Each of these components is adjusted to domestic shadow price units, CFs of 0.888 and 0.755 are used for transport and distribution, respectively (Table 6A.1). The non-traded inputs into construction, of local materials and other items of capital costs, are not revalued as a CF of 1.0 is used. Labour used in construction is converted using the CF for labour applied elsewhere in the case study, and all transfers are omitted.

The domestic price analysis of the PSF project is given in Table 6A.4 for Cases (1) and (2). In both the NPVs are negative at 10 per cent, and the IRRs are 8.4 and 9.0 per cent, respectively. In Case 2 the analysis is directly equivalent to that of the world price analysis of the previous chapter; although the NPV results of Rs − 24.50 million in the domestic and Rs − 21.62 in the world price system differ slightly due to rounding. (Rs − 21.62 × 1.111 = Rs − 24.02). The results of Cases (1) and (2) in the domestic price analysis whilst close, differ because of the greater detail used in the treatment of some non-traded items in the latter.

Table 6A.4 Resource statement at shadow prices (domestic price system Rs million)

	Present values at 10%				
		(Case 1)		(Case 2)	
	Domestic market prices	CF	Shadow prices	CF	Shadow prices
Benefits					
1. Sales revenue					
PSF	1404.38	0.754	1058.90	0.754	1058.90
Costs					
1. Investment					
Equipment	201.96	1.093	220.74	1.093	220.74
Construction	43.53	1.000	43.53	0.819	35.65
Others	13.95	1.000	13.95	1.000	13.95
2. Working capital					
PSF	24.27	0.754	18.30	0.754	18.30
TPA	10.88	0.919	10.00	0.919	10.00
EG	4.78	0.884	4.22	0.884	4.22
3. Operating					
TPA	503.41	0.919	462.64	0.919	462.64
EG	220.43	0.884	194.86	0.884	194.86
Electricity	80.09	1.003	80.33	0.915	73.28
Skilled labour	18.29	1.000	18.29	1.000	18.29
Packing materials and others	31.47	1.000	31.47	1.000	31.47
Net Resource Flow	251.31		-39.43		-24.50
IRR (%)	19.0		8.4		9.0

However, the greater detail has not had a major impact on the results, because the two non-traded inputs, construction and electricity, are not sufficiently important in the costs of the project. The more approximate analysis of Case 1 gives an IRR 0.6 percentage points lower than the more accurate analysis of Case 2.

Resource Disaggregation of the Project

The difference between the treatment of cases (1) and (2) can be illustrated by disaggregating the benefits and costs of the project into the following categories (Table 6A.5):

(a) foreign exchange (F)
(b) unskilled labour (LU)
(c) skilled labour (LS)
(d) transfers (T)
(e) domestic resources (N)

Table 6A.5 Disaggregation of benefits and cost into resource categories

	F	*LS*	*LU*	*T*	*N*	*Total*
PSF[a]	0.676		0.006	0.318		1.000
TPA	0.816		0.023	0.161		1.000
EG	0.786		0.019	0.195		1.000
Equipment	0.972		0.023	0.005		1.000
Construction						
(Case 1)	0.283	0.267	0.039	0.011	0.400	1.000
(Case 2)	0.408	0.050	0.261	0.111	0.170	1.000
Other Capital Cost					1.000	1.000
Electricity						
(Case 1)					1.000	1.000
(Case 2)[b]	0.496	0.277	0.097	0.096	0.034	1.000
Packing materials and others					1.000	1.000

Notes

[a] For the traded items PSF, TPA, EG and Equipment, foreign exchange is the cif value of these goods, plus the foreign exchange content in the transport and distribution costs associated with these items. The unskilled labour and transfer categories are from the transport and distribution costs involved.

[b] For Construction and Electricity costs of production are decomposed into the five categories. Foreign exchange costs are the cif and fob value of traded inputs plus the foreign exchange content of non-traded inputs. Labour and Transfers cover either direct inputs, or inputs into inputs into these sectors. Non-traded inputs are direct inputs that are not decomposed further.

Using the symbols in brackets the NPV of the project at market prices will be

$$NPV = F + LU + LS + T + N$$

where each category is discounted at 10 per cent with benefits having a positive and costs a negative sign. The NPV at shadow prices can be found by applying CFs to each of the five resource categories. In this example the CFs used are for F 1.111 (the conversion factor for foreign exchange), for LU 0.555 (the conversion factor unskilled labour), for LS 1.00 (on the assumption that the market wage equals the shadow wage at domestic prices), for T zero (as these are transfers), and for N 1.00 (on the assumption that for this residual item domestic market and domestic shadow prices are equal).

Table 6A.5 gives the breakdown of each project item into these categories. Foreign exchange is the cif or fob element of all traded goods; where non-traded items are disaggregated into traded, non-traded and labour costs the foreign exchange element of traded good inputs into these items is entered under foreign exchange. Unskilled and skilled labour are shown as separate categories, although they could be disaggregated further into traded and non-traded elements depending on how their output foregone is defined. In this example, the only unskilled labour identified is part of construction costs. As in Case (1) construction is not broken down in detail, so here there is no unskilled labour element shown. Transfers are taxes, subsidies and surplus profits. Transfers identified in the cost structure of non-traded inputs used by the project, for example the surplus profits and taxes in construction, are included here, as well as tariffs on imported inputs either used directly by the project or in the production of its non-traded inputs.

Table 6A.6 Disaggregation of project NPV by resource categories: domestic price system

	Case 1			*Case 2*	
			Present values at 10% (Rs million)		
	Domestic market prices	*% of NPV*		*Domestic market prices*	*% of NPV*
F	117.310	46.7	F	82.490	32.8
LS	−39.677	−15.8	LS	−42.654	−16.9
LU	−15.596	−6.2	LU	−31.602	−12.6
T	310.266	123.4	T	298.626	118.8
N	−120.989	−48.1	N	−55.546	−22.1
NPV	251.314	100.0		251.314	100.0

The category N refers to those non-traded items that are not broken down into foreign exchange, labour and transfers. All non-traded items to the project with a CF of 1.0 fall into this category, as well as non-traded inputs into construction and electricity, such as local materials, which are not disaggregated. This is a residual category and the larger it is the greater will be the approximation in the analysis.

Table 6A.7 PSF case study disaggregated into resource categories (Present value at domestic market prices at 10% discount rate. Rs million)

			(Case 1)			
	F	*LS*	*LU*	*T*	*N*	*Total*
Benefits						
1. Sales revenue						
PSF	949.358		8.426	446.591		1404.375
Costs						
1. Investment						
Equipment	196.301		4.645	1.010		201.956
Construction					43.529	43.529
Others					13.954	13.954
2. Working capital						
PSF	16.406		0.146	7.717		24.269
TPA	8.879		0.250	1.752		10.881
EG	3.756		0.091	0.932		4.779
3. Operating						
TPA	410.786		11.578	81.050		503.414
EG	173.254		4.188	42.983		220.425
Electricity	22.666	21.385	3.124	0.881	32.037	80.093
Skilled labour		18.292				18.292
Packing materials and others					31.469	31.469
Total	117.310	−39.677	−15.596	310.266	−120.989	251.314

Value at shadow prices (domestic price numeraire)

F × 1.111 =	(117.310 × 1.111)	=	130.331
LS × 1.000 =	(−39.677 × 1.000)	=	39.677
LU × 0.555 =	(−15.596 × 0.555)	=	−8.656
T × 0.000 =	(310.266 × 0.000)	=	0.000
N × 1.000 =	(−120.989 × 1.000)	=	−120.989
		NPV	−38.99
		IRR =	8.4%

Note
Due to rounding there is a small difference between the NPV results here and in Table 6A.4.

Using these categories, Table 6A.6 gives the summary breakdown of the PSF project for Cases (1) and (2). Resources for which the project is a net user have a negative sign to signify costs. The NPV of the project can be found in two alternative ways, either by applying CFs to each item of costs and benefits as in Table 6A.4, or alternatively by disaggregating all cost and benefit items into the five resource categories identified, and revaluing each category by its appropriate conversion factor (Tables 6A.7 and 6A.8). Apart from some minor errors of rounding the results are identical for the two alternative approaches.

In this case study the crudest treatment is of the residual category N, covering non-traded items that are not broken down to find a more detailed shadow price. The difference between Cases (1) and (2) lies in the size of this residual, and the greater it is the more approximate will be the calculations. In Case (1) N is 48 per cent and in Case (2) 22 per cent of the NPV at market prices.

Conclusion

The analysis of the PSF project in Case 2 shows how a domestic price numeraire can be applied at the same level of detail as used in the world price illustration of Chapter 5. A simpler analysis that does not attempt to trace through as many indirect foreign exchange effects is given in Case 1. For the PSF project examined here the simplified treatment for electricity and construction in Case 1 does not have a major impact on the project's IRR. Where non-traded inputs are a relatively small part of the total costs, the simplifying assumptions implied by the use of a CF of 1.0 will not have a significant effect on the overall accuracy of a project analysis.

Table 6A.8 PSF case study disaggregated into resource categories (present value at domestic market prices at 10% discount rate. Rs million)

			(Case 2)			
	F	*LS*	*LU*	*T*	*N*	*Total*
Benefits						
1. Sales revenue						
PSF	949.358		8.426	446.591		1404.375
Costs						
1. Investment						
Equipment	196.301		4.645	1.010		201.956
Construction	17.760	2.176	11.361	4.832	7.400	43.529
Others					13.954	13.954
2. Working capital						
PSF	16.406		0.146	7.717		24.269
TPA	8.879		0.250	1.752		10.881
EG	3.756		0.091	0.932		4.779
3. Operating						
TPA	410.786		11.578	81.050		503.414
EG	173.254		4.188	42.983		220.425
Electricity	39.726	22.186	7.769	7.689	2.723	80.093
Skilled labour		18.292				18.292
Packing materials and others					31.469	31.469
Total	82.490	−42.654	−31.602	298.626	−55.546	251.314

Value at shadow prices (domestic price numeraire)

F × 1.111 =	(82.490 × 1.111)	=	91.646
LS × 1.000 =	(−42.654 × 1.000)	=	−42.654
LU × 0.555 =	(−31.602 × 0.555)	=	−17.539
T × 0.000 =	(298.626 × 0.000)	=	0.000
N × 1.000 =	(−55.546 × 1.000)	=	−55.546
	NPV		−24.093
	IRR	=	9.0%

Note

Due to rounding there is a small difference between the NPV results here and in Table 6A.4.

APPENDIX 6.2 DOMESTIC RESOURCE COST (DRC) RATIO

An indicator of economic efficiency that has a close link with the domestic price system is the DRC. For projects producing traded goods this estimates the domestic resources required to earn or save a unit of foreign exchange. Such projects will use both foreign exchange with traded inputs into their production, and domestic resources of labour and non-traded inputs, including the non-traded elements of capital cost. The DRC compares domestic resources with the net foreign exchange effect of the project, where this net effect is the difference between the world price value of output and the cost of traded inputs at world prices. Domestic resources should be at shadow prices to reflect their cost to the economy.

Expressed in this form the DRC is an intuitively clear indicator of a project's impact in terms of trade efficiency. If the project's cost in domestic resources is greater than the value to the economy of the foreign exchange it generates, it will be an inefficient participant in foreign trade. Efficiency in trade requires that the domestic resource costs of a project be below the value of foreign exchange, given by either the SER or where there is no premium by the OER.

The DRC ratio is often calculated for an individual year of operations, however, to be comparable with the measures of project worth discussed in Chapter 3, all flows of domestic resources and net foreign exchange should be identified annually and discounted to the present at the economic discount rate.

There are two alternative ways of presenting the DRC ratio, although each give identical project decisions. It can be given as an exchange rate for an individual project. In this approach domestic resources are expressed in domestic currency and net foreign exchange in foreign currency. Using the domestic price system formally the DRC can be expressed as

$$DRC_i = \frac{PV\left(\sum_j a_{ji} . DPSP_j + \sum_L a_{Li} . DPSWR_L\right)}{PV\left(\mathrm{WP_i} - \sum_n a_{ni} . WP_n\right)} \quad (6A.1)$$

where

PV is present value

j, L, and n are non-traded, labour and traded inputs respectively into traded activity i,

a_{ji} is the number of units of non-traded input j per unit of i,

a_{Li} is the number of workers of category L per unit of i,

a_{ni} is the number of units of traded input n per unit of i,

$DPSP_j$ is the shadow price of non-traded input j,

$DPSWR_L$ is the shadow wage for labour category L,

WP_i and WP_n are the world prices in foreign currency of output i and input n.

In this form efficiency requires for activity i that $DRC_i < SER$.

Alternatively both domestic resources and net foreign exchange can be given in domestic currency, so that the DRC becomes a ratio of costs to benefits. Here

$$DRC_i = \frac{PV\,(\sum_j a_{ji}.DPSP_j + \sum_L a_{Li}\,DPSWR_L)}{PV\,(WP_i - \sum_n a_{ni}.WP_n\,).SER} \qquad (6A.2)$$

where all terms are as in (6A.1) and SER is the shadow exchange rate. In this approach efficiency requires that $DRC_i < 1.0$.

Where the official exchange rate is a reasonable indicator of the value of foreign exchange, so that $CF_F = SER/OER = 1.0$, conditions for efficiency using the DRC indicator change.

With equation (6A.1) efficiency requires

$DRC < OER$, where $SER = OER$,

and with equation (6A.2) efficiency requires

$DRC < 1.0$, where OER is used in the denominator.

Further complications arise once it is recognized that non-traded goods and labour can have an opportunity cost in foreign exchange. Where possible non-traded goods should be decomposed into foreign exchange and local (non-traded and labour) costs. Only the local element of their costs should be kept in the numerator of the ratio, with the foreign element added to the traded inputs in the denominator. Where labour has a foreign exchange element in its SWR, and if equation (6A.2) is used the SWR must be calculated converting this foreign exchange into local currency at the SER.

As a form of cost–benefit ratio the DRC should not normally be used for ranking activities, but for accept or reject decisions on individual projects. Provided identical assumptions are adopted results from an NPV and DRC calculation will give identical recommendations on projects. An acceptable project with an NPV > 0 at a particular discount rate, will have a DRC < SER (from equation 6A.1) or a DRC < 1.0 (from equation 6A.2) at the same discount rate. The advantage of the DRC indicator lies in its presentation of results, since where trade efficiency is the main concern of decision-takers, knowledge of a project's own exchange rate is a useful piece of information. Also the DRC can be used simply in short-cut calculations to assess efficiency in a single year of operations.

DRC FOR PSF PROJECT

The analysis of the PSF project can be readily converted to a DRC calculation using the resource categories in Tables 6A.5 to 6A.8. Domestic resources in the numerator of the ratio will be skilled labour (LS), unskilled labour (LU) and domestic resource (N), which are not broken down further. Foreign exchange (F) is the denominator of the ratio. It is already a net figure being the difference between foreign exchange benefits from the production of PSF and foreign exchange costs due to the project's direct and indirect use of traded inputs.

To apply equation (6A.2) to the PSF project requires that all domestic resources are converted to shadow prices using their respective conversion factors, and that foreign exchange (F) which is initially expressed at the OER be converted to shadow prices by the conversion factor for foreign exchange of 1.111.

Table 6A.9 DRC calculations: PSF project (present values at 10% (Rs million))

Domestic resources	*Case 1* *Domestic market prices*	*CF*	*Shadow prices*	*Case 2* *Domestic market prices*	*CF*	*Shadow prices*
LS	39.677	1.000	39.677	42.654	1.000	42.654
LU	15.596	0.555	8.656	31.602	0.555	17.539
N	120.989	1.000	120.989	55.546	1.000	55.546
Total	176.262		169.322	129.802		115.739
Net foreign exchange F	117.310	1.111	130.331	82.490	1.111	91.646
DRC			1.299		1.263	

For the PSF project the DRC can be expressed as

$$DRC = \frac{(LS.DPCF_{LS}) + (LU.DPCF_{LU}) + (N.DPCF_{N})}{(F.CF_{F})}$$

where LS, LU and N are the present values of skilled labour, unskilled labour and domestic resources respectively, at domestic market prices from Tables 6A.7 and 6A.8, $DPCF_{LS}$, $DPCF_{LU}$ and $DPCF_{N}$ are their respective conversion factors in the domestic price system, F is the present value of foreign exchange at the OER from Tables 6A.7 and 6A.8 and CF_{F} is the conversion factor for foreign exchange .

Using values of $DPCF_{LS}$ = 1.0, $DPCF_{LU}$ = 0.555, $DPCF_N$ = 1.0, and CF_F = 1.111, gives a DRC of 1.26, for Case 2, and a DRC of 1.30 for Case 1. (Table 6A.9).

The results are compatible with the earlier NPV analysis. At a 10 per cent discount rate both Cases 1 and 2 are unacceptable by the NPV criteria since they have a negative NPV. They are also unacceptable by the DRC criteria with a DRC of above 1.0.

Further Reading

The seminal statement of the domestic price approach is UNIDO (1972), with further discussion and some minor modification in UNIDO (1978b) and (1980). Londero (1987) is an example of a detailed analysis using a domestic price numeraire. The equivalence of the two price systems is demonstrated in Lal (1974); Weiss (1976); Gittinger (1982), chapter 7; and Irvin (1978), chapter 5. Baldwin (1972) gives a helpful analysis of the approximation in the two systems. For specific discussion of the shadow exchange rate, see Balassa (1971) and (1974), Scott (1974) and Bacha and Taylor (1971). Beyer (1975) is a case study of different approaches to its estimation for one country.

7 Non-traded Outputs and External Effects

This chapter surveys the key issues relating to several project effects which are generally difficult to incorporate within an analysis. Initially there is a discussion of the procedures for valuing outputs from projects in non-traded sectors. As pointed out earlier, the treatment of their benefits is less straightforward than where traded output is involved. The procedures for estimating non-traded benefits utilizing a demand curve for the good concerned are discussed, and examples of transport and irrigation projects are considered. The second part of the chapter focuses on external effects and the related concept of linkages.

BENEFIT VALUATION IN NON-TRADED ACTIVITIES

The characteristic of non-traded production is that the goods concerned are net additions to domestic supply. This is in contrast with production of traded goods which affect the trade balance. Goods can be non-traded for a variety of reasons. Thus non-traded output can vary, covering, for example, capital equipment protected from import competition by trade policy, public utilities like water, transport and power that are physically difficult to trade, and social sectors, like education and health.

Where non-traded output is sold on a market, benefit valuation can be based on what consumers are willing to pay to obtain it. This can exceed significantly what they actually pay, where additional supply from a new project causes a substantial fall in price. Estimation of willingness to pay requires a demand curve for the good concerned, with willingness to pay given by the area under the demand curve for the output produced by a new project.

However, not all non-traded activities can be valued in this way. Social sector output is not normally sold in a market. Even where a private health or education sector exists, it is not appropriate to base valuation of such social goods on individual preferences. How much education or health services a society provides should be decided by government on the basis of long-run development objectives. There are limits, therefore, on the extent to which the principles of benefit valuation can extend within the non-traded part of an economy.[1]

WILLINGNESS TO PAY

In theory, for all non-traded activity sold in a market that operates without controls there will be a demand curve which reflects the price consumers are willing to pay for additional units of the good. In Appendix 7, a simple treatment of demand curve estimation for the purpose of benefit valuation is discussed, with the aim of illustrating the general procedures.

Once a demand curve can be identified the area under that curve, denoting a specific additional quantity produced by a project, measures in monetary terms what consumers are willing to pay for that additional quantity. For example, in Figure 7.1, a new water project expands output for a village from Q_1 to Q_2, and this additional supply lowers price charged from P_1 to P_2. Actual willingness to pay for the additional output is the area under the curve relating to $Q_2 - Q_1$, which is $GQ_1\ Q_2F$.

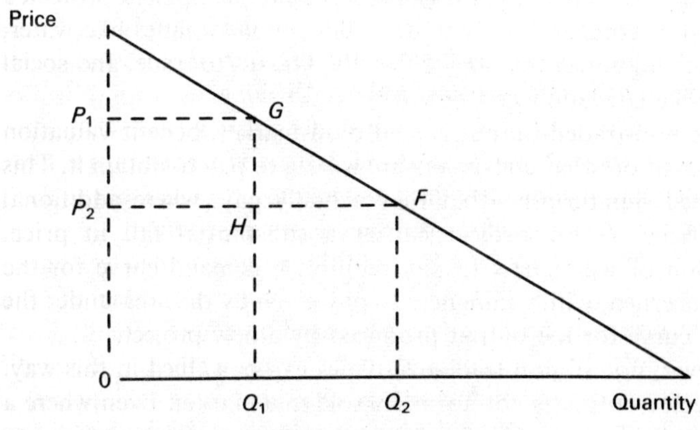

Figure 7.1 Willingness to pay

Total revenue actually paid to the project for the additional output is the price P_2 times the quantity involved $(Q_2 - Q_1)$. This is the area HQ_1Q_2F. However, there is an additional gain to new consumers of the triangle GHF – conventionally termed consumer surplus – which represents the excess of what consumers are willing to pay for $(Q_2 - Q_1)$ over what they actually pay. For linear demand curves this consumer surplus is $0.5\ (P_1 - P_2) \times HF$, and it must be added to revenue actually paid by consumers to reflect their full gain from the production of $(Q_2 - Q_1)$. Where non-linear demand curves are involved, the mathematical technique of integration will be required to identify the area under the curve.

A simple numerical example may illustrate the point. Assume that existing output Q_1 is 100, and new output Q_2 is 150, so that the net expansion in output is 50. If the original price P_1 is Rs20, and the new lower price P_2 is Rs15, total revenue collected from the sale of the additional output will be $50 \times 15 =$ Rs750. This is the area HQ_1Q_2F in Figure 7.1. Assuming a linear demand curve consumer surplus for new consumers will be $.5\ (5 \times 50) =$ Rs125. This is the area GHF in Figure 7.1.

So far the discussion has only considered new consumers. However, there is also a larger consumer surplus, given by the area $P_1\ P_2\ HG$, for those who bought the water originally at the old price P_1. This arises because with the new project existing consumers receive water at a lower price P_2, whilst they were previously willing to pay more than P_1 for their consumption.[2] In this example, where previous consumption was 100, and the price fall with the project is Rs5, this second surplus is Rs500. Total consumer surplus of Rs500 + Rs125 is now nearly as high as the revenue of Rs750 collected from sales by the new project, and total willingness to pay will be revenue actually paid plus total consumer surplus (Rs1375). Omission of willingness to pay in assessing large non-traded projects can thus understate significantly their impact on consumers, particularly where price is highly responsive to increases in supply.

Once willingness to pay for additional non-traded output is known this becomes a measure of the economic value of that output at domestic prices, since it is based on prices actually faced by consumers. This is an adequate measure for analysis at domestic prices, but where the numeraire is measured at world prices, a further adjustment is required which involves converting benefits to consumers to an equivalent value at world prices. This requires an aggregate CF for consumption expenditure, the consumption conversion factor (CCF), which compares the cost of a unit of consumption at world prices and domestic prices.

In other words, if Rs10 of consumption expenditure when spent domestically on traded goods can purchase items worth only Rs8 internationally, the CCF will be 0.8.[3] When applied to the consumption benefits from production of a non-traded good, a CCF provides an approximate means of converting these to an equivalent gain in foreign exchange. For example, in the illustration used above total consumer willingness to pay is Rs1375 at domestic prices. If the CCF is 0.8 this means that in a world price calculation such benefits would be Rs1100 (Rs1375 × 0.8).

Willingness to pay gives a measure of annual benefit. However, over time with changes in demand willingness to pay can itself change. For instance, an upward shift in the demand schedule raises willingness to pay for output ($Q_2 - Q_1$). It is necessary to include this new measure of annual benefit in future years provided it is at constant prices.

BENEFIT VALUATION – AN EXAMPLE FROM TRANSPORT

If one considers a road project there are three main sources of benefit:

(1) Lower vehicle and other operating costs for traffic that had previously used the road system prior to the improvements introduced by the new project; these gains relate to existing traffic.
(2) Lower vehicle and other operating costs for traffic that had previously used another transport system, for example, either a different road network or another transport mode such as rail, but which now shifts to the new road system as a result of the project: these gains relate to diverted traffic.
(3) The net value of additional output carried on the road, whose production had previously been constrained by the availability of transport services, so that in the absence of the road project this additional output would not have been produced; here gains relate to generated traffic.

It is clear that not all road projects will generate these benefits; category (1) are relevant only where there is an existing road that is improved by a new project. Here care should be taken in ensuring that the correct comparison of vehicle operating costs with and without the new project is made. This is important if the existing road network is becoming overcrowded or is poorly maintained. Failure to improve the road network may lead to sharply rising costs per vehicle in the future, and the gains from a new project must be based on a comparison between costs with the project and future costs on the unimproved road, not with current costs on the road.

Under categories (1) and (2) the main savings in costs will be in terms of lower vehicle maintenance and fuel costs, and in savings in travelling time. Where the latter cover vehicle operators travelling for business reasons, the gain will be in terms of lower wage costs which can be valued either at market or shadow prices. However, where leisure is involved, there is a difficulty in valuing travel time for leisure as opposed to productive purposes. Normally, some proportion of the daily wage is used.

It should be noted that category (3) relating to generated traffic stimulated by a new project is potentially very important, particularly where the new road gives access to a market that was previously inaccessible, but also often very difficult to quantify. What is involved is first to estimate the rise in output in the area linked with a market by the new road project. This output must be attributable to the new project, however, so that it would not have been forthcoming without the road. In practice it may be difficult to estimate with accuracy how much of a projected rise in output would have been forthcoming without a new road.

Once a projection of additional output has been made it must be converted to a net benefit figure. This requires placing a shadow price on the output and subtracting from this the shadow price of the inputs required to produce this output. These inputs will include both intermediates and labour, and where additional investment is required for the output expansion, all such investment costs must also be included. For example, if a new road links farmers with a new urban market, the gain in terms of generated traffic will be the value of their additional output, that is the addition to what they would have produced without the road, minus the value of the inputs used to produce this additional output; such inputs will include seed, fertilizer, pesticides, the farmer's own time, the cost of purchase or hire of oxen for ploughing, and any capital cost of land clearing or other infrastructure facilities.

The demand for transport can be viewed as a function of the cost of using the service. Costs on alternative modes of transport or other roads determine the maximum that users are willing to pay to use a road. With a demand curve of DD^1 in Figure 7.2 a new project improves an existing road and lowers costs per vehicle from OC to OC^1. There are gains to both existing traffic Q and new traffic diverted to the road $(Q_1 - Q)$. The gain to the former is the unit cost saving for existing traffic and is shown by the shaded area CPP^1C^1. Diverted traffic $(Q_1 - Q)$ gains the difference between what users are willing to pay for the services of the road PEQ_1Q, and what they actually pay P_1EQ_1Q.

In practice these two categories of benefit – for existing and diverted traffic – can be approximated by a simple comparison between average costs per vehicle mile on the unimproved and improved road, without resort to a detailed specification of the position of the demand schedule, provided one can make the assumption that it is linear. This is clear for existing traffic since benefit is defined as average cost savings per vehicle mile. For diverted traffic benefit is given by the willingness of new users to

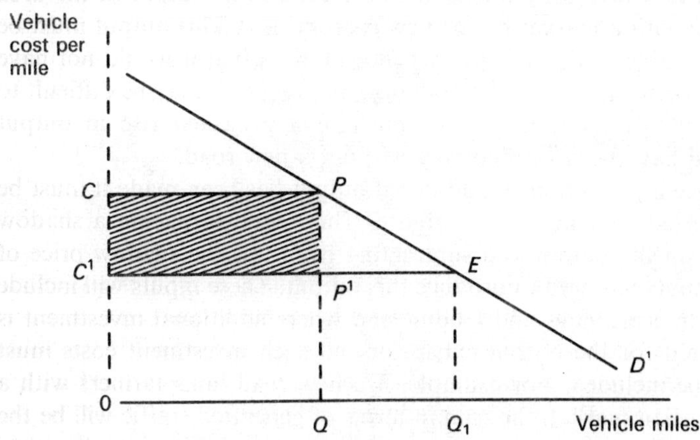

Figure 7.2 Demand for transport

pay for the services of the improved road minus what they actually pay. However, the cost of providing transport services on alternative roads or modes of transport defines how much these new users are willing to pay to use a new route; for example, in Figure 7.2 for $(Q_1 - Q)$ vehicle miles of diverted traffic alternative costs are given by PEQ_1Q. The net gain to new users is thus the difference between alternative costs and costs with the new project; this consumer surplus triangle PEP^1 is equivalent to the new vehicle miles $(Q_1 - Q)$ multiplied by the average saving per mile $(C - C_1/2)$.

In principle cost savings of this type can be valued at either market or shadow prices. The procedure for estimating such cost savings is illustrated in Table 7.1. It is assumed that a road of 30 miles has a current use of 50 000 vehicles per year, of which 60 per cent are trucks and buses and 40 per cent are cars. Improvements to the road due to a new project result in cost savings of 26 pesos per vehicle mile for the former and eight pesos for the latter. Total annual benefits in cost savings are 23.4 million pesos and 4.8 million pesos respectively. In addition, the cost reductions generated by the road will divert traffic from other roads; estimates of this diversion are 6000 trucks and buses and 2000 cars. A comparison between average vehicle costs on the other roads and the improved new road gives a cost saving of 34 pesos per vehicle mile for trucks and buses and 6 pesos for cars. Total savings for diverted traffic are therefore 6.1 million pesos for trucks and buses and 0.4 million pesos for cars. In summary, benefits as approximated by vehicle cost savings are as follows:

Pesos million	*Existing traffic*	*Diverted traffic*
Trucks and buses	23.4	6.1
Cars	4.8	0.4
Total	28.2	6.5

Where it is clear that a new road project stimulates additional output that would not otherwise have been generated, the net economic value of this output becomes an additional benefit that must be included in the appraisal.[4] Normally, one would expect this form of benefit to arise gradually as producers respond to the situation created by a project. This means that the share of generated benefits in total annual benefits is likely to rise over the life of a project.

Table 7.1 Average cost savings existing traffic (pesos per vehicle mile)

	Trucks and buses		*Cars*	
	Old road	*New road*	*Old road*	*New road*
Fuel and oil	50	50	32	32
Tire wear	40	34	10	8
Vehicle maintenance	80	64	32	26
Wages[a]	25	21		
Total	195	169	74	66
Savings		26		8

Average cost savings diverted traffic (pesos per vehicle mile)

	Other Road	*New Road*	*Other Road*	*New Road*
Fuel and oil	55	50	20	18
Tire wear	38	25	8	8
Vehicle maintenance	82	70	40	36
Wages	25	21		
Total	200	166	68	62
Savings		34		6

Note

[a] Car driver and passenger time not valued.

BENEFITS FROM GENERATED OUTPUT – AN ILLUSTRATION FROM IRRIGATION

Generated output will be relevant for some transport, and for most irrigation projects; in fact it forms the main objective of the latter. Estimation of the economic benefit from generated output is illustrated here for an irrigation project, although the procedure is equally relevant for a transport scheme that links farmers with a new market and thus stimulates additional production. For illustration we take an irrigation scheme with a cost of Rs100 million, and a working life of thirty years with normal maintenance expenditure. The objective is to supply irrigation water to farmers in a previously rainfed area to raise farm yields. The water will be sold at a nominal charge that covers only running not investment costs of the scheme. Here the economic benefits of the project will be the additional net agricultural output arising from the availability of irrigation water.

For simplicity, the farmers affected by the scheme can be divided into two groups – medium- and small-scale farmers – with the latter having holdings up to 5 hectares, and the former up to 50 hectares. These groups grow combinations of cotton, wheat and sorghum. Table 7.2 summarizes the cost of the irrigation project, whilst Table 7.3 gives data on farm operations both with and without the new project; the data are in present values discounted at 10 per cent over the life of the project. It is predicted that with additional supplies of fertilizer and pesticides the availability of irrigation water will raise agricultural yields considerably.

Table 7.2 Irrigation project: present value of costs at 10 per cent (Rsmillion)

	Present value at market prices	*CF*	*Present value at shadow prices*
Capital cost			
Equipment	50.00	0.92	46.00
Construction	30.00	0.70	21.00
Others	20.00	0.90	18.00
Operating cost			
Electricity	7.00	0.95	6.65
Maintenance			
Labour	2.00	0.50	1.00
Others	1.00	0.90	0.90
Extension services	5.00	0.90	4.50
Total	115.00		98.05

The total area reached by the project is 9000 hectares of which 3000 are farmed by medium-size and 6000 by small farmers. The farm budget figures in Table 7.3 are averages for each group, and from these the incremental income for medium-size farmers is Rs36.9 million (Rs12 300 × 3000) and for small farmers Rs53.4 million (Rs8900 × 6000). In total these additional income figures are below the project cost of Rs115 million.

However, to find the economic benefits of the project requires estimation of additional agricultural output minus additional input costs with both at shadow prices. The tariff charges for use of the irrigation water is simply a transfer between the farmer and the project and not part of the economic benefit from the water. Table 7.4 gives revised net benefit figures using a set of conversion factors to revalue output and inputs, and excluding water tariffs.[5]

Table 7.3 Farm budgets per hectare at market prices: present values at 10 per cent (Rshundred)

	Small farmers			*Medium farmers*		
	Without project	*With project*	*Incremental income*	*Without project*	*With project*	*Incremental income*
1. Revenue						
Cotton	50	150	100	60	180	120
Wheat	30	60	30	40	80	40
Sorghum	20	40	20	30	60	30
2. Costs						
Labour[a]	20	30	10	30	45	15
Hired tractor	10	15	5	12	18	6
Fertilizer	10	30	20	12	32	20
Pesticides	5	15	10	6	16	10
Seed	10	15	5	10	15	5
Materials	5	6	1	5	6	1
Water tariff		10	10		10	10
Net Income	40	129	89	55	178	123

Note

[a] For small farmers this covers the cost of farmers' own time, whilst for medium farmers it covers wages of hired workers in addition to the cost of the time of family members.

In economic terms benefits are now Rs48.21 million (Rs16,070 × 3000) for medium-size farmers, and Rs71.16 million (Rs11 860 × 6000) for small farmers. These total benefits of Rs119.37 million must be compared with total costs of the irrigation project at shadow prices of Rs98.05 million (Table 7.2). Using shadow prices at 10 per cent the NPV is Rs21.32 million.

Table 7.4 Economic benefits per hectare: present values at 10 per cent (Rshundred)

	Small farmers			*Medium farmers*		
	Incremental Income at market prices	*CF*	*Shadow price value*	*Incremental Income*	*CF*	*Shadow price value*
1. Revenue						
Cotton	100	1.10	110	120	1.10	132
Wheat	30	1.10	33	40	1.10	44
Sorghum	20	1.25	25	30	1.25	37.5
2. Costs						
Labour	10	0.5	5	15	0.5	7.5
Hired tractor	5	0.9	4.5	6	0.9	5.4
Fertilizer	20	1.10	22	20	1.10	22
Pesticides	10	1.25	12.5	10	1.25	12.5
Seed	5	0.9	4.5	5	0.9	4.5
Materials	1	0.9	0.9	1	0.9	0.9
Net benefit			118.6			160.7

For irrigation projects this direct estimate of generated benefits is an alternative to specification of a demand curve for irrigation. In theory, with full knowledge of the gains from irrigation water, farmers' willingness to pay should equal their additional real income at market prices. However, lack of information on the part of farmers, and of the data necessary to specify a demand curve for irrigation water, make this direct approach easier to apply in project analysis.

The sectors of transport and irrigation provide some of the clearest examples of benefit valuation for non-traded activities. However, in education, health and housing, for example, it is far more difficult to establish a link between additional investment and higher incomes due to greater productive activity.

EXTERNAL EFFECTS

External effects can be defined broadly as unintended income or income equivalent welfare changes for others in the economy for which the project that generates the effect neither receives nor makes a full financial payment. By definition, therefore, such effects will not be internalized in that they do not appear in the financial statement of the project from which they originate. By stressing the unintended nature of these effects, which are a by-product of other activity, this definition means that the benefits of infrastructure projects, such as cost savings or generated output for others, do not fall under the heading of externalities, despite the fact that infrastructure projects will not normally receive full financial payment for these effects. For this type of project, gains for others provide their central economic justification and are clearly intended.

Although there is no dispute that external effects should be included in economic analysis, there is still disagreement concerning their significance for the overall results. This disagreement arises at least in part from the difficulty in quantifying their impact. This section first discusses linkages between economic activities before turning to three main examples of external effects of projects in terms of labour training, technical progress and the environment.

Linkages

Linkages are important for the present discussion because they are one of the most important mechanisms through which a new project can transmit external effects. Linkages refer to production interrelations between industries. Backward linkages arise when a project purchases inputs from domestic suppliers and forward linkages arise when it sells its output to domestic users for further processing. Linkages generate external effects when incomes of users and suppliers are changed as a result of a project. For example, with a supplier industry subject either to economies of scale or to excess capacity, additional demand from a new project can raise wage and profit income in supplier firms. Similarly, if a project supplies goods that were previously unavailable or available only at a higher price, higher incomes may result for user firms and their employees.

Linkages will normally only transmit external effects in the case of non-traded goods, since by definition where a project produces or uses traded goods this will affect the foreign trade balance not domestic production and income. However, shadow prices for non-traded inputs and outputs should already capture these additional income effects, so that separate identification of this form of external effect will be double counting.

As we have seen in Chapter 5, the shadow prices of most non-traded inputs to a project are determined by the opportunity cost of all items that go into their production. Labour is valued at a shadow wage that represents its opportunity cost, so that the difference between the market and shadow wage measures approximately what workers gain from employment. Similarly, the capital charge for a non-traded input refers only to normal profits that would have been earned in the absence of the demand from the new project under consideration. Therefore, all labour and profit income in excess of what would have been earned elsewhere are excluded from the costs of the non-traded input supplied to a new project. Since reduction in costs is equivalent to increasing benefits by the same amount, this treatment is identical to attributing as a benefit to a new project the extra income generated for workers and capitalists in activities that supply the project.

Similarly, in the case of non-traded project output, valuation is on the basis of what users are willing to pay for this output. If the price at which it is sold to them falls as a result of a new project coming into production, the total benefit for the user will be revenue actually paid (at the new lower price) plus the additional benefit as reflected in the consumer surplus involved. Hence this definition of benefit already incorporates the external gain to existing and new users in the form of lower prices.

There are, nevertheless, several cases where shadow price valuations of particular project outputs and inputs do not include extra benefit or cost terms. Hence it is necessary to value these effects and include them as separate benefits or costs in a project resource flow statement. Three examples of these cases are discussed.

Labour Training

A labour training externality is one cited frequently in relation to new projects, particularly in manufacturing. It arises whenever a project trains unskilled workers who leave after a time and use their newly acquired skills on another project that obtains the benefit of their enhanced productivity. The gain to others generated by the original project can be defined as the difference between the productivity of the workers with and without training, during the period of their working lives after they have left employment on the original project. Practical estimation of this external effect requires a forecast of the number of newly trained workers leaving each year, the length of their working lives, and their additional productivity due to training. An approximation for productivity differentials is often based on estimates of their earnings. Once assumptions on these points have been made, it is not difficult to produce quantitative estimates for this externality which should be included as an additional benefit in the resource statement. It should be noted, however, that the absolute value of this external effect is rarely sufficiently high to be critical to the viability of projects.

Technical Progress

An external benefit can arise when the introduction of a new technology or improvements to a known technology by one project lead to cost reductions or quality improvements when other projects adopt the same technology. For this to be an external as opposed to an internal benefit, the original project must not license the technology for a royalty, or if it does so, it must charge a fee that only partially reflects the additional income to be derived from the use of the technology. An informal process of technology transfer may be easier in agriculture than in industry, for example, with farmers outside a project area copying the improved farming practices adopted by those in an agricultural improvement project. In industry more secrecy is likely to be involved with production processes. Some of the main mechanisms of informal transfer are likely to be workers leaving and passing on information or setting up their own production facilities (which could be seen as another aspect of the labour training externality); buyers of project output passing on information on design or other specifications to other producers; local equipment manufacturers who through designing machines for a project learn the specifications of a technology, which they can then pass on to others through the machinery they supply.

This last mechanism may provide one of the important explanations for productivity growth in the currently industrializing countries. However, putting quantitative estimates on such effects can be very difficult. One can use sensitivity analysis (as discussed in Chapter 8) to test how benefits from different assumed rates of productivity growth in other projects, due to externally induced technical progress, affect the appraisal of a project deemed to have instigated the externality. Even so, it is difficult to do more than this.

Environmental Effects

It is now accepted that new projects in a range of sectors may have an important impact on the environment that will affect production and consumption levels – and thus ultimately income – elsewhere in the economy. For example,

- an industrial plant may discharge waste into a river and thus reduce the fish population; this will lower the production and income of fishermen in the area;
- an irrigation scheme, if inadequately drained, may increase soil salinization, which in the long run might adversely affect agricultural yields and farm income on the surrounding lands;
- a power project may create air pollutants with long-run consequences for human health in the area of the project;
- widening of a road may increase traffic use, and reduce what is considered to be the quality of life of domestic residents close to the road by ruining their views and raising noise levels.

All effects noted here can be seen as unintended negative consequences of projects designed for other purposes. Some projects can, of course, have positive environmental effects, but normally these will not be unintended, but will provide the initial rationale for the project and are thus not included in our definition of externalities; for example, a forest management project designed to prevent deforestation and the consequent soil erosion and timber depletion.

It is clear that in project studies all environmental effects, both costs and benefits, should be identified and where possible put in numerical terms. Where quantification is not possible environmental consequences should be stated clearly for comparison with the quantifiable economic and financial effects of the project. Whilst it is recognized that there will be some environmental effects which of their nature do not lend themselves readily to quantification – for example, the destruction of countryside of scenic beauty or of a rare breed of wildlife – there are techniques that can be applied to derive approximate numerical estimates for a range of effects. The discussion here cannot be comprehensive, but it notes briefly a number of possible approaches, each of which may be applied depending on the circumstances.

Environmental effects may result in a change in output elsewhere in the economy, so that this output change becomes a measure of the environmental effect. For instance, where pollution of a river by a factory results in death of fish and a lower catch, the economic value of this drop in fish output gives the negative externality to be attributed to the factory. Although in principle this is the easiest type of externality to quantify two qualifications should be noted. First, what must be estimated is the net loss in output, assessing whether any reduction in input cost will also result. If the catch is reduced but fishermen also now fish for less time, there will be lower running costs of the boats partially to offset the lower catch; net loss is therefore reduction in output minus any reduction in input costs. Secondly, the important comparison is between output with and without the project. If the river was already polluted, it is only the cost of the additional pollution that must be attributed to the factory.

Loss of earnings by workers can be used as a proxy for lower productivity due to a negative environmental effect; for example, if workers' health is adversely affected by air pollution or water contamination. It is recognised, though, that this approach has a number of drawbacks. Its basic assumption that earnings can be used as a proxy for productivity can be overcome by valuing working time at a shadow not a market wage. More significantly, it requires that there is a clear link between the environmental effect and time away from work, and thus loss of earnings. Where illness can be due to a number of factors it may be inaccurate to attribute all of the loss of productivity to a particular environmental effect. Further, it runs into serious difficulties where loss of life is involved, since such a loss is of such significance that it is contentious to value it in terms of opportunity cost.

Alternative projects, one with serious environmental consequences and the other which avoids these, can be compared to determine the best alternative. If the latter is the least-cost alternative there will be no ambiguity as to which is to be preferred. However, in the more typical case the environmentally more suitable project will be more expensive. In this approach the decision-taker will be presented with information as to how much more expensive is the environmentally preferred solution. This gives a monetary cost to compare with intrinsically unquantifiable benefits, and the decision-taker can then decide if the latter are sufficiently important to outweigh the former. For example, there may be two routes for a road, one which destroys good farm land whilst the other does not but is more expensive. The additional cost of the latter route is the opportunity cost of preserving farm land. However, this approach does not provide a simple numerical comparison of benefits and costs, but rather draws attention to the costs of decisions. Where a number of such decisions have been taken in the past, it may be possible to identify the implicit value that decision-takers place on environmental effects through the extra costs that they are willing to incur.

Particular environmental effects may also be valued on the basis of what groups affected are willing to pay to prevent them from occurring. For example, an irrigation scheme may lead to eroded soil carried by the water causing siltation in fields and crop damage. If farmers affected by a similar project were willing to pay a certain sum to construct diversion dikes to prevent the water reaching the fields, this can be taken as an approximate estimate of farmer's valuation of the cost to them of this effect. Since the rich will be willing to pay more than the poor to prevent certain effects, this approach could lead to environmental decisions favouring higher income groups.

Having noted briefly various approaches to the quantification of environmental effects, it remains to be stressed that all externalities of whatever type become equivalent once they have been quantified. External benefits and costs should be entered into a project resource statement in the year in which they arise, and thus be included in the net benefit figure for that year. In an economic analysis strictly for comparability with other direct effects, where possible, externalities should be valued at shadow prices. For instance, in the environmental case, using the change in productivity approach output foregone should be valued at shadow prices. Similarly, loss of earnings should be at shadow not market wages. If willingness to pay to avoid specific environmental effects is estimated in a domestic price shadow pricing system, no further adjustment is required; in a world price system, a CCF for the group concerned is required to convert the willingness to pay measure to an equivalent figure at world prices.

Illustration of Externalities

As a simple numerical illustration one can take an industrial project with two external effects – a labour training effect which is positive, and an environmental effect which is negative. The project employs 200 workers, of which all receive training, whilst ten leave each year over a fifteen year period. Workers who leave have to be replaced and these new workers need further training. As a result of their training workers are taken to have an extra productivity 50 per cent of their market wage and for those who leave this is a gain to their new employers. Wages per worker are 10 000 pesos per year. The annual external benefit for other producers is 50 000 pesos (10 × 10 000 × 0.5 = 50 000). The environmental externality arises because the project pollutes a stream leading to a loss in catch of 5000 fish per month. There is no saving in operating costs of

Table 7.5 Illustration of externalities (pesos thousand)

	Internal effects		
Costs *Year*	*0*	*1---------- 15*	*16*
Investment[a]	10 000		(1000)
Operating			
Labour		2000--------- 2000	
Raw materials		2000--------- 2000	
Others[b]		800--------- 800	
Benefits			
Sales		8000--------- 8000	
Net benefits	(10 000)	3200--------- 3200	1000
	External effects		
Year	*0*	*1---------- 15*	*16*
Labour training		50---------- 50	
Environmental[c]		(1200)--------(1200)	(2200)
Adjusted net			
Benefits	(10 000)	2050--------- 2050	(1200)

Notes

[a] Including initial cost of training; terminal value of assets shown as a negative cost.

[b] Including cost of training to replace workers who leave.

[c] Including negative environmental terminal value shown in year 16.

All negative items in brackets.

fishing. The shadow price of fish is 20 pesos each, so the annual external cost is 1.2 million pesos (5000 × 12 × 20 = 1 200 000). Pollution of the stream causes lasting damage to the fish population, so that even when the project ceases production in year 15 there is a continuing negative effect – shown as a negative external terminal value of 2.2 million pesos. This is estimated as an annual cost of 1.0 million pesos over an infinite period starting in year 16, and discounted to the present at 10 per cent. For simplicity, the construction period of the project is one year, and all costs and revenues are constant during the fifteen years of operations (see Table 7.5).

In this example the NPV at 10 per cent is 14.56 million without the externalities and 5.33 million when they are included. The labour training externality here is only small, whilst the environmental effect is much larger.

CONCLUSION

This chapter has examined some of the more difficult aspects of project analysis; the valuation of benefits from non-traded output, and of external benefits and costs. Here only approximate estimates may be possible in both these cases.

Willingness to pay forms the measure of value for non-traded project output in both domestic and world price systems. However, the world price system involves an additional adjustment since willingness to pay at domestic prices is converted to a foreign exchange equivalent. Furthermore, benefits from some non-traded activities, particularly social sectors like health and education, are not adequately captured in monetary terms at any set of prices. For other sectors, like power, transport and water, benefits may be difficult to measure fully. Where benefit estimates are illustrative rather than definitive cost-minimization criteria may have to replace standard benefit–cost comparisons.

Externalities, particularly environmental, are potentially of considerably importance. Again it is difficult to incorporate these fully although this is an area where one would expect current research to lead to improvements in techniques for the future.

APPENDIX 7.1 DEMAND CURVE ESTIMATION FOR BENEFIT VALUATION

The simplest procedure is to work with a linear demand curve of the type illustrated in Figure 7.1. For an urban water project, for example, this will show the quantity of water consumed for different water tariffs charged. Initially, the position of the current tariff and water consumption will be known. If a new project both expands the supply of water and lowers the tariff charged, one needs to know the demand curve to establish what consumers are willing to pay to receive the extra water supplied by the project.

Price elasticity of demand is the relationship between the proportional change in price of a good and the proportional change in demand that results. An elasticity of – 0.5, for example, means that for every 1 per cent rise in price there is a 0.5 per cent fall in quantity demanded. Price elasticities can be estimated from econometric studies, although they will generally only be approximate for most non-traded activities. However, if one assumes that the demand curve is linear, then with an estimate of the price elasticity of demand relevant at current price and output levels, the position of the demand curve can be specified fully.

This follows since price elasticity of demand (e) can be defined as

$$e = \frac{\Delta Q_1}{Q_1} \div \frac{\Delta P_1}{P_1}$$

where

Q_1 and P_1 are current quantity demanded and price,

and

ΔQ_1 and ΔP_1 are changes in quantity and price.

Rearranging gives $e = \dfrac{\Delta Q_1}{\Delta P_1} \cdot \dfrac{P_1}{Q_1}$

and $\dfrac{\Delta P_1}{\Delta Q_1} = \dfrac{P_1}{Q_1} \cdot \dfrac{1}{e}$

However, $\dfrac{\Delta P_1}{\Delta Q^1}$ is the slope of the demand curve.

Therefore as one knows P_1 and Q_1, and if one estimates e, the slope of the demand curve will be defined. By extrapolating this slope to the vertical and horizontal axes one can fully define the demand curve.

In Figure 7A.1 current price and demand are at point A on the demand curve. The slope of the line is $\Delta P_1 / \Delta Q_1$ and once this is identified points B and C on the vertical and horizontal axes can be found. BAC is therefore the full current demand curve.

It is also useful to estimate future demand curves, since over a project's life quantity demanded at a particular price will change. One simple approach is to assume that for a given price over time the price elasticity of demand remains constant. To specify a new future demand curve in this situation requires a forecast of what demand will be in a later period at the existing price.

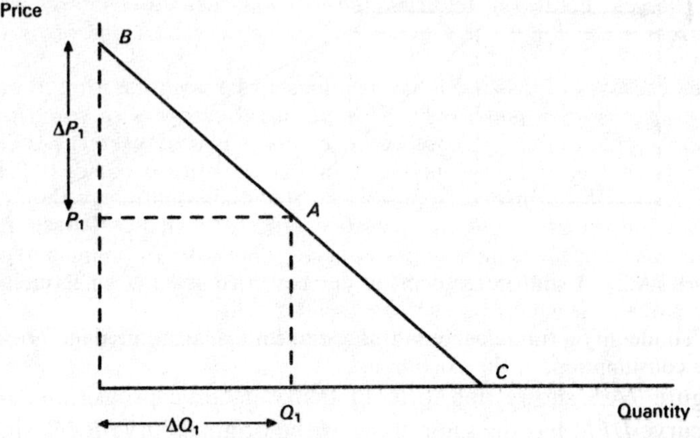

Figure 7A.1 Identifying a demand curve from the price elasticity

If the future consumption level can be forecast at the existing price the relation between price elasticity, and price and demand at a point in time, can be used to find the new slope of the demand curve.

$$\text{Now } e = \frac{\Delta Q_2}{\Delta P_1} \cdot \frac{P_1}{Q_2}$$

where e and P_1 remain as before, whilst Q_2 is forecast independently. However, provided Q_2 can be forecast reasonably accurately the new slope will be specified.

This is illustrated in Figure 7A.2 where F is the future price-consumption point, and Q_2 is future demand at price P_1. The intercept B remains as before but the slope of the curve now differs from that initially.

This approach to estimating a future demand curve has the limitation that it assumes a constant price elasticity at a given price level. An alternative is to assume a changing price elasticity but a constant slope of the demand curve, so that over time perhaps in response to rising incomes, the demand curve shifts outwards by the same absolute rise for each price

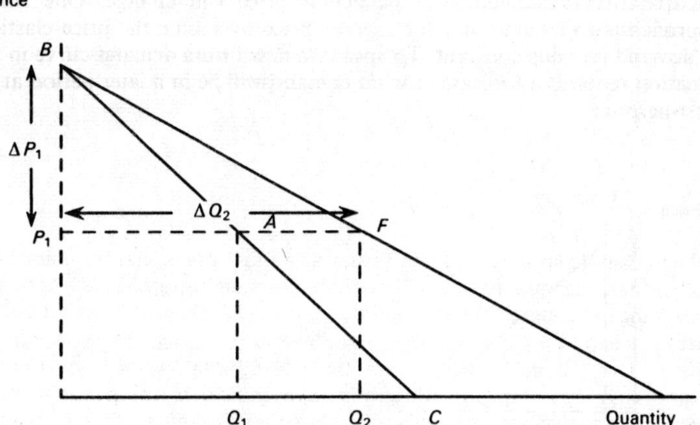

Figure 7A.2 A shift in the demand curve at a constant price elasticity

level. To identify a future curve in this approach one again needs to project future consumption, at the existing price.

Figure 7A.3 shows this form of demand curve projection. The new curve *DFE*, has the same slope as the original curve *BAC*, since

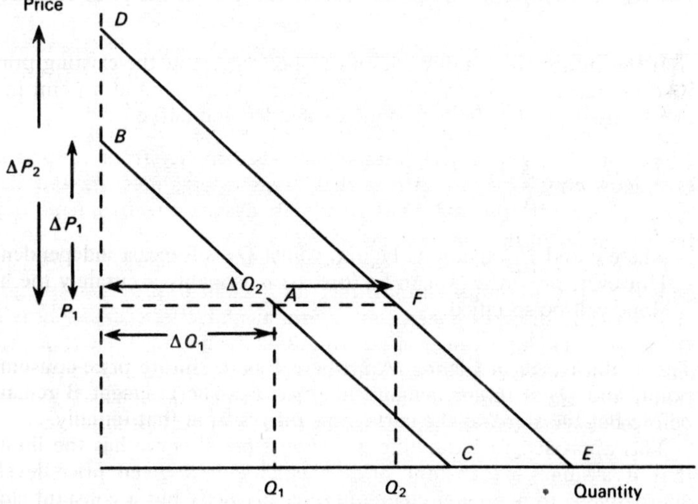

Figure 7A.3 A shift in the demand curve with a constant slope

it is parallel to it. However, price elasticity at P_1 is lower than for the original curve. This follows, since Q_2 is greater than Q_1, and e varies inversely with Q.

Now if the slope of the demand curve remains unchanged, so that $\Delta P_1/\Delta Q_1 = \Delta P_2/\Delta Q_2$, one can determine the new price elasticity at price P_1, where

$$e = \frac{\Delta Q_1}{\Delta P_1} \cdot \frac{P_1}{Q_2}$$

These simple specifications of future demand – price relations have been used in the water supply sector. The first approach, using the assumption of a constant price elasticity of demand, is normally taken to cover situations where per capita income is stable, but demand grows as new users join the system. The second approach, on the other hand, where the elasticity changes but the slope of the curve is constant, is taken to be more appropriate where income per capita is rising leading to higher demand at all price levels.

Neither approach is free from difficulty, however. Theoretically both are crude in that there is little evidence to suppose that linear relations reflect future demand conditions. Furthermore, both require estimates of current price elasticity of demand, and a projection of how consumption at a given price grows over time. None the less, they reflect a short-cut approximation that may be used in practice.

Further Reading

The discussion here of benefit valuation in the Appendix draws heavily on Powers (1977). For transport projects Adler (1987) is an updated comprehensive survey, and Harberger (1972), chapter 10 is an important early article. Karatas (1989) is a case study of benefit valuation in transport. Cook and Mosley (1989) discuss various benefits from infrastructure projects, although many effects they term externalities are not defined here as such. Walsh and Daffern (1990) discuss the treatment of non-traded output in the UK context.

For externalities in general see Weiss (1990a), chapter 3; Weiss (1989) considers the potential importance of technical progress for project analysis. The discussion here on environmental effects draws heavily on Dixon *et al.* (1986). Cooper (1981) discusses the link between appraisal and environmental issues at a more theoretical level. Pearce and Turner (1990), chapters 9 and 10 discuss measures of environmental damage. Van Pelt *et al.* (1990) survey environmental issues from a project perspective.

8 Uncertainty

The techniques of project analysis have been considered so far as if the basic data which they have used are known with certainty. However, both technical and economic information is used in the form of forecasts and is subject to considerable uncertainty. It is possible to conceive of different values, based on experience, for the fundamental technical relations in any productive process, and for the project costs and benefits at either market or shadow prices. For most project data, a range of values can be found or predicted, yielding the possibility of different conclusions in the application of project worth measures.

Variation in some technical or economic values will be more significant than others. Moreover, some will be subject to greater uncertainty or a greater range of likely values. An initial attempt to identify those variables that are likely to affect most the project outcome is provided by sensitivity analysis. By varying values one at a time, as explained in the first section below, the effect on the project worth measures can be calculated, and for each variable the range of variation within which the project decision remains the same can be identified.

In implementation, a number of variables is likely to vary simultaneously, in either complementary or contradictory fashion. Moreover, they will do so with different likelihood. A second technique of risk analysis, explained in the second section below, investigates the effects of combinations of events with different probabilities. This technique can be applied particularly to the most significant variables identified through sensitivity analysis.

Both sensitivity and risk analysis provide additional information for decision-taking. An apparently acceptable project may appear risky, if small variations in the predicted values cause the project decision to change; other projects yielding a lower rate of return may appear more robust in the sense that the project decision is unaffected by changes in key variables. However, these forms of analysis only identify the likely origin and extent of uncertainty. It is also desirable to try to reduce or control uncertainty. Brief mention is made in the third section of how this might be done at the analysis as well as implementation stages of projects.

SENSITIVITY ANALYSIS

Measures of project worth are first calculated using the best estimate of inputs and outputs and the discount rate. The project decision will be based on these best estimates. However, what would be the effect on the project worth measure of variation in the estimates? By how much would a project item have to vary before the project decision is changed? These are the questions that sensitivity analysis is designed to address, in order to identify the variables to which the project is most sensitive.

For any project statement, some items will have a significant effect on the project outcome. Where discounting is applied, variation in items occurring in earlier years will have a greater effect than variation in items in later years. It is common, for example, to investigate the effects of investment cost overruns or delays in construction that lengthen the investment period. Other items liable to have a major impact include the prices of the main inputs and outputs. Looking outside the productive process to the relevant economic parameters, the project decision may be sensitive to the choice of discount rate or the premium on foreign exchange built into conversion factors.

The application of sensitivity analysis involves varying one project item at a time and measuring the effect on project worth. Because this is easier to interpret in absolute terms, the project worth measure generally employed in sensitivity analysis is the net present value (NPV). This is illustrated in Table 8.1 which contains the resource flow for an agro-processing project. At a discount rate of 10 per cent the best estimate of the NPV at market prices is 163.7. The items in each row of the resource flow have been varied by 10 per cent; cost items have been increased (and the terminal values where appropriate), whilst revenue has been decreased. The first column of Table 8.1 shows the resulting absolute value of the NPV whilst the second column gives the percentage change in the NPV. Other project effects also varied are the technical ratio between materials and output, the length of the construction period and the discount rate.

The variation in many project items could come about through variations in quantities or prices, or a combination of both. At this stage of the analysis, the source of variation is not as important as its likely effect. Table 8.1 shows that some items have a very

Table 8.1 Resource flow: best estimates (effects of 10 per cent change on NPV[1])

New NPV	*% change in NPV*		*0*	*1*	*2*	*3*	*4*	*5*	*6*	*7*	*8*	*9*	*10*
83.7	49	Investment: Construction	1000										(500)
63.7	61	Equipment	1000										
143.7	12	Working capital	200										(200)
(329.8)	301	Materials	0	450	675	900	900	900	900	900	900	900	900
108.8	34	Power	0	50	75	100	100	100	100	100	100	100	100
136.2	17	Transport	0	25	38	50	50	50	50	50	50	50	50
71.5	56	Skilled labour	0	150	150	150	150	150	150	150	150	150	150
54.0	67	Unskilled labour	0	100	150	200	200	200	200	200	200	200	200
(838.4)	603	Revenue	0	900	1350	1800	1800	1800	1800	1800	1800	1800	1800
		Net resource flow	(2200)	125	262	400	400	400	400	400	400	400	1100
42.5	74	Discount rate	0.10										
		Net present value	163.7										
		Other effects											
57.9	65	Investment spread over 2 years. Working capital built up in second investment year. Residual values unchanged.											
(329.8)	301	Ratio of materials to revenue 0.55 rather than 0.50 (same as 10% increase in materials).											

Notes

[1] Increase for costs, decline for revenues.

Figures in brackets are negative.

substantial effect on the NPV, particularly the revenue, the cost of materials, and the technical ratio between them.

On the basis of best estimates, this is close to a marginal project since the NPV, although positive, is not very high at the given discount rate. The resource flow has also been converted into shadow prices. Each project item is disaggregated into the resource categories foreign exchange (covering traded goods), skilled labour, unskilled labour, transfers and domestic costs (covering non-traded goods that are not decomposed further). Each category is converted to shadow prices by a different conversion factor. The CFs used can be seen as national parameters relevant across all projects (see Chapter 11).

The analysis is in world price units so foreign exchange has a CF of 1.0. For both skilled and unskilled labour output foregone in their alternative employment defines their opportunity cost. However, the ratio of output foregone at domestic prices to the market wage differs for these two types of labour. For skilled labour it is 1.20 and for unskilled 0.65. In this case, for simplicity, output foregone for both is converted to world prices using the Average Conversion Factor of 0.77. Variation in the ACF therefore alters the value of both types of labour. Transfers have a CF of zero, and domestic costs covering non-traded goods are also converted at the ACF of 0.77.

Table 8.2 shows the cost breakdown for each project item and the national parameter values that have been applied to them. Applying the resulting set of conversion factors, and an economic discount rate of 9 per cent, yields a NPV at shadow prices of minus 79.0. At prices that reflect opportunity costs, the project should be rejected.

Variation in project items, as discussed above, can also be investigated at shadow prices. However, the additional information used in making shadow price estimates gives rise to additional uncertainty. The sensitivity of this result to the ACF, the opportunity cost of unskilled labour at domestic prices, and the discount rate has been investigated by calculating the effects of a 10 per cent variation in each. In this case, the effect of a change in a national parameter is not entirely predictable as it enters into the specific conversion factors for both cost and revenue items; however, declines in national parameter values improve the NPV at shadow prices, as shown in the lower section of Table 8.2. Variation in the ACF in particular has a very substantial impact on the NPV.

Table 8.2 Percentage cost breakdown and conversion factors

National Parameters	*1.0*	*1.20 × 0.77*	*0.65 × 0.77*	*0.0*	*0.77*	
	Foreign exchange	*Skilled labour*	*Unskilled labour*	*transfers*	*Domestic costs*	*Conversion factors*
Investment: Construction	.7		.1	.05	.15	0.87
Equipment	.9		.05		.05	0.93
Working capital	.7		.1	.1	.1	0.83
Materials	.7		.1	.1	.1	0.83
Power	.4	.2	.2	.2		0.84
Transport	.4	.1	.2	.2	.1	0.67
Skilled labour		1.0				0.92
Unskilled labour			1.0			0.50
Revenue	.7		.05	.2	.05	0.78

Effects on NPV at shadow prices — *NPV at Shadow Prices* (79.0)

NPV	*%*	*10% change in:*
207.7	363	Average Conversion Factor change from 0.770 to 0.693.
44.5	156	Unskilled labour, ratio of opportunity cost at domestic prices to market wage for unskilled labour, change from 0.650 to 0.585.
18.4	123	Discount rate changed from 9% to 8.1%.

An alternative way to present the results of sensitivity analysis is to ask by how much a project item needs to change before the project decision is affected. It can then be asked whether such a variation in the project item is likely. The so-called switching values for each project item are presented in Table 8.3. Items with a relatively low switching value indicate that the project decision is very sensitive to changes in the item. In this example, at market prices the project decision is very sensitive to variation in revenue and material costs; very small percentage changes in these items result in a negative NPV rather than a positive one. The results at shadow prices are also very sensitive to the national parameter estimates, since small variations produce a positive rather than a negative NPV.

Table 8.3 Switching values (%)

	Market prices (NPV = 163.7)[1]		*Shadow prices (NPV = (79.0))*
Investment: Construction	+ 16.4	Discount rate	−8.1
Equipment	+ 16.4	Average Conversion Factor	−2.8
Working capital	+ 83.3	Opportunity cost of unskilled labour to market wage	−6.4
Materials	+3.3		
Power	+ 29.4		
Transport	+ 58.8		
Skilled labour	+ 17.9		
Unskilled labour	+ 14.9		
Revenue	−1.7		
Materials ratio[2]	+ 3.3		
Discount rate	+ 13.5		

Notes
[1] Delay of investment of more than one year not investigated.
[2] Value of raw material divided by value of total revenue.

Other project items also need to be assessed. The project result is sensitive to the materials ratio, and quite sensitive to cost overruns in the investment period. At both market and shadow prices, the results are sensitive to changes in the discount rate.

Given the sensitivity of the project worth measure to variation in different project items, it needs to be asked how likely is it that the decision to accept or reject the project would be wrong. An assessment of this risk can be based on the project items to which the result is most sensitive; at market prices, the investment costs, material costs, materials ratio and revenue; at shadow prices, these same items plus the ACF and the estimate of output foregone for unskilled labour. Moreover, a fuller statement of the risks involved in deciding on the project should include an assessment of the possibilities of simultaneous variation in these project items.

RISK ANALYSIS

Risk analysis involves a fuller assessment of possible variation. Its purpose is to provide a probability estimate of how likely a project decision is to be wrong. Risk analysis begins from the best estimates contained in the initial resource flow and from the effect of variation given by sensitivity analysis; but now different variables are considered simultaneously.

The actual outcome for a project may vary from the original best estimates. A range of values above and below these best estimates can be defined: for example, in the illustration below values 10 and 20 per cent above and below the best estimates are used. This is a relatively conservative range for variation.

Some project items can be estimated with greater certainty than others. Although it is convenient to use the same range of variation for each variable considered in risk analysis, the probability of the different values in the range occurring will differ. For example, given the optimism with which projects are often prepared, some items like investment costs are more likely to vary upwards rather than downwards from the best estimate, whilst others like revenue are more likely to be below rather than above the best estimate. A probability should be attached to the best estimate and each variation, to reflect the likelihood with which the different values in the range will occur. The sum of these probabilities must total 1.0 for each variable.

The effect of varying values within a range can be calculated through sensitivity analysis. It is the additional probability estimates associated with each variation that represent the essential feature of risk analysis. Where do these probability estimates come from? For some variables they may come from past evidence, for example, of fluctuations in prices, outputs, or of material ratios in different production processes. For other variables, intuitive guesses may have to be made on the basis of experience.

For this example, Table 8.4 summarises the effect on the NPV of variation in each variable, presents the probabilities associated with each variation, and also converts these to a set of two-digit random

Table 8.4 Risk analysis: basic data

	Variation	*−20%*	*−10%*	*0*	*10%*	*20%*
(a) *Market Prices*						
Investment cost	Probability	.1	.1	.4	.2	.2
	Change in NPV	+200	+100	0	−100	−200
	Range	00–09	10–19	20–59	60–79	80–99
Materials cost	Probability	.1	.1	.6	.1	.1
	Change in NPV	+988	+494	0	−494	−988
	Range	00–09	10–19	20–79	80–89	90–99
Materials ratio	Probability	.05	.05	.8	.05	.05
	Change in NPV	+988	+494	0	−494	−988
	Range	00–04	05–09	10–89	90–94	95–99
Unskilled	Probability	.1	.1	.8	.1	.1
labour	Change in NPV	+200	+110	0	−110	−220
	Range	00–09	10–19	20–79	80–89	90–99
Revenue	Probability	.1	.2	.5	.1	.1
	Change in NPV	−1974	−987	0	+987	+1974
	Range	00–09	10–29	30–79	80–89	90–99
(b) *Shadow Prices*						
Average						
Conversion	Probability	.1	.1	.8	.1	.1
factor	Change in NPV	+574	+287	0	−287	−574
	Range	00–09	10–19	20–79	80–89	90–99
Opportunity cost	Probability	.1	.1	.8	.1	.1
unskilled	Change in NPV	+248	+124	0	−124	−248
labour	Range	00–09	10–19	20–79	80–89	90–99
Change in NPV[1]						
Investment cost		+324	+162	0	−162	−324
Materials cost		+762	+381	0	−381	−762
Materials ratio		+762	+381	0	−381	−762
Unskilled labour		+102	+51	0	−51	−102
Revenue		−1614	−807	0	+807	+1614

Note

[1] Probabilities and range as for Market Prices.

numbers. The random numbers are a means of making random choices within the range for each variable. The probabilities for a particular variable, which sum to 1.0, are associated with numbers between 00 and 99. For investment cost in Table 8.4, for example, the probability of 0.1 for investment cost being 20 per cent less than the best estimate is associated with the ten values 00–09; the probability of 0.1 for investment cost being 10 per cent less than the best estimate is associated with the ten values 10–19, and so on. A randomly selected two-digit number then identifies a particular value for investment cost. This information is presented for five variables at market prices and for seven variables at shadow prices. At market prices, risk analysis now proceeds by the selection of sets of five two-digit random numbers, identifying the variation in each variable to which they relate, and adding up the total effect on the NPV. This has been done 100 times to yield 100 estimates of the NPV. At shadow prices, sets of seven two-digit random numbers have been chosen and applied in a similar way. This selection process has also yielded 100 estimates of the NPV.

These 100 estimates in each case are distributed around the best estimate of the NPV (and around their own mean value). The results of the risk analysis are presented in Table 8.5. At market prices, the expected NPV by this process is larger than the best estimate and positive; at shadow prices, it is still negative and well below the best estimate. These expected values confirm the earlier decision that the project could be accepted at market prices but rejected at shadow prices.

However, there is a very large range of values around the best estimate and the expected NPV, implying considerable risk. Owing to the selection process in risk analysis, both distributions of the NPV values are approximately normal, and because of the large range both distributions contain many negative and positive values.[1]

The proportion of negative and positive values can be calculated. At market prices, 39 per cent of the NPV values are negative. If the project is accepted because of its positive NPV at best estimates, there is a 39 per cent chance that the decision will turn out wrong. At shadow prices, 31 per cent of the NPV values are positive. If the project is rejected because of its negative NPV at best estimates, there is a 31 per cent chance that the decision will turn out to be wrong.[2]

Table 8.5 Results of risk analysis

A.	*NPVs*	*Market prices* (NPV = 164)	*Shadow prices* (NPV = −79)
Sample Range:	Highest	+2852	+2618
	Lowest	−3786	−2896
Expected value		+ 369	−890
Standard Deviation		779	721
B. Distribution of NPVs			
	3000+	0	0
	2500 – 2999	2	1
	2000 – 2499	10	0
	1500 – 1999	5	4
	1000 – 1499	11	6
	500 – 999	8	7
	0 – 499	25	13
	−499 – −1	12	20
	−999 – −500	14	17
	−1499 – −1000	8	13
	−1999 – −1500	3	10
	−2499 – −2000	1	6
	−2999 – −2500	0	3
	−3000 –	1	0
Probability:	Positive NPV	61	31
	Negative NPV	39	69

These are the essential results of the risk analysis. They contain more information than simply the best estimate, but also provide a dilemma for those who have to decide. For this project, whether market prices or shadow prices are chosen as the basis of decision, there is a substantial chance of being wrong. It may be thought unacceptable to risk the 39 per cent chance of a negative NPV at market prices; this would reinforce the shadow price calculation that yields a negative NPV anyway, although there is considerable uncertainty with this calculation also.

Risk analysis is most important for marginal projects, with a rate of return just above the discount rate. For projects with a much larger rate of return the probability of a negative NPV with variation in the major variables is likely to be small. The main effect of risk analysis is thus likely to be on decisions among alternative marginal projects. If all project analyses include a risk analysis conducted on similar lines to that in the illustration above, then the less risky among the marginal projects can be chosen.

REDUCING RISK

Identifying the effects of variation in major variables, and investigating the likelihood of their combined variation, provides considerable information on the risks associated with a project. It indicates where the risk might be reduced.

Risk can be reduced at both the analysis and implementation stages of a project. An analysis carried out using the most pessimistic estimates for each variable shows the amount that has to be available as a contingency reserve in the worst case. Reducing risk should aim at improving the project results at least to this extent so the reserve is no longer necessary.

The project results in many cases can be improved by a redesign of the project. Alternative technologies, locations, output mixes and scales should be investigated. Redesign can also include the phasing of investment so that the production lessons learnt in early phases can be applied in later phases, improving the overall performance. Each course of action will have its own risks; lower expected NPV results will probably have to be traded off against lower risks.

Risk reduction can also be achieved by choosing projects for which there are well-known precedents. Replication of small-scale projects rather than commitment to a few large-scale projects can reduce risk. Investment decisions can be seen in terms of programmes of investments rather than one-off projects. Copying and adapting from imported technologies under supply and management contracts can also reduce production and marketing risks. These forms of dealing with risk, however, cannot easily be incorporated into project analysis calculations or decisions on individual projects. Moreover, such approaches lose the potential benefits of developing new technologies or learning-by-doing.

For projects where there are several sources of risk, a different approach may have to be adopted. The illustration above revealed a project highly sensitive both to changes in revenue and in the materials ratio. Where considerable uncertainty attaches both to output sales and technology then the best approach may be to initiate pilot production on a small scale. Pilot production will allow the technical ratios and the output to be tested and improved. It will allow a re-estimation of the main project variables and a reduction in risk for a full investment. However, this does not mean that the full investment will necessarily become acceptable; a reduction in risk may be associated with a smaller estimate of the project net benefits.

A better design for the project may result from these actions; but in practice there will still be considerable uncertainty about project effects. A major tool to use in project implementation to reduce risk is contracting. Generally, the longer for which a contract runs, the more certain the elements contained in the contract. Long-term contracting can be applied both to the purchase of inputs and to the distribution of outputs. It can be applied in management and technical and marketing agreements, to encompass pricing, profit sharing and exchange rate calculations. Again, however, achieving greater stability, or less uncertainty, in project effects may be purchased at a lower level for the net benefits.

CONCLUSION

Measures of project worth are based initially on the best estimates of inputs and outputs. Sensitivity analysis identifies the project variables which affect the best estimate most, both production variables and significant economic parameters. Risk analysis takes the variables to which the project is most sensitive and simulates simultaneous variation in each, using the probability that such variation will occur, and resulting in a statement about the risk of taking a wrong decision. There are different strategies for reducing risk; but in both project decision-taking and implementation, lower risk may have to be traded off against a lower expected NPV.

Further Reading

Little and Mirrlees (1974), chapter XV provides a general description of uncertainty in project analysis and some methods of dealing with it. ODA

(1988), chapter 6 outlines the role of sensitivity analysis and methods for risk reduction. Irvin (1978), chapter III outlines the role of a probability distribution in project decisions using expected values and a measure of dispersion. Brent (1990), chapter 11 has a summary of risk analysis similar to that given here. Pouliquen (1970) outlines the theory of risk analysis and provides some illustrations.

9 Income Distribution Effects of Projects

As is discussed in Chapter 5 projects can be analysed from different perspectives. So far the discussion has focused on their effects in terms of resource use. Projects are assessed on the efficiency with which they use existing resources; an acceptable project being one which generates more total national income than could be obtained by committing the same resources elsewhere.

However, this is only one perspective from which to appraise projects. Two others that have been discussed extensively relate to the impact of projects on the distribution of income and the long-run growth of the economy. This chapter focuses on the first of these, showing how it is possible to trace through the distributional effects of projects and to identify gaining and losing groups. This should be an important piece of information for decision-takers, since most projects will have negative as well as positive income effects. Estimates of income changes created by a project can be given as additional information alongside the standard indicators of project worth from market and shadow price calculations. However, as an alternative, a methodology has been developed to incorporate distributional and growth effects of projects into NPV and IRR calculations. This alternative is discussed in Chapter 10.

This chapter begins by discussing the income changes created by the financing arrangements of a project. It then considers how information from an economic analysis on divergences between market and shadow prices can be used to identify income changes. Income changes are discussed at three levels; between classes and individuals, between regions of an economy, and between nationals of an economy and foreigners. A case study using the world price system illustrates the principles involved. Finally, there is a discussion of the type of project likely to create significant changes in the distribution of income.

ESTIMATING INCOME FLOWS FROM FINANCIAL STATEMENTS

The starting point for an analysis of the income effects of projects must be the results of analysis at market prices, since market prices determine the actual money revenues and costs of projects. The important income flows from financial statements will be the profits received by project owners, taxes paid by a project to the government or subsidies received by it, and any income transfers arising from the financing arrangements of a project.

In terms of the mechanics of tracing distributional effects, it is easier to work with discounted present values for income flows to allocate both the market and shadow price NPV of a project into flows to different groups. This means that instead of calculating the income effects for an individual year, all annual project costs and benefits are converted to a present value by discounting. This greatly simplifies the treatment of distributional issues, although it will not be strictly accurate where the relationship between market and shadow prices for individual items changes over time, so that the CFs involved are not constant. However, provided one can assume constant CFs, the conversion of all cost and benefit streams to present values will be the appropriate starting point for distributional analysis.

The exact income groups used for the identification of income flows can vary between projects but it is desirable to have some consistency, so that the comparative position of different projects can be assessed. Normally, it would be desirable to include the following groups:

- the government, as the origin of taxes and subsidies and the owner of public sector projects. There is an ambiguity regarding the treatment of government income, since in principle if additional income changes for the government are large enough they could affect tax payments, with higher government income used to reduce taxes, and lower income causing a rise in tax rates. Where tax changes follow a change in government income the ultimate gainers and losers will be tax payers. However, if one assumes that no individual project is large enough to affect tax policy this complication can be avoided, and all changes in government income can be treated as income effects for the government;

- equity owners of projects, who in some cases will be the government;
- the rest of the private sector, that is capitalists other than project equity owners, who may supply a project with inputs or use its output;
- various households distinguished by income level, or region of location, who will be affected directly or indirectly as suppliers of labour to a project or as purchasers of output;
- lenders of financial capital, who could be either the banking sector or private depositors. Which group is relevant depends on who bears the cost or receives the benefit of the income transfers that arise from the financing of a project. For example, where the real interest rate of a loan to a project is below the financial opportunity cost discount rate, and where the banks pass on this low interest charge to savers as a low deposit rate, this will be a cost to depositors. Alternatively, if in these circumstances savers receive a real deposit rate equal to the financial discount rate the banks themselves will be meeting the cost of supplying cheap credit to a project;
- foreign income recipients, such as foreign equity holders or foreign workers.

Use of these various groups is illustrated for a simple example of an import substitute project, producing an output steel, with two purchased inputs iron ore and coal, and labour. Coal is imported but local iron ore is non-traded since its poor quality means it has no export market. The market price NPV of the project (discounted at 10 per cent) showing the returns to an equity investment of 100 million pesos and their distribution, is given in table 9.1.[1]

At market prices the net gain to the economy from the project is calculated excluding transfers so that the profits tax and financing elements are omitted from the calculation to give a net NPV of 170 million pesos (400 – 180 – 50 = 170). However, from a distributional viewpoint these transfers must be included.

The equity owners have a net gain 103 million, whilst the government gains the profits tax of 80 million. This is a transfer between the project and the government. The other transfer shown is between the project and the lenders of its loan capital. The net

Table 9.1 Market price NPV at 10 per cent (pesos millions)

	Project owners	*Equity*	*Government*	*Lenders*
1. Benefits				
1.1 Operating profit (before tax)	+400			
1.2 Profits tax	−80		+80	
2. Costs				
2.1 Investment	−180			
2.2 Working capital	−50			
3. Financing				
3.1 Loan	+100			−100
3.2 Repayment	−87			+87
	+103		+80	−13

transfer in favour of the project of 13 million, and the equivalent net loss for the lenders, is derived as follows. The original loan is 100 million (assumed to be received in year zero); the loan is repaid in four annual instalments at a real interest rate of 4 per cent, which gives an annual repayment of 27.5 million (Capital Recovery Factor at 4 per cent × 100). Discounting at the financial discount rate of 10 per cent in present value terms this annual loan repayment is 87.2 million. (Annuity Factor at 10 per cent for four years × 27.5). The difference between the present value of the loan and that of the repayments of principal and interest is the net transfer to the project, or in other words the subsidy from the lenders to the project.

ESTIMATING INCOME FLOWS FROM RESOURCE STATEMENTS

In addition to the flows created at market prices, it is also necessary to identify the transfers arising as a result of divergences between market prices and shadow prices. This is because shadow prices reflect the opportunity cost of utilizing resources on a project, and the benefits of producing output. In other words, shadow not market prices cover the real income effect of a project. If an input costs more at market than at shadow prices, for example because of a tax, the real income loss to the economy due to the use of the input is less than the value placed on it in financial analysis. A project which pays the market price for the input loses this market value, so that someone else must gain the difference between the full opportunity cost and that met by the project. Where a tax is involved this will be a gain to the government. Similarly, if the shadow price of an output is above its market price, there will be an income gain to the economy not captured in the financial calculations. Again some group must gain this additional value.

Identifying the difference between shadow and market prices is relatively straightforward for traded goods and will be caused by trade taxes and controls, which create gains to the government and traders who have access to scarce imports. However, it can be considerably more complex for non-traded goods.

For non-traded inputs in variable supply as discussed in Chapter 5, their cost must be decomposed and inputs valued at shadow prices. Divergences between economic and market values will arise through the effect of taxes and controls on trade, through the existence of surplus profits, and through the payment of market wages above the productivity of workers in alternative occupations. These divergences will create income changes for the government, traders, private capitalists and labour.

Where non-traded outputs and inputs in fixed supply are involved, as discussed in Chapter 7, in theory valuation should be based on consumer willingness to pay. Where the latter exceeds the market price there is an extra gain (for an output) or cost (for an input) not reflected in the financial calculations. A detailed distributional analysis would try to identify the pattern of use of the non-traded goods concerned, and attribute these additional gains or losses to different groups.

Finally, it must be stressed that often the most important direct income effect created by the divergence between market and shadow prices is through the employment effect of projects. Where there is significant underemployment of labour, opportunity cost measured by output foregone in a worker's alternative activity will generally be below the market wage on new projects. This implies that workers will experience an income gain as a result of moving to a new project, given by the difference between their new wage and their previous income. In addition government income can also be affected by additional employment. Where workers previously produced traded goods, so that their output foregone is in terms of traded commodities, it is often assumed that the drop in domestic output that occurs when workers move to employment on a new project is made up by expenditure on additional imports. Thus the government will gain from the tariffs collected on the imports.

The logic of these arguments can be illustrated by extending the previous example of the production of steel. Now more information is given on Operating Profit and Working Capital to show how differences between market and shadow prices can create income changes. The main item of capital cost is equipment, that is imported duty free, and there are very low transport and distribution costs in moving the equipment to the steel project. Under these circumstances for simplicity, it is assumed that all capital costs have an equal value at market and at shadow prices, so that no income effects are created through capital expenditure. A similar assumption is made for terminal value. Table 9.2 summarizes the position on the income changes created by the price divergences relating to Operating Profit and Working Capital.

In deriving these income flows some additional simplifications are adopted. First, for traded inputs to a project or sector all transport and distribution costs from port to user are ignored. A more detailed analysis can incorporate these by treating them as non-traded costs to be decomposed in the same way as the costs of other non-traded inputs used by a project.

Secondly, it is assumed that wherever domestic and world prices (at the official exchange rate) of traded goods diverge, with the former exceeding the latter, this is due to government taxes on trade. Where import controls in the form of licensing and quota restrictions are also in force, the divergence will be partly due to surplus profits of traders, who obtain licences and as a result of the scarcity of imports can charge domestic prices in excess of world prices plus the import tariff. Here part of the divergence will go to importers as surplus profits, and if state trading corporations are not involved these will be gains to the private sector. In economies where this form of import control is important, the assumption that the divergence between domestic and world prices is due only to trade taxes will be misleading, and will have to be dropped in favour

Table 9.2 Income changes (present values at 10 per cent. pesos millions)

	Project market prices	*CF*	*Government*	*Project users*	*Labour*	*Project suppliers*	*Shadow prices*
Operating Profit							
Output							
steel	+700	0.800	−224.0	+84.0			+560.0
Inputs							
coal	−50	0.800	+10.0				−40.0
iron ore	−160	0.551	+24.9		+23.0	+24.0	−88.1
Labour	−90	0.320	+7.2		+54.0		−28.8
	400		−181.9	+84.0	+77.0	+24.0	403.1
Working Capital							
Output							
steel	−20	0.800	+6.4	−2.4			−16.0
Inputs							
coal	−15	0.800	+3.0				−12.0
iron ore	−15	0.551	+2.3		+2.2	+2.2	−8.3
	−50		+11.7	−2.4	+2.2		−36.3

of an attempt to allocate the divergence between taxes and surplus profits to traders. This further complication is not introduced here.

Thirdly, the economic discount rate is taken to be 10 per cent; that is the same as the financial rate.

Steel is an import substitute sold at 100 pesos per kilogram. The alternative source of supply is imports which cost Pesos 80 per kilogram (cif prices at the OER) plus a 40 per cent import duty, to give a landed cost price of 112 pesos per kilogram. Since transport and distribution costs port to users, and project to users, are ignored the shadow price of steel in a world price analysis is 80 pesos per kilogram, compared with the domestic market price of 100 pesos; total output value at shadow prices is 560 million pesos. The distributional effects from the production of steel are two-fold. First, since imports no longer take place the government loses the import duty of 32 pesos per kilogram. Second, domestic users of steel gain due to the fact that domestic supply is cheaper than imports at the import duty-inclusive price; their gain is 12 pesos per kilogram. (112 – 100). Together these twin effects account for the difference between the world and the domestic price. As a percentage of the market price the government loses 32 per cent and users gain 12 per cent. Since the total value of steel at market prices is 700 million pesos, 32 and 12 per cent represent income changes of 224 million pesos and 84 million respectively.

Coal is imported by the project with an import duty of 25 per cent. Its shadow price is 80 per cent of its market price (since 100 / 125 = 0.8) and its total cost at shadow price is 40 million pesos. As a result of the project more imports of coal take place thus raising additional tax revenue for the government through the import duties paid on coal. These duties are the remaining 20 per cent of the domestic price. The total value of coal at domestic market prices is 50 million pesos, so that 10 million pesos goes to the government as tax.

Iron ore is non-traded and as its supply is expanded to meet the needs of the project, its treatment is more complicated. The CF for iron ore is 0.551 and its derivation is given in Table 9.3. The use of each item in the production of iron ore causes income flows. Each input valued at market prices is shown with a negative sign indicating that its use is a cost. However, where the shadow price of inputs is below their market price there will be gains to other groups, in addition to the cost met by the steel project when it uses iron ore. In the case of the traded raw material inputs, these are imported and subject to a 33 per cent import duty giving a CF of 0.75 (100 / 133 = 0.75). This means that of any one unit of expenditure on these raw materials 25 per cent goes to the government as taxes. Hence the government gains 25 per cent of 60 million pesos, that is 15 million pesos.

Capital costs refer to traded capital assets in iron ore production, subject to an import duty of 11 per cent. Under the same assumptions as for traded raw materials this gives a CF of 0.9 (100 / 111 = 0.9). Here the government gains 10 per cent of these capital costs at market prices in the form of additional taxes.

Labour employed in producing iron ore also gains. The market wage is 8 pesos per day, whilst at domestic prices output foregone is 4 pesos per day. The latter is taken as a measure of a worker's

Table 9.3 Conversion factor for non-traded input iron ore (present value at 10 per cent pesos million)

Costs	*Project cost at market prices*	*%*	*CF*	*Government*	*Labour*	*Project suppliers*	*Shadow prices*
Traded raw material inputs	−60.0	37	0.750	+15.0			−45.0
Capital costs	−30.0	19	0.900	+3.0			−27.0
Labour	−46.0	29	0.350	+6.9	+23.0		−16.1
Surplus profits	−24.0	15	0.000			+24.0	0
	−160.0	100	0.551	+24.9	+23.0	+24.0	88.1

income without employment in iron ore production. The gain per day is therefore 4 pesos or 50 per cent of total wages paid. Labour therefore gains 50 per cent of the wage bill of 46 million pesos; that is 23.0 million pesos. However, there are further income changes arising from employment in iron ore, due to the fact that labour's output foregone is traded goods, subject to import tariffs. The CF for the output workers employed in iron ore would have produced is 0.70. This means that at world prices output foregone is 2.80 pesos per day and the conversion factor for labour is 0.35 (2.80/8.00 = 0.35). The difference between these opportunity costs at world and domestic prices, of 1.20 pesos per day, is due to trade taxes and will accrue to the government, since if workers move to employment in iron ore and the fall in output of the goods they were previously producing is made up by additional imports, the government will gain the tariff revenue on these new imports. This tariff gain of 1.20 pesos per day is 15 per cent of the daily market wage, and in total is 15 per cent of the wage bill; that is 15 per cent of 46 million pesos, or 6.9 million pesos.

Finally, the surplus profits earned in the production of iron ore by definition are profits in excess of those that can be earned elsewhere in the economy. They are therefore a gain to the owners of capital who produce iron ore, termed here the project suppliers, since iron ore is an input to the steel project.

The analysis of supply conditions in iron ore reveals that three groups gain from the expansion of iron ore as follows:

	(Pesos millions)
government	24.9
labour	23.0
project suppliers	24.0
	71.9

The total gain of 71.9 million pesos equals the difference between the cost of iron ore at market prices and its shadow price value. In other words, whilst iron ore costs the project 160 million pesos, the cost to the economy is only 88.1 pesos million, so that there is a gain of 71.9 million pesos to other groups, distributed in the manner described above.

For labour employed in the production of steel there will be a significant income gain. The daily wage rate is 10 pesos per day. The workers concerned would have been producing other commodities worth 4 pesos per day, at domestic prices, and this is taken to reflect their alternative earnings. The net gain to workers is thus 6 pesos per day, or in total 60 per cent of the market wage bill. The output steel workers would have produced is a non-traded good, and expenditure that would have been made on this is diverted to other commodities. The tax component of expenditure on these goods is 20 per cent, so that for every 4 pesos per day of diverted expenditure there is a tax gain to the government of 0.8 pesos, and an opportunity cost of 3.20 pesos, so that the conversion factor for labour is 0.320. This tax element is 8 per cent of the total wage bill, so that through the loss of output arising from workers shifting to employment in the production of steel the government gains 7.2 million pesos, which is 8 per cent of the total wage bill.

The outcome of all these adjustments is that whilst the Net Operating Profit figure is very similar at market prices and shadow prices, this hides significant distributional shifts, caused by divergences between market and shadow prices for individual items. The government is the main loser because steel, previously imported, is now produced domestically and the import tariffs on steel are lost. There are other small tax gains on direct and indirect inputs into steel, but these do not offset this loss of import tariffs. However, if the government is the owner of the project the income from its financial operations will more than offset this loss of tariff revenue. Other affected groups are users of steel, who will get the good at a lower price when it is produced domestically rather than imported, workers employed in steel and also in the production of iron ore, and project suppliers who produce iron ore and earn surplus profits.

Table 9.2 also shows the income flows associated with inventories held as working capital. The principle of adjustment is identical to that discussed for Operating Profit and the CFs involved are the same. Thus the gains and losses for the various groups are the same percentage of value at market prices as in the case of Operating Profit. The one difference is a change of sign for all income flows associated with steel. In Working Capital steel is held as a stock. It has a negative sign indicating that it is a cost to the project, since some output is held back from sale thus reducing the revenue of the project. Lower sales of steel mean that the government will gain tariff revenue from additional imports hence the positive sign for the government income flow. Also users of steel will lose if sales of steel are reduced and hence the negative sign for user income.

Table 9.4 sets out the full set of income changes incorporating those from the analysis at market prices (Table 9.1) with those arising from the divergences between market and shadow prices (Table 9.2). Several points can be noted.

- The main divergence between the NPV in the market price analysis (103.0 million pesos) and that of the economic analysis (186.8 million pesos) is caused by the adding back of Profits Tax in the latter; in other words as a transfer, taxes on profits have no opportunity cost, although they create an income flow between the project and the government.
- The divergences between shadow and market prices have only a small impact overall on the NPV, but none the less as we have seen create a number of important income effects.
- The loan financing arrangements create a net gain to the project of 13 million pesos, however, as they relate to transactions between domestic lenders and borrowers they are a transfer not a resource cost. Hence the financing effects of the project have a zero value in the economic analysis. As we shall see below, where foreign financing is involved this may not always be the appropriate treatment.
- The actual income groups affected by a project can be specified in different ways. In Table 9.4, since steel is an intermediate good, if no public sector firms are involved project users and suppliers can be grouped under a single heading of the private

Table 9.4 Summary of income changes of market price and shadow price analysis (pesos millions)

	Project NPV market prices	*Government*	*Project users*	*Project suppliers*	*Labour*	*Lenders*	*Project NPV shadow prices*
1. Benefits							
1.1 Operating profit	+400.0	−181.9	+84.0	+24.0	+77.0		+403.1
1.2 Profits tax	−80.0	+80.0					0
2. Costs							
2.1 Investments[a]	−180.0						−180.0
2.2 Working capital	−50.0	+11.7	−2.4	+2.2	+2.2		−36.3
3. Financing							
3.1 Loan	+100.0					−100.0	0
3.2 Repayment	−87.0					+87.0	0
	+103.0	−90.2	+81.6	+26.2	+79.2	−13.0	+186.8

Note

a For simplicity it is assumed that for investment costs market prices and shadow prices are equal.

sector. Where it is possible to break down users and suppliers into public and private firms, the income changes for the former can be added to the government category. Also where data are available it may be helpful to distinguish between various groups of workers differentiated by income level or perhaps region. It should be stressed that in practice inevitably there will be some approximations regarding the categorization of the groups affected by a project. Analysts will be doing well if they can specify groups in the broad categories illustrated here.

REGIONAL INCOME EFFECTS

The discussion so far has focused on the distribution of income between different groups in the economy regardless of location. However, the generation of employment opportunities in backward regions is a common element of policy in many countries, so that information on how residents of a region are affected by a new project can be important.

Residents of a particular region can be affected by a new project in a variety of ways. If they are owners of equity in the project they will receive a proportion of the profits; if they are employed as workers they will receive some of the wage income, and if they supply the project with inputs their profits and wage income may be raised. Finally, as users of a project's output their income may be changed by the pricing policy of the project.

Once the national position on income changes is estimated, deriving a distribution for the region of location requires estimates of

(a) the distribution by location of shareholders of the project;
(b) the proportion of its workers who come from the region of location and the proportion of the wage bill they receive;
(c) the domestic inputs supplied to the project that are produced within the region;
(d) the extent to which output of a project is used within the region.

All these characteristics will vary between projects depending upon financing arrangements, choice of technology, the availability of labour, and the productive structure of different regions. Of these the direct regional employment effect is the most certain and the easiest to estimate. For certain types of project, particularly infrastructure schemes for irrigation and transport, the use of project output within a region may have a major effect in terms of additional incomes for users, and may provide the main rationale for locating a project in the region concerned.

The principle of regional income effects can be illustrated by reference to the previous example of the steel project. To introduce a regional dimension to the distributional analysis the following assumptions are made:

- equity owners of the project are all resident outside the region of location, so that no profits accrue to residents of the region;
- all workers employed in the production of steel come from the region of the project; all the gain to workers employed in steel is therefore a regional gain;
- production of the input iron ore is a local activity within the region, and workers and capitalists involved in supplying iron ore are all residents of the region, so that their gains are regional;
- distribution of output steel is nation-wide, but residents of the region take 10 per cent of project output, so that 10 per cent of the gains to project users are a regional gain;
- residents of the region are not involved as lenders of funds to the project.

Based on these assumptions Table 9.5 sets out the regional income effects of the project. It can be seen that whilst the economy gains 186.8 million pesos (the shadow price NPV at 10 per cent discount rate), the region in which the project is located gains 113.6 million pesos, or just over 60 per cent of the addition to national income. This is largely through the gains of workers employed by the project itself or in the production of the iron ore used by the project.

A further point worth commenting on is that from a regional point of view the multiplier concept can be introduced at the project level. The multiplier relates to the total income change generated by an increase in expenditure, when there are idle resources that can be put to productive use. In other words, higher incomes for residents

Table 9.5 Regional income effect (pesos millions)

	Economic NPV
National income gain	186.8
Regional income gain	
Labour[a]	79.2
Project suppliers[b]	26.2
Project users[c]	8.2
	113.6

Notes
[a] 54.0 million pesos in the production of steel itself, and 25.2 million pesos in the production of iron ore (from both Operating Profit and Working Capital).
[b] Surplus profits from the production of iron ore.
[c] 10% of the total user gain of 81.6 million.

of a region lead to higher expenditures which stimulate additional production and income. This means that the total income gain to a region may be considerably more than the direct gains in wage and profit income going to workers and capitalists associated with a new project. The multiplier concept is normally excluded from analyses of individual projects on the grounds that even if there is excess capacity within the economy to respond to an increase in demand, any equivalent investment expenditure would generate the same growth in total income. In other words, if a deficiency in demand is the problem, it can be made good by spending resources on any project not on one in particular. If the multiplier effect cannot be attributed to any individual project, it is argued, it cannot legitimately be included as an additional benefit of a project. These objections to the inclusion of multiplier effects in project analysis are less convincing at the regional level, since whilst a given expenditure may lead to the same national income increase regardless of which project it is spent on, the regional distribution of the increase is likely to vary with the region of location of the project.

However, capturing the regional multiplier effect of a new project is very demanding in terms of data, since it involves the concept of the marginal propensity to spend within a region; that is the proportion of additional income spent on goods and services produced within the region in which a project is located.[2] This requires not just an estimate of expenditure patterns, but also of supply responses, so that one can identify how far demand can be met by additional production from within the region. In backward regions, which are those most likely to be favoured by government regional policy, by definition the level of economic development will be low, so that the capacity to meet additional demand from region-based production will in turn be low. Furthermore, an assessment of the regional effect of projects should be done systematically, not carried out in isolation for an individual project.

FOREIGN PARTICIPATION IN PROJECTS

Up to this point the discussion of income distribution effects has not distinguished between nationals and foreigners. However, foreigners, for example banks, transnational firms, governments or foreign workers, can all be involved with projects. The difference of principle in the treatment of income flows to foreign as opposed to national groups is that income received by foreigners will be a cost to the economy, since it is an income outflow, whilst income losses to foreigners will be a gain or form of income inflow to the national economy.

Apart from the trading links in supplying imports or buying exports, which are handled through the valuation of traded goods, there are four main ways in which foreign groups will be involved with projects:

(1) through supplying loan or aid finance;
(2) through direct foreign investment in some or all of the equity of a project;
(3) through the employment of foreign labour;
(4) through supplying services, such as management, or technology.

The distributional aspects of these links will be discussed in turn.

As discussed in Chapter 2, a key issue in relation to foreign financing is whether the inflow of funds is linked specifically with the project under consideration. If it is not, for example if there is a general aid budget or loan programme available for any project not just one in particular, then all the financial transactions involved, both inflows and outflows, will occur regardless of which project is selected. This means that any gain or loss to the economy resulting from foreign financing arrangements cannot be treated as a benefit or cost linked with an individual project. In our example of the steel project, one can change the original assumption and now assume that the loan of 100 million pesos is from a foreign source. The project gains as a result of the loan finance since the discounted flow of repayments (87 million pesos) is less than the present value of the original loan (100 million pesos). Where domestic lenders provide the loan, which is the assumption used in Table 9.4, the gain of 13 million pesos is a domestic transfer, since it is a gain to the project owners, but a loss to another domestic group. As a transfer it is not included as a benefit in the shadow price NPV calculations. Similarly, if the loan comes from a foreign source, but is not tied to a specific project, the net gain of 13 million pesos will again not be included as a benefit.

However, in this example if the loan is tied specifically to the project, so that it would not be available for other projects, the financing arrangements with foreign creditors cannot be ignored. The net gain of 13 million pesos arising from the difference between the discounted value of the loan and the outflows associated with it becomes a net gain to the economy and a loss to foreigners. Losses to foreigners have no social value in an analysis from the national perspective, so that the net value of the project in economic terms is now increased by 13 million to 199.8 million pesos. The logic of this is that the economy has gained by receiving a loan greater than the value of repayments associated with it; or, in other words, it has gained from a loan whose real interest rate is below the economic discount rate reflecting returns available on other investments.[3] Including foreign financing with the other income flows gives a new set of income changes, set out in Table 9.6.

Similar procedures apply to aid flows, although given its concessional element one would expect higher net transfers to be involved with such flows, so that repayments are below the value of the inflow by a higher proportion than in the case of commercial credit. The ratio of discounted repayments to the present value of the aid inflow is what is termed the grant element of aid.

The principles involved for foreign equity participation in projects are similar to those for loan finance, although it is likely that more foreign investments than foreign loans will be linked specifically to particular projects. Where investment is not linked, so

Table 9.6 New income changes with foreign financing (tied to the project)

	Project NPV market prices	Domestic income groups				Project NPV shadow prices	Foreigners
		Government	Project users	Project suppliers	Labour		
1. Benefits							
1.1 Operating profit	+400.0	−181.9	+84.0	+24.0	+77.0	+403.1	
1.2 Profits tax	−80.0	+80.0				0	
2. Costs							
2.1 Investment	−180.0					−190.0	
2.2 Working capital	−50.0	+11.7	−2.4	+2.2	+2.2	−36.3	
3. Foreign loan financing							
3.1 Loan	+100.0					+100.0	−100.0
3.2 Repayment	−87.0					−87.0	+87.0
	+103.0	−90.2	+81.6	+26.2	+79.2	199.8	−13.0

that the same investment inflows of equity and outflows of repatriated profits would arise regardless of what project is selected, the foreign investment arrangements of a project can again be ignored.[4]

Foreign investment projects will often be package deals put together by host governments and investors, reflecting sets of incentives, marketing and management arrangements. Such deals will often be unique, in the sense that only this particular set of arrangements will attract the foreign investor concerned. In this type of situation analysis of the project proposed must assume that in the absence of this package, or a version of it, the foreign investment involved would not be forthcoming. This does not mean that the sensitivity of the project analysis to changes in the package, such as tax concessions, local content requirements, marketing arrangements, royalty payments and so forth, should not be tested. However, it will be appropriate to treat the foreign funds as specific to the project under scrutiny. The financing arrangements then become part of the economic analysis since the economy will gain from the inflow of the equity investment, and lose from the outflows of repatriated profits. This is in addition to outflows and inflows arising from foreign loan finance.

Other specific effects arising from the involvement of foreign investors, such as transfer prices for equipment and raw materials supplied by the foreign investor, and any external effects on local competitors, should be included in the assessment of the project's economic costs and benefits.[5] In the discussion of our steel project, though, such issues are ignored to allow a focus simply on the financial effects of foreign investment.

Now of a total capital of 200 million pesos, divided equally between loan end equity finance, it is assumed that whilst 100 per cent of the loan is from foreign sources, 60 per cent of the equity capital is also foreign. Therefore, the foreign investment participation of 60 million pesos (which is assumed to be received in year zero and therefore has a present value of 60 million) creates a benefit for the economy in the form of an inflow of income, but also a cost when 60 per cent of profits that accrue to foreign equity owners are repatriated. It is assumed that all such profits are repatriated in the year in which they are received rather than reinvested.

The NPV at market prices accruing to the owners of the project is 103 million pesos, which can be interpreted as the present value of equity income in excess of the normal rate of profit given by the 10 per cent discount rate; that is a form of surplus profit. In other words the steel project can generate income to recover the initial investment of 100 million pesos, earn a return of 10 per cent on this investment and still have a surplus of 103 million pesos for distribution to equity holders. With foreign equity representing 60 per cent of the equity capital, 60 per cent of these surplus profits, or 61.8 million pesos, will go to foreign investors. Foreign investors will therefore put in 60 million pesos in equity, recover this 60 million pesos with a 10 per cent rate of profit, and still gain extra profits of 61.8 million pesos. This high profitability reflects the fact that the project has an IRR well above the 10 per cent discount rate. Assuming that the entire loan of 100 million pesos is foreign, but now introducing a 60 per cent foreign share of equity, the income flows of table 9.6 become those of Table 9.7.

Now the shadow price value of the project has fallen from 199.8 million pesos (Table 9.6) to 138.0 million pesos (Table 9.7). The difference is due to the surplus profits of 61.8 million pesos repatriated by foreign investors. The project is still highly profitable, but with foreign equity involvement foreigners now gain some of these profits which they take out of the economy. The gain to the economy is therefore correspondingly lower.

Foreign workers employed on a project will experience an income gain if their earnings in their new employment exceed what they could have earned in their alternative occupation in their country of origin. However, following the procedure that only income changes for nationals are relevant in a national cost–benefit calculation, income gains to foreign workers are not incorporated as a benefit of a project. As is discussed in Chapter 5, the cost to the economy of employing foreign labour is the proportion of their income sent home as remittances, a direct foreign exchange cost, plus the cost of their local consumption expenditure, which can be translated into an indirect foreign exchange cost.

These procedures can be illustrated by assuming that in the production of steel, some of the workers employed are foreign immigrants. These workers receive 10 pesos per day in wages, and remit 60 per cent or 6 pesos to their home countries. The remainder, 4 pesos per day, is spent domestically on consumption goods. These on average have an import tariff of 35 per cent, so that their CF is 0.74 (100 / 135 = 0.74). This means that the 4 pesos daily

Table 9.7 New income changes with foreign financing and foreign investment (tied to the project. pesos millions)

	Project NPV market prices	Domestic income groups: Government	Project users	Project suppliers	Labour	Project NPV shadow prices	Payments to foreigners
1. Benefits							
1.1 Operating profits	+400.0	−181.9	+84.0	+24.0	+77.0	+403.1	
1.2 Profits tax	−80.0	+80.0				0	
2. Costs							
2.1 Investment	−180.0					−180.0	
2.2 Working capital	−50.0	+11.7	−2.4	+2.2	+2.2	−36.3	
3. Foreign loan financing							
3.1 Loan	+100 .0					+100.0	−100.0
3.2 Repayment	−87.0					−87.0	+87.0
4. Foreign investment financing							
4.1 Equity Inflow	+60.0					+60.0	−60.0
4.2 Equity recovery[a]	−60.0					−60.0	+60.0
4.3 Surplus profit[b]	−61.8					−61.8	+61.8
	41.2	−90.2	+81.6	+26.2	+79.2	+138.0	+48.8

Notes

a Discounted at 10% with 10% rate of return on equity.

b Discounted value of profits above those at 10% rate of return.

consumption expenditure per worker has an equivalent foreign exchange cost of 2.96 pesos (4 × 0.74 = 2.96). The full cost to the economy of employing such a worker on a daily basis is therefore direct remittances (6 pesos) plus the foreign exchange value of local consumption (2.96 pesos), which totals pesos 8.96.

In addition to the gain to workers themselves the government will gain tax revenue from import tariffs on the goods the workers consume. These tariffs are 26 per cent of the market price of the consumption, since the relevant CF is 0.74. On a daily basis the tax gain for the government is 1.04 pesos per day (4 pesos × 0.26).

Therefore, from the employment of an individual foreign worker paid 10 pesos per day, the government gains pesos 1.04, whilst the economic cost of employing the worker is 8.96 pesos. This opportunity cost is 89.6 per cent of the market wage (CF for foreign labour = 0.896), whilst the government's gain through tax revenue is the remaining 10.4 per cent. These income flows can be incorporated in the analysis of the steel project by adjusting the data from Table 9.2 to allow for the employment of some foreign labour. In Table 9.8 it is assumed that 30 per cent of the wage cost in operations represents a bill for foreign workers. For simplicity no foreign labour element is included in working capital.

If Table 9.8 is compared with table 9.2 it can be seen that there is a slightly lower value of Operating Profit caused by the higher valuation of labour due to the inclusion of foreign workers. The only income change for domestic groups caused by the employment of foreign workers is the tax gain to the government of 2.8 pesos million (10.4 per cent of the market wage bill of 27 million).

The results of Table 9.7 are amended in Table 9.9 by incorporating this treatment of foreign labour employed in the steel project.

Now in comparison with the earlier results the NPV has at shadow prices fallen further to 122.4 million pesos, with foreigners receiving a total of 75.8 million pesos.

Payments to foreigners also arise through management service contracts and royalties for technology. These are direct expenditures of foreign exchange and like imports are a cost to the economy. Their treatment can be illustrated by modifying the steel project example still further. In Table 9.10 a management fee, set at 5 per cent of operating profits before tax, is added to the data from Table 9.9. This management fee is an additional payment to foreigners, that reduces the project NPV at both shadow and market prices. As

Table 9.8 Income changes operating profit with foreign labour (pesos millions)

	Project market prices	CF	Domestic income groups: Government	Project users	Labour	Project suppliers	Shadow prices	Payments to foreigners
Output								
steel	+700.0	0.800	−224.0	+84.0			560.0	
Inputs								
coal	−50.0	0.800	+10.0				−40.0	
iron ore	−160.0	0.551	+24.9		+23.0	+24.0	−88.1	
Labour: domestic	−63.0	0.320	+5.0		+37.8		−20.2	
foreign	−27.0	0.896	+2.8				−24.2	+27.0
	400.0		−181.3	+84.0	+60.8	+24.0	387.5	+27.0

Table 9.9 New income changes with foreign financing, foreign investment and foreign labour

		Domestic income groups					
	Project NPV market prices	*Government*	*Project users*	*Project suppliers*	*Labour*	*Project NPV shadow prices*	*Payments to foreigners*
1. Benefits							
1.1 Operating Profits	+400.0	−181.3	+84.0	+24.0	+60.8	387.5	+27.0
1.2 Profits Tax	−80.0	+80.0					
2. Costs							
2.1 Investment	−180.0					−180.0	
2.2 Working capital	−50.0	+11.7	−2.4	+2.2	+2.2	−36.3	
3. Foreign loan financing							
3.1 Loan	+100.0					+100.0	−100.0
3.2 Repayment	−87.0					−87.0	+87.0
4. Foreign investment financing							
4.1 Equity inflow	+60.0					+60.0	−60.0
4.2 Equity recovery	−60.0					−60.0	+60.0
4.3 Surplus profit	−61.8					−61.8	+61.8
	41.2	−89.6	81.6	26.2	63.0	122.4	75.8

Table 9.10 New income changes with foreign financing, foreign investment, foreign labour and foreign management

		Domestic income groups					
	Project NPV market prices	*Government*	*Project users*	*Project suppliers*	*Labour*	*Project NPV shadow prices*	*Payments to foreigners*
1. Benefits							
1.1 Operating profits	+400.0	−181.3	+84.0	+24.0	+60.8	387.5	+27.0
1.2 Profits tax	−80.0	+80.0					
2. Costs							
2.1 Investment	−180.0					−180.0	
2.2 Working capital	−50.0	+11.7	−2.4	+2.2	+2.2	−36.3	
3. Foreign loan financing							
3.1 Loan	+100.0					+100.0	−100.0
3.2 Repayment	−87.0					−87.0	+87.0
4. Foreign investment financing							
4.1 Equity inflow	+60.0					+60.0	−60.0
4.2 Equity recovery	−60.0					−60.0	+60.0
4.3 Surplus profit	−61.8					−61.8	+61.8
5. Foreign management fee	−20.0					−20.0	+20.0
	21.2	−89.6	81.6	26.2	63.0	102.4	95.8

a direct expenditure of foreign exchange it has a CF of 1.0. The new NPV at shadow prices is 102.4 million pesos, with foreigners receiving a total payment of 95.8 million pesos from the projects financing, employment of labour and use of management services.

PROJECTS WITH IMPORTANT DISTRIBUTIONAL EFFECTS

The procedures outlined above can be applied to any type of project. Projects which have a positive impact on the distribution of income are those where net benefits are distributed in a more egalitarian manner than is average income. Such projects will be those for which a significant part of benefits go to lower income and underprivileged groups, such as unskilled workers, small farmers, artisans, small traders and low income consumers. The type of project likely to have this impact will possess several characteristics such as

(a) employment of relatively large numbers of unskilled workers, in either operations or construction;
(b) production of consumption goods for low-income groups, which were either previously unavailable, or only available at a higher price;
(c) production of intermediate inputs used by low income producers that were again either previously unavailable or available only at a higher price;
(d) generation of backward linkages so that additional jobs, and thus higher incomes, can be created for unskilled workers in domestic activities that supply inputs to the new project.[6]

From this list of characteristics it should be clear that what is important from a distributional point of view is not the sector of investment, but the type of project involved. For example, although it is sometimes implied that investment in agriculture has more beneficial distributional effects than investment in industry, this is not at all inevitable. Investment in a mechanized or estate farming system may be less progressive in distributional terms than investment in industrial projects for relatively simple low-income goods and utilizing labour-intensive techniques of production.

CONCLUSIONS

In principle it is possible to go into considerable detail in tracing through the income effects of projects, particularly those arising from divergences between market and shadow prices. However, in practice it will be difficult to go much beyond the stage of identifying in broad terms the main groups affected. A typical breakdown could be between government, private producers, skilled and unskilled labour. It is also possible to estimate the income inflows and outflows arising from foreign involvement in projects. Failure to go beyond these aggregate groupings is largely due to the crude assumptions required to allocate income changes between different groups. However, whilst limited this information may none the less be an important input into project decision-taking, particularly if it is possible to estimate how the poorest groups are affected.

Further Reading

Relatively little has been written on the problems of tracing through the income effects of projects. By far the most detailed discussion is Londero (1987), which is a rigorous and advanced text. There distributional analysis is based on economic analysis at domestic not world prices, so that there are some differences between the discussion and that given here. There are very detailed case studies of an industrial project (chapter 9), an electricity project (chapter 10) and an irrigation project (chapter 11). Other case studies are found in UNIDO (1972), chapters 19 to 22. The regional multiplier is discussed in UNIDO (1972), chapter 7, pages 80–2. UNIDO (1980) examines actual projects from Pakistan with chapter 4 on a textile project, illustrating the regional dimension with a crude estimate of the regional multiplier, and chapter 5 on a sugarmill, showing a full application of the procedures discussed here. ODA (1988) has a brief distributional case study (detailed case study), Weiss (1980) discusses the economic analysis of foreign investment projects. MacArthur (1978) and Phillips (1986a) survey some of the principles of distributional analysis discussed here.

10 Savings and Income Distribution

As noted earlier projects can contribute to different objectives. The shadow pricing system discussed so far uses a definition of opportunity cost based on income foregone from the use of existing resources. However, in the 1970s considerable attention was given to showing how the effects of projects on the growth of income over time and on living standards of poorer groups could be incorporated in project analysis.

If projects are to be assessed quantitatively in terms of their contribution to different objectives, numerical weights will be required to combine these various effects. These weights should capture the potential conflict or trade-off between objectives; for example, an efficient project in terms of resource use may have a weak impact on the income of the poor, or a project that employs many poor people may have a weak contribution to growth. This chapter discusses the derivation of weights required to produce a single measure of project worth (NPV or IRR at shadow prices) when project effects are assessed from a wider range of perspectives.

The chapter begins by discussing the rationale for incorporating additional objectives. It then considers how different specifications of the numeraire affect this type of analysis. Two alternatives for incorporating weights for growth and distributional effects are noted. Problems in specifying the relevant weights are considered, and their application is illustrated with a simple example. The chapter concludes with a discussion of the practical applicability of the methods.

CONSTRAINTS AND OBJECTIVES

If governments have a strong degree of control over the economy they can intervene directly in pursuit of growth and distributional objectives; for example, they could raise the rate of savings by taxation or by bond issues to the private sector, and improve income distribution by asset redistributions, such as land reform and nationalization, and various subsidy programmes targeted at the poor. Wherever such direct interventions are feasible they are likely to be the most effective means of meeting such objectives. However, the incorporation of growth and distributional considerations in the process of project selection was justified originally in terms of the constraints on government capacity to pursue such direct measures. Project selection was therefore to be a backdoor policy instrument that would be less obvious in its effects than the alternatives, and thus less likely to run into opposition from class and vested interests. This view of constrained governments is somewhat inconsistent with the picture of widespread government interventions often drawn in discussions of developing countries. Even where direct measures are feasible, provided they alone are insufficient to meet what the government considers to be adequate savings and distributional targets, there should still be scope for using project selection as a complement to these other measures.

Projects are seen as contributing to higher growth by increasing income that is saved, and thus available for investment. This follows from a view of capital-scarce LDCs, implying that government growth targets for national income are frustrated by low domestic savings and that additional savings will automatically be invested. A project which contributes to additional savings via the income changes it creates, will help to raise the rate of growth. The extent of the growth effect will depend on the productivity of the investment that the additional savings finance.

Projects will improve the distribution of income and consumption by employing the poor or involving them as either suppliers of inputs or users of project output. There can be a conflict here since the poor often save proportionately less of their income than do richer groups, so that income changes that are desirable from one perspective may not be so from another. Hence the need for weights that attempt to balance gains in terms of different objectives; for example, such weights would compare the worth of Rs1 of income saved against Rs1 of income going as consumption to a poor group.

THE NUMERAIRE

Thus far the unit of account in which project effects have been calculated is income, measured either at world or domestic prices.

However, once savings and distributional effects are incorporated into the calculations one must distinguish how this income is used – whether it goes to the government or the private sector, whether it is saved or consumed, and which groups or individuals receive the consumption. These different dimensions of the numeraire can be summarized in Figure 10.1.

Income	Prices	
	World prices	Domestic prices
Government	saving	saving
Private	consumption	consumption

Figure 10.1 Dimensions of the Numeraire

In principle, as we have stressed earlier, the choice of numeraire *per se* is a matter of presentation or convenience. However, the two original main texts have used different specifications of the numeraire. One uses private consumption (for the average consumer) at domestic prices; that is the bottom right-hand box in Figure 10.1. The other uses government savings at world prices, the top left-hand box.[1]

As we have seen in Chapter 5, use of different prices to measure income will create differences in NPVs. A further difference is created when one uses savings or consumption in the numeraire. If there is a premium on savings relative to consumption due to the fact that savings are below the government's desired level, this can be handled in two equivalent ways. Where savings are the numeraire, as the unit in which other effects are expressed, they must have a value of 1.0. Consumption will be expressed in the numeraire by reducing its value in relation to savings. For example, if savings are twice as valuable as consumption, implying a savings premium of 100 per cent, a project with a NPV of 100, 30 of which will be saved and 70 of which will be consumed, will be worth 65 in the savings numeraire (30 + 70 / 2 = 65). This follows since the consumption component of the NPV is worth only 35 in terms of savings.

Alternatively, where consumption is the numeraire and savings are worth more than consumption, savings must be increased in value to express them in terms of the numeraire consumption; with the same numerical example the NPV increases from 100 to 130 [(30 × 2) + 70 = 130] since the savings component is worth 60 in terms of consumption.

Thus with a premium on savings, either consumption is reduced in value using a weight of below 1.0 (the savings numeraire) or savings are raised using a weight of above 1.0 (the consumption numeraire). It is clear that provided identical assumptions are made these adjustments are logically equivalent.

MECHANICS OF SAVINGS AND DISTRIBUTIONAL ADJUSTMENTS

There are two approaches to the mechanics of incorporating savings and distribution weights into project analysis. One is to adjust individual shadow prices, and thus CFs, to allow for savings and distributional effects. The other is to break down a project NPV at shadow prices into gains for different groups in the manner described in Chapter 9. The savings and consumption for the groups arising from these income changes can then be revalued and a new NPV estimated.

Using the first approach of adjusting shadow prices often the key price is the shadow wage for unskilled labour. Much of the discussion focuses on the treatment of labour on the grounds that the main income effect of most projects will be through the employment of unskilled workers, who will experience a significant income increase as a result of finding permanent work on a new project. This income will have effects in terms of savings and distributional objectives that must be incorporated in a new expression for the shadow wage. The following equation illustrates the procedure in general terms.

$$\text{SWR} = \begin{array}{l}\text{Output}\\ \text{foregone at}\\ \text{world prices}\end{array} + \begin{array}{l}\text{Cost of additional}\\ \text{consumption of}\\ \text{unskilled worker}\\ \text{at world prices}\end{array} - \begin{array}{l}\text{Benefit of}\\ \text{additional}\\ \text{consumption of}\\ \text{unskilled worker}\\ \text{at world prices}\end{array} \qquad (10.1)$$

The first term is equivalent to the SWR discussed in Chapter 5, whilst the second and third terms reflect the incorporation of savings and distributional objectives. Additional consumption by workers is a cost in terms of raising the level of savings since resources are diverted to consumption; hence the second term has a positive sign. However, additional consumption will also be a benefit from a distributional point of view if workers are a low-income group. This benefit will lower the cost of their employment, hence the negative sign on the third term. The trade-off between these two objectives is reflected in the weight given to additional consumption.

Use of a new SWR alters the shadow prices of all commodities, and thus all CFs. This follows since labour enters into the production of all non-traded goods, and even traded goods, valued primarily at their world market prices, have an element of their shadow prices determined by transport and distribution margins, the value of which will be influenced by the SWR. Therefore, in theory a full set of new CFs will be required whenever savings and distributional adjustments are incorporated in an analysis.

However, many types of income effects are created by projects in addition to those experienced by project workers, and it may be very complicated to capture all of these through the adjustment of individual prices. Chapter 11, Appendix 11.2 shows how an adjusted set of CFs can be obtained using the technique of semi-input-output analysis.

The alternative procedure for incorporating growth and distributional objectives involves identifying the income flows for different groups, and is easier to apply in a detailed analysis. It requires estimates of marginal propensities to save for the different groups. Once savings and consumption changes have been estimated they can be adjusted by the weight appropriate for the numeraire and the groups affected.

As a simple numerical example of the procedure a project with an NPV of 100 million pesos creates the income effects shown in Table 10.1.

Out of the total income increase of 100 million pesos, savings rise by 20 and consumption by 80 million. The weights given to the additional savings and consumption should reflect the trade-offs between growth and distribution and the following sections discuss their derivation.

Table 10.1 Project example: income flows (pesos millions)

	NPV	*MPS*[a]	*Consumption*	*Savings*[b]
Project owners	40	0.30	28	12
Government	10	0.40	6	4
Consumers of output	−10	0.20	−8	−2
Workers	60	0.10	54	6
	100		80	20

Notes

[a] Marginal propensity to save (MPS) is the proportion of extra income saved.

[b] Savings = income changes × MPS.

THE SAVINGS PREMIUM

Savings are assumed to lead to additional investment. The extra weight given to savings relative to consumption arises in a situation where the rate of return obtainable on additional investment is greater than the rate of discount which society (or the government as its representative) applies to future income and consumption to express it in terms of the present.

For example, assume one unit of additional investment generates a return of 10 per cent for each of twenty years, all of which is consumed, whilst the government chooses to discount future benefits at 5 per cent. By saving and postponing one unit of consumption in the present, society as a whole gains 0.10 units of consumption in each of twenty years. This annuity discounted at 5 per cent over twenty years gives a present value of approximately 1.25.[2] In other words, by postponing one unit of consumption and diverting it to investment, a future stream of consumption has been created which in present terms is worth 25 per cent more than the original postponed consumption. This example implies that post-poned consumption, that is savings, is worth 25 per cent more than present consumption, so that one unit of income saved is worth 1.25 units of present consumption. In an analysis where consumption is the numeraire, savings will have a weight of 1.25, whilst where savings are the numeraire one unit of consumption will be worth 0.80 units of savings (1/1.25 = 0.80).

The principle behind this simple example can be generalized to give the most common formulae for the savings premium. Where it is assumed that all benefits from an investment are consumed so that there is no reinvestment, and the investment has a long life, that can be approximated by a perpetual stream of consumption, and where all consumption generated by investment goes to average consumers, the formula for the value of savings relative to consumption, is

$$v = \frac{q}{i} \tag{10.2}$$

where v is the number of units of consumption that are equivalent to one unit of savings, q is the return on a marginal unit of investment at domestic prices and i is the social or government discount rate to reduce future benefits to the present, conventionally termed the consumption rate of interest discount rate. Finally $v - 1$ gives the savings premium, the extra weight on income saved. In our simple example, if the investment has an infinite rather than a 20-year life, with $q = 0.10$, and $i = 0.05$, v will rise to two (0.10/0.05 = 2.0), and the savings premium is 100 per cent.

Equation (10.2) is a simplification, however, because of the assumption of no reinvestment out of returns. If one introduces a positive marginal propensity to save out of returns (represented by the symbol s), and assumes that all parameters remain constant over perpetuity, there is a new expression for v

$$v = \frac{(1 - s)q}{i - sq} \tag{10.3}$$

Equation (10.3) implies that the value of savings is given by project returns consumed, divided by the discount rate for consumption minus project returns that are saved.

In our example, if s is 0.20, so that 20 per cent of returns from the investment are reinvested to add to the original assets and create further consumption in future, v rises to 2.67.

$$v = \frac{(1 - 0.2)\ 0.10}{0.05 - 0.02} = \frac{0.08}{0.03} = 2.67$$

and the savings premium becomes 167 per cent.

Using the project data from Table 10.1, where domestic prices are the numeraire, and the project NPV of 100 million pesos is composed of 80 million additional consumption and 20 million additional savings, if $v = 2.67$, and all extra consumption has a weight of 1.0, the project NPV rises to 133.4 million [(80) + (20×2.67)].

The revised expression for v in equation (10.3) is still a simplification as it assumes an infinite life of assets, and constancy of all parameters in the formula. Further, it will only give a meaningful result where the rate (i) used to discount the stream of future consumption is greater than the rate at which capital accumulates due to reinvestment out of profits (sq). Given the assumptions they involve, equation (10.2) is considered a lower-bound and (10.3) an upper-bound estimate for v.

In this example, the parameter v is used to adjust all savings. Use of a single value for v implies that all savings are part of a common pool of funds for investment. However, where funds are not mobile between the government and the private sector, there will be different values of v for public and private savings.[3] A further simplification is the assumption that government capital and current expenditure are allocated rationally, so that at the margin they are equally valuable. Where this holds, all uses of government income are equally valuable and can be treated as equivalent to savings.[4]

The main difficulty in applying equations (10.2) and (10.3) is that whilst two of the parameters involved, q and s in principle can be estimated objectively even if with difficulty, the third, i, the consumption rate of interest, is subjective. It reflects a preference for consumption now rather than in the future. In theory individuals will have their own rate of discount or time preference, which can differ from society's collective view. If it is assumed that the government acts on behalf of society, i will be simply what the government feels it ought to be. An expression for i that is used frequently is

$$i = ng + p \qquad (10.4)$$

where n is elasticity of the government utility function for consumption (in other words, the rate at which the government's valuation of additional units of consumption declines as the consumption level of the recipient rises), g is the per capita growth of consumption, and p is pure time preference (or the rate at which future consumption declines in value because it arrives in the future).

Equation (10.4) bases the government's lower valuation of future as opposed to present consumption on two factors; first, that average incomes are growing over time, so that consumption gains in the future will go to consumers with an average higher living standard than consumers in the present; second, that consumption in the future is less valuable simply because its arrival is delayed – a pure time preference rate based on delay alone. Whilst use of equation (10.4) may give an appearance of precision, it simply substitutes direct value judgements for i, by judgements on n and p, which determine it. As we shall see, the elasticity parameter n plays a key role in savings and distributional weighting analysis, and n is required not just for a value for savings, but also for deriving consumption weights.

Uncertainty over i creates significant uncertainty regarding v. Table 10.2 illustrates the sensitivity of v to i.

Table 10.2 Sensitivity of v to i (using equation 10.3)

	$i = 0.125$	$i = 0.075$	$i = 0.05$	$i = 0.04$
$s = 0.30$ $q = 0.125$	$v = 1.00$	$v = 2.33$	$v = 7.00$	$v = 35.00$

It can be seen that estimates of the savings premium rise rapidly as i falls. The common sense of this is that a given return on investment is being discounted at a progressively lower rate, so that with a falling i the future consumption generated by investment is worth increasingly more in present terms. As i and sq move closer together the savings premium becomes increasingly high. Given the intrinsic uncertainty over the true value of i, and the obvious sensitivity of the results to the choice of i, it is difficult to argue that either of the equations for v can be applied operationally in a meaningful way.[5]

CONSUMPTION WEIGHTING

Savings are valued on the basis of the productivity of the investment they finance. However, consumption changes created by projects are approached from the viewpoint of their impact on current living standards. It is through their consumption effects that projects are seen as contributing to government distributional objectives, so that additional consumption will have a different value to governments depending on whose consumption has increased. Consumption represents expenditure on goods that go to different individuals, groups or classes. Different weights can be placed on consumption varying with the position of the recipient. For operational purposes it is necessary to view consumers in groups, distinguished by their income level or some other common characteristic (such as large farmers, unskilled labour or private capitalists). The national average level of per capita consumption is an intuitively obvious reference point, so that groups can be given weights depending upon both their average per capita consumption in relation to the national average, and the commitment of the government to redistribution in favour of poorer groups.

The commitment of government is approximated numerically by the elasticity parameter *n* that we have encountered in equation (10.4) for the consumption rate of interest. There *n* related to comparisons between present and future consumers, but it can also be used in comparisons between contemporaries, since it is the standard of living (as measured by the level of consumption) of different groups that is the key issue. If governments prefer consumption going to poorer rather than richer groups, implicitly they place higher weights on consumption going to the former, with such weights declining as consumption goes to increasingly better-off recipients. If one assumes that the rate of decline of the weights is constant, for a given percentage increase in the consumption level of recipients, a simple formula can be used to specify consumption weights. This constant elasticity weighting formula is

$$d_i = \frac{(\bar{c})^n}{c_i} \qquad (10.5)$$

where

n is the constant elasticity of the government utility function for consumption,
$\bar{c}$ is the national average per capita consumption level,
c_i is the average consumption of group i,

and

d_i is the weight placed on consumption to group i in comparison with consumption going to average consumers.[6]

Table 10.3 shows different values for *di*, varying with $\bar{c}/ci$ and n. The intuitive meaning of these weights is that if a group (say unskilled labour) has weight of 1.5 this means that a peso of consumption going to this group in the eyes of the government is worth 50 per cent more than a peso going to someone with the national average level of consumption. Equation (10.5) is an attempt to interpret government preferences on how consumption should be distributed. Once these weights are estimated they can be used to revalue the consumed income created by a project.

Table 10.3 Consumption weights for different values of n and $\bar{c}/c_i$

	n				
	0.0	0.5	1.0	1.5	2.0
Relative consumption level					
$(\bar{c}/c_i)$					
10.00	1.0	3.16	10.00	31.62	100.00
4.00	1.0	2.00	4.00	8.00	16.00
2.00	1.0	1.41	2.00	2.83	4.00
1.33	1.0	1.15	1.33	1.53	1.77
1.00	1.0	1.00	1.00	1.00	1.00
0.66	1.0	0.81	1.66	0.54	0.44
0.33	1.0	0.57	0.33	0.19	0.11
0.17	1.0	0.41	0.17	0.07	0.03
0.10	1.0	0.32	0.10	0.03	0.01

The stronger is a government's commitment to income redistribution the higher will be n, that is the faster the government's valuation of additional consumption will decline in response to a rise in the consumption level of the recipient. As Table 10.3 shows, where $n = 0$, all weights are 1.0, and no distinction is drawn between consumption to different groups. However, whenever $n >$ 1.0, setting the national average consumption as the norm with a weight of 1.0, any consumers with a consumption level greater than the average will have a weight of < 1.0, and those below the national average a weight of > 1.0. The higher is *n* the greater will be the disparity between the weights on the rich as compared with those on the poor. It can be seen that weights on groups at the top and bottom of the consumption scale can become very low and very high respectively. For example, where $n = 2.0$, someone with a consumption three times the national average ($\bar{c}/c_i = 0.33$) will have a weight of only 0.11, and someone with a consumption one quarter of the average ($\bar{c}/c_i = 4.00$) will have a weight as high as 16.0. Use of such weights would imply that projects with strongly negative returns in terms of their resource use, could still be socially acceptable provided their cost was borne by the rich and all the benefits went to the poor.

The simplest form of equation (10.5) is where *n* is 1.0; here the weights for different groups are determined directly by their standard of consumption relative to the national average; for example, someone with a consumption twice the national average will have a weight of 0.5 ($\bar{c}/ci = 0.5$). Whilst $n = 1.0$ has the advantage of simplicity, and is often seen as a reasonable figure, a range of $n = 0.5$ to 1.5 has also been suggested with the former reflecting a weak preference for income redistribution and the latter a much stronger one.[7]

WEIGHTS AND THE NUMERAIRE

Having discussed how values can be found for the savings and consumption effects of projects, it is necessary to draw the discussion together by relating these weights to the alternative specifications of the numeraire. The consumption weights from equation (10.5) are determined by the elasticity parameter n, and the relative values of c_i and $\bar{c}$. It does not matter whether these consumption figures are measured at world or domestic prices, since it is the ratio $\bar{c}/c_i$ which is important. Use of different price units will not affect the consumption weighting system. The important distinction is the choice of a consumption or savings numeraire.

With the consumption numeraire the adjustments are more straightforward. All project effects must be converted to an equivalent figure in units of consumption (going to average consumers). The income effects of a project are broken down into savings and consumption. The former are multiplied by v to convert flows of savings into average consumption units. The latter are multiplied by the relevant set of weights that convert consumption to particular groups to a figure equivalent to consumption to average consumers.

The procedures involved can be illustrated with reference to the example in Table 10.1. For simplicity the question of the use of world or domestic prices to measure income changes is ignored (implying $CF_F = 1.0$) to allow a focus on the savings–consumption dimension of the numeraire. The income changes created by the project go to four different groups – project owners, government, consumers of project output, and workers. Each group has a different average consumption prior to the project. Table 10.4 gives average consumption for each group and their consumption weights applying equation (10.5) with $n = 1.0$. Here all government income is not treated as being equally valuable. Its consumption or current expenditure is assumed to go to average consumers, whilst its savings is taken to be as valuable as private savings. It is assumed that $v = 2.50$ so that a unit of income saved has a 150 per cent premium relative to a unit of income spent by an average consumer. Table 10.5 illustrates the adjustments from using savings and consumption weights. The new project NPV is 127.52 million pesos. The interpretation of this result is that allowing for growth effects (via savings) and distributional effects (via consumption) has raised the projects NPV by 27.52 million pesos in comparison with the initial result. In other words, the growth and distributional effects of the project are equivalent to 27.52 million pesos of consumption going to average consumers.

Where the savings numeraire is used the equivalent adjustments are slightly less obvious. Savings as the numeraire have a weight of 1.0 and are not adjusted. Consumption changes for different groups are adjusted twice – first, to convert consumption to a particular group into a figure equivalent to consumption for average

Table 10.4 Project beneficiaries consumption weights

	Group average consumption (pesos)	*National average consumption (pesos)*	*Consumption weight* (d_i)
Project owners	2500	350	0.14
Consumers of output	350	350	1.00
Workers	250	350	1.40

Table 10.5 Income adjustment: consumption numeraire (pesos milions)

Group	*Income change*	*Income flows* *Consumption*	*Savings*	
Project owners	40	28	12	
Government	10	6	4	
Consumers of output	−10	−8	−2	
Workers	60	54	6	
NPV	100	80	20	
		Adjusted income flows (*Consumption* × d_i)	(*Savings* × v)[a]	*Total*
Project owners		28 × 0.14 = 3.92	12 × 2.5 = 30.0	33.92
Government		6 × 1.0 = 6.00	4 × 2.5 = 10.0	16.00
Consumers of output		−8 × 1.0 = −8.00	−2 × 2.5 = −5.00	−13.00
Workers		54 × 1.40 = 75.60	6 × 2.5 = 15.00	90.60
NPV		77.52	50.00	127.52

Note

[a] $v = 2.50$.

consumers, and secondly, to convert units of average consumption into a figure equivalent to units of savings.

If a particular group, for example low-income consumers, gains 100 pesos of additional consumption and from equation (10.5) their consumption weight d_i is 1.5, then 100 pesos to the group are worth 150 pesos going to average consumers. If however, one unit of savings is worth two and a half units of average consumption, so $v = 2.50$, then in terms of savings the original pesos 100 of extra consumption are worth Rs150 / 2.5 or Rs60. These two adjustments mean that the full weight used to convert the consumption of a group to the savings numeraire is d_i/v; in this example 1.5/2.5 or 0.6.

The example from Table 10.1 is recalculated with a savings numeraire in Table 10.6. The set of consumption weights d_i are those given in Table 10.4, and v remains at 2.50. The new NPV is now 51.01 million pesos.

Table 10.6 Income adjustment: savings numeraire (pesos millions)

Group	*Income change*	*Income flows* *Consumption*	*Savings*
Project owners	40	28	12
Government	10	6	4
Consumers of output	−10	−8	−2
Workers	60	54	6
	100	80	20

	Adjusted income flows *Consumption* × d_i/v		*Savings* × 1.0		*Total*
Project owners	28 × 0.14/2.50 =	1.57	12 × 1.00 =	12.00	13.57
Government	6 × 1.00/2.50 =	2.40	4 × 1.00 =	4.00	6.40
Consumers of output	−8 × 1.00/2.50 =	−3.20	−2 × 1.00 =	−2.00	−5.20
Workers	54 × 1.40/2.50 =	30.24	6 × 1.00 =	6.00	36.24
NPV		31.01		20.00	51.01

This NPV is below that in Table 10.5, but they are still directly comparable. Table 10.5 is in units of average consumption whilst Table 10.6 is in units of savings. The link between the two results is the parameter v. Since $v = 2.50$, one unit of income saved is worth 2.50 units of income consumed by average consumers. Hence the NPV in table 10.5 is 2.5 times that in Table 10.6 ($51.01 \times 2.50 = 127.52$).

Application of this form of weighting analysis changes a project's NPV and IRR, since its effect on growth and distribution objectives are incorporated quantitatively in these measures of project worth. However, since project benefits and costs are now redefined, the test of whether a project is acceptable must also be changed. Acceptability now requires a positive NPV at a discount rate adjusted for the incorporation of these additional objectives, and similarly an IRR above this adjusted discount rate.

ADJUSTED DISCOUNT RATE

Once consumption or savings are introduced as additional dimensions of the numeraire there is a potential divergence between the discount rate in the alternative systems, since theoretically the discount rate should measure the fall in value of the numeraire over time. The discussion in Chapter 5 defined the discount rate as the cost of the savings used to finance a project, either in terms of income foregone from other investment or of the cost of increasing savings. However, once savings and distributional effects are allowed for, the opportunity cost of the funds committed to a project will change.

For example, using the savings numeraire and defining the discount rate as the return on a marginal project, returns must now be recalculated to include the effect of the marginal project on savings and distribution. This adjusted opportunity cost discount rate is often termed the Accounting Rate of Interest (ARI). If q is the return on the marginal project then the ARI can be expressed as $q + h$, where h is the net effect of the adjustments for savings and consumption weights. Normally, h will be negative, so that the discount rate relevant for a weighting analysis will be below that used in efficiency calculations.[8] Hence although weighted project NPVs may be below those from efficiency calculations, this need not be a cause for concern, since where weights are used the basis for the calculation and the test of acceptability are different.

With a consumption numeraire the discount rate should be the consumption rate of interest which is intrinsically subjective. However, under the simplifying conditions that v, the weight on savings, remains constant the fall in value of savings over time will equal the fall in the value of consumption. The common sense of this at first sight surprising result is that the discount rate must reflect the fall in value of the chosen numeraire over time. The fall in the consumption numeraire is given by i, the consumption rate of interest, and the fall in the savings numeraire by the ARI. Provided the relative value of savings and average consumption remains the same over time – which implies a constant v – both numeraires must be declining at the same rate; therefore, a constant v requires that i = ARI.

Having noted the formal specification of the new discount rate in this weighting system, it must be pointed out that practical applications have had great difficulty in providing estimates of this adjusted discount rate. This is in part due to the difficulty of identifying a meaningful estimate for v, for the reasons noted earlier, and in part also due to the problem of estimating accurately the distribution of returns from marginal investments.

LIMITATIONS OF WEIGHTING SYSTEMS

The types of projects which will look better relative to others as a result of applying these weights are those with either one or both of two characteristics;

(1) those with high savings effects, generating income potentially available for investment;
(2) those that redistribute income to poor groups.

In many instances, these effects may be incompatible so that projects that are effective by one criteria perform poorly by the other. The exact outcome for particular projects will depend upon their respective savings and distributional effects, and the numerical trade-off between objectives reflected in the weights on savings (v) and consumption to different groups (d_i).

However, it must be stressed that whilst the theoretical framework for this form of analysis has been available since the mid-

1970s, practical applications of this type of weighting have been infrequent. Where governments and donor agencies have wished to formalize the examination of the income effects of projects, they have generally preferred to simply identify the main gaining and losing groups in the manner discussed in Chapter 9, rather than weight these income flows to derive new NPV and IRR estimates. Several factors account for the relative neglect of this type of weighting analysis.

One of these is the change in intellectual climate from the mid-1970s to the present. In the earlier period direct interventions to meet employment and distributional objectives were at the forefront of the debate on aid effectiveness. The use of weights that allowed the selection of new investments that contributed to such objectives was a natural extension of this emphasis. During the 1980s, though, perceptions shifted away from this interventionist scenario. Questions of macroeconomic policy and overall economic efficiency have come to the forefront of thinking, with the emphasis on measures that raise overall efficiency, which in the longer term it is argued will benefit all, the poor included. Such a view implies that economic analysis focusing on efficiency considerations will be more appropriate than the use of weights which might lead to the acceptance of projects that perform poorly in terms of their immediate impact on national income. This objection is strengthened by the fact that the weighting system discussed here can produce very wide disparities in consumption weights for the rich and the poor. This implies that some highly inefficient projects, in terms of their resource use, might be socially acceptable, once weights are introduced. It has been argued that in such circumstances it would be preferable to devize a system of income transfers or subsidies for the poor groups involved, rather than invest in inefficient projects that create a net loss of national income, as a means of affecting the desired income changes.

Practical concerns have also been raised about the feasibility of conducting a full distributional analysis, setting out accurately the income flows from projects. This is perhaps less critical than the theoretical point that the weighting system discussed here is subjective. Initial judgement on basically one parameter, n, which is to reflect the government's commitment to income redistribution as an objective, is sufficient to create a complex set of distributional weights. It is conventional to assume that n is constant over time and relevant over all levels of consumption, and that it lies in a range of 0.5 to 1.5, with the top and bottom of the range reflecting weak and strong commitments to redistribution, respectively. However, n is essentially an unknown which need not be constant. Choosing a different value for n will alter the weight on savings (through the effect of i on v) and the discount rate (through the effect of v on the ARI), as well as the consumption weights (d_i). The fact that such a complex system of weights can be derived from a number of simplifying assumptions and subjective judgement casts severe doubt on its operational effectiveness.

CONCLUSION

The weighting system discussed here emerged from a rigorous theoretical examination of these issues in the 1970s. The aim was to provide a framework for assessing quantitatively the impact of projects on growth and distribution, as well as the short run use of resources. However, there are both practical and theoretical difficulties with this weighting system and examples of operational work are rare.

Further Reading

The seminal texts are UNIDO (1972) and Little and Mirrlees (1968) and (1974), whilst Squire and van der Tak (1975) synthesize much of the earlier discussion. In turn their work is surveyed and summarized in Brent (1990).

The approach of adjusting individual shadow prices to incorporate savings and distributional effects is used in Little and Mirrlees (1974) and Squire and van der Tak (1975). The alternative of identifying income flows and adjusting their savings and consumption elements is used in UNIDO (1972) and UNIDO (1980).

Little and Mirrlees (1974), chapter 13 give a slightly different approach to consumption weights to that discussed here. Stewart (1975) discusses the rationale for savings and distribution weights in terms of constraints on more direct government actions to raise savings or redistribute consumption. Marglin (1967) and UNIDO (1972), chapters 13 and 14 derive the formulae for the savings premium. Weiss (1979), Irvin (1978), chapter 8, UNIDO (1978) chapters VI and VII, and ODA (1988) chapters 4 and 5 survey the use of savings and distributional weights. Ray (1984), particularly chapters 2, 3, 5 and 6, is a rigorous and demanding exposition of these issues.

Linn (1977) and UNIDO (1980), chapter 5 are applied studies using a weighting system. Harberger (1984) and (1978) are critiques of the use of consumption weights of the type discussed here. OECD (1989) discusses how far this type of weighting system has been used in practice.

11 National Economic Parameters

This chapter discusses the national economic parameters (NEP) required for project analysis. Such parameters are national in that they apply to all projects regardless of their sector, and they are economic because they reflect the shadow price of the items concerned. A typical set of NEP covers CFs for unskilled and skilled labour, some of the main non-traded sectors, some aggregate CFs, such as a consumption conversion factor (CCF) and a standard or average conversion factor (ACF), and the discount rate. A project analyst can apply these parameters directly to the project under analysis so that, for example, the discount rate or a conversion factor for electricity does not need to be re-estimated for every project. Some shadow pricing will still need to be done at the project level, relating to the main project output and key inputs, and probably also to labour. However, the existence of a set of NEP allows the project analyst to focus on parameters that are treated most accurately on a specific project-by-project basis.

In the last fifteen years considerable progress has been made in refining techniques for estimating NEP. This chapter examines the approach of semi-input-output (SIO) analysis, which is designed to derive a consistent set of NEP estimates, and discusses the results of studies that use this approach. Most NEP calculations tend to employ a world price numeraire so that the discussion here is in terms of this unit. Indeed, as we have seen earlier, where equivalent assumptions are adopted world and domestic price systems are directly comparable, and CFs derived from one system can be transformed readily into the other.

Theoretically, national CFs should not be estimated in isolation. For example, electricity will be an input into construction, and the latter an input into electricity. The two CFs will therefore be interdependent. SIO analysis can cope with a major part of this interdependence, but some calculations must be exogenous, relying on data that are external to the SIO model. The main example of a parameter that must be estimated externally is the discount rate, and reference is made also to approaches to its estimation.

CONVERSION FACTORS IN A SEMI-INPUT-OUTPUT (SIO) APPROACH

The semi input output method requires the building of a SIO table that covers the main sectors of an economy and allows a simultaneous solution for valuation of commodities, sectors and factors of production. A SIO framework is particularly important for the treatment of non-traded activities that are in variable supply, since it can assess the total factor requirements per unit of non-traded output. This allows an estimate of total income gains for previously underemployed factors. In terms of its coverage a SIO table can be comprehensive, in the sense of covering all production sectors in an economy, or it can be more limited focusing on sectors which are linked closely with new investment projects. The aim is to establish the main economic effects of new investment, so that there is less need to incorporate sectors that are affected in only a minor way. Outputs from sectors covered in the table that are used as inputs into other economic activities can be termed produced inputs, in that they come from sectors covered by the SIO system. This is in contrast with inputs supplied exogeneously, either from abroad, or from domestic activities not shown as productive sectors in the table.

The SIO table is composed of two distinct matrices. What is conventionally termed the A matrix shows the produced inputs into sectors; what is termed the F matrix gives inputs of primary factors, that are exogenous to the system. To solve the system direct coefficient matrices are required which show inputs per unit of sector output. The structure of the direct coefficient matrix of a SIO table can be illustrated in Figure 11.1.

In Figure 11.1 the table has n columns, so that the A matrix is $n \times n$ in size. There are g primary factor inputs so that the F matrix is $g \times n$. Since all entries are direct coefficients, each column in the table must total 1.0; a_{1n}, for example, is the value of inputs from sector 1 into one unit of sector n; f_{gn} is the value of primary factor input g per unit of sector n.

Sectors 1 to n will be productive sectors, both traded and non-traded, plus aggregate CFs that are weighted averages of the CFs for individual sectors in the table. Primary factors 1 to g can vary with the level of detail and assumptions adopted. However, as a minimum requirement there needs to be primary factors for foreign

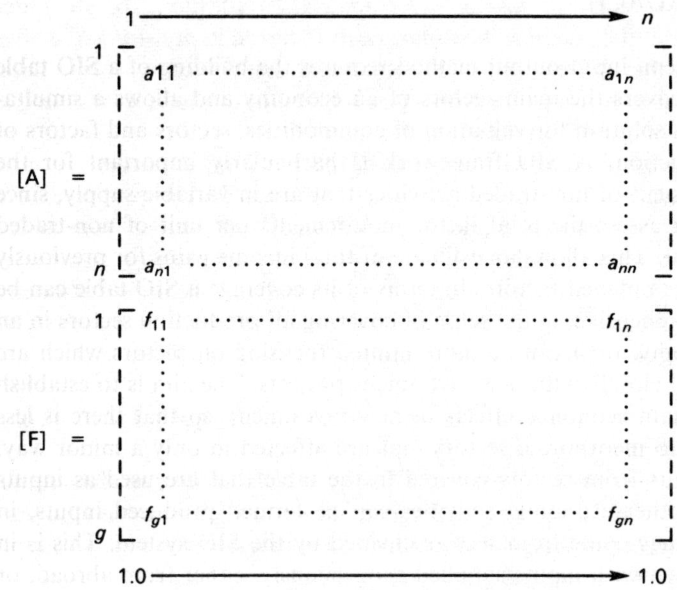

Figure 11.1 SIO table – direct coefficients

exchange, transfer payments (covering taxes, subsidies and surplus profits), labour, possibly distinguishing between skilled and unskilled workers, and capital inputs.

The direct coefficients of the A matrix are given by expressing all entries in a column as a proportion of the market value of output in each sector. An important practical issue is what level of market prices are used to value output. The chief alternatives are producer's or purchaser's prices. In practice most SIO analyses work with the latter and this example also uses purchasers prices as the reference price level. This means that for each sector market prices include distribution margins, transport costs in moving goods from producers to purchasers, and retail and producer-level indirect taxes.

In a SIO analysis the aim is to assess the consequences of additional expenditure on each of the sectors in the table. For traded sectors the main effect will be in terms of foreign exchange, with more imports if the goods consumed are imported at the margin, and less exports if they are exported. The foreign exchange effects as a proportion of the market price will be shown in the foreign exchange row of the F matrix. In addition, for all traded commodities there will be some costs incurred in non-traded sectors, since they have to be transported and distributed to users. These costs are shown in the relevant rows for non-traded sectors, such as Transport and Services.

The distinction between traded and non-traded sectors is crucial because output in each is valued differently. The principles discussed in Chapters 5 and 6 are followed, with output from traded sectors valued at border prices plus adjustments for non-traded costs, and from non-traded sectors normally at the opportunity cost of domestic production. For non-traded sectors it is necessary to distinguish three possible situations:

(1) where output can be expanded in the short run due to surplus capacity;
(2) where in the short run capacity is fully utilized so that output can only be expanded in the longer-run after new investment;
(3) where no additional production is possible due to rigid supply constraints.

In the first two cases, additional expenditure induces additional production and opportunity cost is given by the resources that go into this production. In the first case, only variable costs are involved and there will be no primary factor input for capital. In the second case, however, both operating and capital inputs must both be reflected in the opportunity cost. The third case, where supply is fixed, will be relatively rare. Such sectors are normally included as an additional row in the F matrix since their supply is not determined within the SIO system. In this approach they are valued by an aggregate CF, often one for consumption.[1]

The logic of the SIO approach is that the value of a sector can be found by decomposing output at market prices solely into primary factors. Total primary factor requirements in each sector are both the direct primary inputs shown in F plus the primary factors that go into the produced inputs from sectors in the table shown in A. Estimation of total primary factors per unit of output in each sector thus requires first identifying total (direct plus indirect) produced inputs into each sector which involves inversion of the A matrix. Total produced inputs must then be decomposed into primary factors. The value of each sector is determined by the sum of the values of the primary factor inputs that are required directly and indirectly by the sector. This is expressed more formally in Appendix 11.1.

The results of a SIO analysis are given typically as a set of conversion factors;

- for all sectors in the table;
- for all primary factor inputs into these sectors;
- for aggregate categories such as consumption expenditure or aggregate output.

ILLUSTRATION OF A SIO APPLICATION

To illustrate the approach it may be helpful to work at a simple level with a small table of only four productive sectors, one aggregate CF, and four primary factors. Although all actual calculations will involve a far larger table this is sufficient for illustrative purposes. In this example the A matrix is composed of four sectors

(1) Industry
(2) Agriculture
(3) Services
(4) Transport

plus an aggregate average conversion factor, that is a weighted average of the CFs for the four productive sectors.

The F matrix has four primary factors

(a) Transfers
(b) Foreign Exchange
(c) Labour
(d) Operating Surplus

All labour is assumed to be unskilled, and all operating surplus (profits before tax, interest and depreciation) to represent opportunity costs associated with the use of capital, so that no surplus profits are involved. Transfers cover taxes and subsidies. Of the four sectors it is assumed that industry and agriculture are traded, with significant imports of the former and exports of the latter. Services and transport are taken to be non-traded.

Table 11.1 gives the direct coefficients for this example. All row entries are proportions of the domestic market price of output. As expected for the traded sectors, industry and agriculture – output value is predominantly foreign exchange. For industry – an importable – the cif value of output is 60 per cent of the market price, with an import tariff of 50 per cent of the cif price; the foreign exchange entry is therefore 0.60 and transfers 0.30. There are small domestic costs of services and transport involved in moving the imported industrial goods to users and consumers; both are 5 per cent of the domestic market price of output. These are shown in the services and transport rows, respectively. For agriculture, an exportable, the fob export price is 90 per cent of the domestic market price, whilst there is an export subsidy of 10 per cent of the fob price. Entries in the foreign exchange and transfer rows are 0.90 and 0.09, respectively. The only relevant transport and service costs will be any additional costs associated with the domestic consumption of agricultural output as compared with export. There is a small additional domestic transport cost of 1 per cent of the domestic market price, so that the transport entry is 0.01.[2]

Table 11.1 SIO table – direct coefficients

	Industry	*Agriculture*	*Services*	*Transport*	*ACF*
Industry			0.10	0.15	0.20
Agriculture					0.45
Services	0.05		0.20	0.05	0.25
Transport	0.05	0.01	0.10		0.10
ACF					
Transfers	0.30	0.09		0.10	
Foreign exchange	0.60	0.90	0.20	0.30	
Labour			0.30	0.30	
Operating surplus			0.10	0.10	
	1.0	1.0	1.0	1.0	1.0

The non-traded sectors services and transport use both produced inputs from other sectors and primary factors. For services produced inputs from industry, services itself and transport are 10, 20 and 10 per cent respectively, of output at domestic market prices. Primary factors foreign exchange, labour, and operating surplus are 20, 30 and 10 per cent respectively of output at domestic market prices. Similarly for transport produced inputs from industry and services are 15 and 5 per cent of output whilst primary factors transfers, foreign exchange, labour and operating surplus are 10, 30, 30 and 10 per cent of output, respectively.

Any aggregate CF will be an average of CFs for particular sectors. In this example the ACF is a weighted average of the CFs for the four productive sectors. The weights used are 0.20, 0.45, 0.25 and 0.10, for industry, agriculture, services and transport, respectively, and can be taken to reflect the relative value added in the different sectors at domestic market prices.

Total primary factors are shown in Table 11.2. In all cases, total primary inputs are greater than the direct inputs shown in Table 11.1 because of the primary factors that go into the produced inputs used in all sectors. This is most obviously the case for the labour and foreign exchange inputs into services and transport. For services, for example, whilst the direct labour input per unit of output is 0.30, the total labour input, allowing for the labour that goes into inputs used by services, rises to 0.42. Even the traded sectors with no direct labour content, have a small indirect input through their use of non-traded transport and services inputs.

Table 11.2 Total primary factors per unit of output in productive sectors

	Industry	*Agriculture*	*Services*	*Transport*
Transfers	0.3103	0.0917	0.0575	0.1494
Foreign exchange	0.6400	0.9041	0.3820	0.4150
Labour	0.0373	0.0032	0.4204	0.3266
Operating surplus	0.0124	0.0010	0.1401	0.1090
	1.0000	1.0000	1.0000	1.0000

Once total primary factor requirements are known they must be revalued with CFs for each primary factor. In Appendix 11.1 it is shown that

$$CF_i = \sum_g b_{gi}.CF_g \qquad (11.1)$$

where

CF_i is the conversion factor for sector i

CF_g is the conversion factor for primary input g

and

b_{gi} is the share of primary input g in a unit of output i.

The weight b_{gi} placed on the conversion factor for a primary factor is the share of total requirements of that factor in output value of i at domestic market prices. In this example, therefore, Table 11.2 gives the weights for the different primary factors.

As far as CFs for primary factors are concerned the example uses the following:

	CF
Transfers	0
Foreign exchange	1.0
Labour	0.5 × Agriculture conversion factor (CF_{AG})
Operating surplus	1.0 × ACF

Transfers have no opportunity cost, so that their CF is zero. Foreign exchange has a CF of 1.0, since here world prices are used as the numeraire.[3] For labour in this example it is assumed that a worker's output foregone at domestic market prices is 50 per cent of the market wage. This is additional information, external to the model, required to derive labour's CF. However, a further step is required since output foregone must be converted to world prices by a CF for the output workers would have produced. From equation (5.4) the shadow wage rate (SWR) can be expressed as

$$SWR = \sum_i a_i m_i . \; CF_i$$

If for simplicity one single source of labour is assumed, $a_i = 1.0$, and $\Sigma \; a_i m_i$ can be rewritten as M, referring one type of output foregone. Then

$$SWR = M \times CF_m \qquad (11.2)$$

where

M is output foregone from a worker's alternative employment at domestic market prices;

and

CF_m is the conversion factor required to convert this output to world prices.

The conversion factor for labour (CF_{LAB}) is the ratio of the shadow to the market wage

$$CF_{LAB} = \frac{SWR}{MWR} \tag{11.3}$$

or substituting (11.2) into (11.3)

$$CF_{LAB} = \frac{M}{MWR} \times CF_m$$

In this example M/MWR is taken to be 0.50, whilst workers for new projects are assumed to be drawn from agriculture, so that the agriculture conversion factor (CF_{AG}) is used for CF_m

CF_{LAB} is thus $\dfrac{M}{MWR} \times CF_{AG}$, or $0.50 \times CF_{AG}$

Labour is thus valued by a combination of external data, necessary for the ratio of output foregone at domestic market prices to the market wage (M/MWR), and a sectoral CF derived from the model (CF_{AG}).

The use of CF_{AG} in the valuation of a primary factor is an illustration of the interdependence of values in a SIO system, since CF_{AG} depends among other things on the value of labour, whilst in turn it is one of the two determinants of labour's value.

Finally, operating surplus is taken to be resource costs reflecting the opportunity cost return on the capital committed to each sector, at domestic market prices. No surplus profits in excess of these resource costs are involved. Operating surplus must still be converted to world prices. It is assumed that capital is mobile within the economy and can thus be employed in any sector. It is therefore appropriate to use the average conversion factor (ACF) to revalue operating surplus, since the ACF is an average ratio of world to domestic prices for the whole economy. Interdependence also arises in the treatment of operating surplus since it is revalued by the ACF, whilst operating surplus itself is one of the influences on the CF for each sector, and the ACF is a weighted average of sectoral CFs.

Using this set of CFs for primary factors and the weights from Table 11.2 gives the results reported in Table 11.3.

Table 11.3 Full CF results

		CF
Sectors	Industry	0.6664
	Agriculture	0.9064
	Services	0.6812
	Transport	0.6476
	ACF	0.7762
Primary factors	Transfers	0.0000
	Foreign exchange	1.0000
	Labour	0.4532
	Operating surplus	0.7762

These results can be illustrated for the ACF and industry. The former is an average of the CFs for the four productive sectors, using the weights from the last column of Table 11.1.

	Weight	*CF*	*Weighted Average*
Industry	0.2000	0.6664	0.1333
Agriculture	0.4500	0.9064	0.4078
Services	0.2500	0.6812	0.1703
Transport	0.1000	0.6476	0.0647
ACF	1.0000		0.7761

ACF = 0.7761, or rounded to 0.78

Industry is an average of the CFs for the total primary factors into the sector using the weights for industry from Table 11.2.

	Weight	*CF*	*Weighted Average*
Transfers	0.3103	0.0000	0.0000
Foreign exchange	0.6400	1.0000	0.6400
Labour	0.0373	0.4532	0.0169
Operating surplus	0.0124	0.7762	0.0096
	1.0000		0.6665

Industry CF = 0.6665, or rounded to 0.67

There is a very slight discrepancy between these calculations for ACF and the CF for industry and the results in Table 11.3, due to minor rounding errors.

ADVANTAGES OF THE SIO APPROACH

Two major advantages can be claimed for this approach. First, there is the advantage of consistency, since SIO analysis is equivalent to the solution of the economic valuation problem through a series of simultaneous equations. There is interdependence in this analysis with values for certain primary factors being some of the determinants of values for productive sectors, but in turn being influenced by the value of those sectors. In this illustration we have seen this for the primary factors labour and operating surplus. In addition, there will be interdependence between the values of productive sectors, since most will be inputs into each other. In this example, services are an input into industry and will thus help determine the value of the latter, but in turn industry is an input into services. Only a simultaneous solution can resolve this interdependence and achieve consistent results.

The second advantage of the SIO approach is that it allows the linkage effects of additional expenditure to be captured. Expenditure on traded sectors by definition falls largely on the trade balance, however, for non-traded sectors in variable supply domestic resources will be mobilized to meet additional demand. The two most important linkage effects are likely to be the generation of jobs, where labour was previously underutilized, and the direction of demand to sectors where there is surplus capacity. Where labour is underemployed, so that output foregone from a previous activity is below the market wage, this is likely to result in a CF for labour of below 1.0. Non-traded sectors, which generate employment effects, thus have the shadow price of their output reduced relative to its domestic market value. The consequence is therefore that use of such non-traded inputs is encouraged in comparison with activities where such employment effects are not forthcoming. A similar analysis applies where demand is directed to non-traded activities with surplus capacity. Here their opportunity cost will include only variable costs of production, so that no charge for capital is relevant. In this case operating surplus, the primary factor reflecting capital charges, will have a CF of zero. This adjustment will again have the effect of lowering the valuation of output from such sectors, thus encouraging its use.

The overall significance of adjustments for such linkages depends on the importance of non-traded sectors in an economy. Where the economy is relatively closed in terms of trade policy, any realistic analysis of new investments will require use of an input–output framework to capture the interrelations between a project and its suppliers and users.

The ability to trace through the additional income generated within an economy due to these interrelations means that SIO analysis can be extended to estimates of shadow prices and conversion factors that incorporate adjustments for savings and distributional effects, as discussed in Chapter 10. Their derivation in a SIO system is illustrated in Appendix 11.2.

SIO analysis is not without difficulties: for example the treatment of labour and capital inputs can be approximate, and sector CFs derived from national data are not always directly applicable at the project level. However, despite these and other limitations it provides the most rigorous approach to estimating NEP.

DATA REQUIREMENTS

Data requirements for a SIO analysis can be considerable. For traded activities the main data required will be on tariffs and quotas, and on transport and distribution margins. For non-traded activities, however, more detailed data will be required to decompose their cost structure. For manufacturing, periodic censuses of enterprises provide one source; for public utilities project documents and sector surveys may be available. For services often relatively little data are available; one source may be the information used to construct the national accounts, where this type of activity has to be quantified, even if approximately. The limitations of data derived from such varying sources must not be overlooked when the consistency and relative rigour of the approach is acknowledged.

In an economy with a relatively up-to-date national input–output table, construction of a SIO table will be relatively straightforward, since data on the average cost structure of produced inputs will already be available. This data should be adjusted to derive estimates of marginal costs where constant costs cannot be assumed. In the absence of a national input–output table information from varying sources will have to be put together.

Classification of sectors as either traded or non-traded can also be a problem. There may be situations where output of a sector is insufficiently homogeneous to be wholly traded or non-traded, so that it is necessary to distinguish between the traded and non-traded components showing its traded and non-traded elements as separate columns in the SIO table.

Another problem relates to the choice of reference price level, normally either producer or purchaser prices. It is essential to use a single reference price level for domestic market prices. This is necessary for consistency so that for all activities domestic prices at one price level can be compared with shadow prices at the same price level. However, whatever level is adopted requires data on distribution and transport costs, and indirect taxes, as a proportion of the market price.

In a national SIO table one will be working with very aggregate data, so that there will normally be only a very vague indication of where the production and consumption activities covered in the table will be located geographically. In these circumstances, it will be difficult to estimate the importance of transport and distribution costs for particular sectors. Most tables will normally use an approximate average proportion of the market price for these costs. How far this is misleading will vary between economies, and within economies between sectors.

A national CF for labour also poses difficulties. As noted above, data on labour's output foregone at domestic prices is needed as an external input into a SIO model. It is generally acknowledged that in all but geographically small economies unskilled labour is best treated as a regional not national parameter, in the sense that there is insufficient mobility for the opportunity cost of employing an unskilled worker to be the same in all regions. However, in a SIO table it is common to find either a single entry for unskilled labour or two entries only for rural and urban labour. In other words, apart from an urban–rural distinction unskilled labour is treated as a nationally homogeneous input and revalued by a national CF, despite the recognition of likely regional variations.

Estimation of capital charges in non-traded sectors is always a problem. As noted in Chapter 5, they can be calculated as an annuity by applying a capital recovery factor, based on the estimated economic discount rate and length of life of the assets, to the value of capital assets. Any profit in excess of this charge will be surplus profit, not an opportunity cost. Each aspect of the information required will be subject to varying degrees of uncertainty. The value of capital assets is a particular problem since historical book values will rarely be a useful guide to current values. Further, the discount rate is a key national parameter that must be estimated outside the SIO calculations.

THE DISCOUNT RATE

Given the importance of the discount rate and the fact that it needs to be calculated separately from other parameters, it is worth commenting on some alternative approaches to its estimation. As Chapter 5 explains, the discount rate can be seen as either the cost of using or supplying capital, depending upon whether or not a fixed budget constraint is assumed. During the 1970s and early 1980s, when many developing countries engaged in heavy external borrowing, it was common to find the cost of foreign borrowing used to measure the supply cost of capital. In other words, if the supply of capital in the economy could be increased by borrowing from abroad, the cost of repaying these loans gives the cost new investments must cover if they are to be justified. This definition of the discount rate requires an estimate if the real cost of borrowing – that is the nominal rate deflated by an index for the price movements of the borrowing country's exports and imports. International inflation reduces the cost of borrowing since a given interest repayment in foreign exchange can be covered by a smaller physical quantity of goods, when export and import prices are rising. However, where countries face negative price trends for their exports, and they repay foreign debts by exporting more rather than importing less, price deflation will raise not reduce the cost of borrowing.

An example of this approach is an estimate of the discount rate for Jamaica in the early 1980s.[4] The nominal cost of foreign borrowing was estimated at about 12 per cent (London Inter-Bank Offer Rate plus a margin for Jamaica's own risk position). Detailed price projections for Jamaica's exports and imports were not available, however, assuming that any new loan would be repaid through equal combinations of higher exports and lower imports, and using crude assumptions about future price trends in world market prices for Jamaica's exports and imports, an average price rise of 2 per cent per year over the 1980s was estimated. This gave a real cost of borrowing of approximately 10 per cent.

The alternative approach focuses on the returns available on marginal investment. Theoretically, where foreign borrowing is possible, and is carried to its optimal level, these two approaches should give the same result, although in practice most estimates based on the domestic opportunity cost of capital find a considerably higher discount rate.

In estimating the domestic opportunity cost of capital a number of alternatives is possible. The most appropriate, where it can be pursued, is to examine actual ex-post returns on a range of projects approved and implemented. These returns should be at shadow prices, so that the data on operating performance of projects must be adjusted by a set of CFs. The bottom of the range of returns on projects gives a measure of the marginal return on investment. This approach, however, requires a detailed project appraisal and monitoring system, and in practice few if any discount rate estimates have been derived in this way.

Another approach is to use macroeconomic data to derive what must be accepted as an approximate return to capital. A simple version of this approach defines the returns to capital q, as the ratio of gross domestic product minus total wages and depreciation to net capital stock; so that

$$q = \frac{(\text{gross domestic product} - \text{wages} - \text{depreciation})}{(\text{capital stock})} \quad (11.4)$$

when all terms are at shadow prices.

This has the limitation of calculating average not marginal returns, of ignoring the contribution of technical change not embodied in new capital assets, and of inevitably utilizing very crude CFs to convert both sides of the ratio to shadow prices. It is normally seen as an upper limit to the economic discount rate, since the first two of these limitations will create an upward bias to the estimate, whilst the last is likely to be largely neutral in terms of the direction of bias. Furthermore, a major difficulty is in obtaining a realistic estimate of capital stock at replacement prices, since most records will be based on historical not replacement prices.

This approach can also be illustrated using estimates from Jamaica. Here, conversion factors from a national economic parameter study are applied to estimate q. The capital stock is revalued by an investment CF which is a simple average of the CFs for construction and manufacturing. The national capital stock is composed approximately of 50 per cent buildings and 50 per cent equipment, and the CF for construction is used to revalue the former component and the CF for manufacturing the latter. Gross domestic product is revalued by the ACF, and wage cost by a weighted average of the CFs for skilled and unskilled labour. The average estimate of q for 1980–2, is 17.3 (see Table 11.4).[5]

Estimates of the discount rate from a range of countries are shown in Table 11.5. Foreign borrowing is likely to be a much less significant option for increasing the supply of capital in the future, so that the relevance of this approach to the discount rate may diminish. It may be that in many countries the best solution is to use the discount rate as a simple rationing measure. This would involve adjusting the rate periodically in the light of the demand and supply of investment funds. If too few projects relative to the funds available are passing the test of acceptability, this implies the rate should be lowered, and vice versa where too many projects are accepted. In the longer term, if project monitoring and evaluation

Table 11.4 Net return to capital (q) Jamaica 1980–2

	Capital stock[a)]			*GDP*[b]			*Wages*[c]			*Depreciation*[d]			*Net surplus*[e]	*Net surplus/ capital stock %*
	DP	*CF*	*SP*	*DP*	*CF*	*SP*	*DP*	*CF*	*SP*	*DP*	*CF*	*SP*	*SP*	
1980	5414	0.76	4115	1837	0.80	1470	944	0.63	595	164	0.76	125	750	18.2
1981	5604	0.76	4259	1898	0.80	1518	1005	0.63	633	155	0.76	118	767	18.0
1982	5810	0.76	4416	1901	0.80	1521	1092	0.63	688	180	0.76	137	696	15.8
														Average 17.3

DP = Domestic market prices
SP = Shadow prices: world price numeraire

Notes

[a] *CF* of 0.76, is $CF_{Inv} = 0.5\ CF_c + 0.5\ CF_{MF}$
where CF_c is conversion factor for construction
CF_{MF} is conversion factor for manufacturing
and CF_{Inv} is conversion factor for investment
The weights are approximate shares of buildings and equipment in Capital Stock.

[b] *CF* of 0.80 is *ACF*

[c] *CF* of 0.63 is $CF_{LAB} = 0.66\ CF_{UL} + 0.33\ CF_{SL}$
where CF_{UL} is conversion factor for unskilled labour
CF_{SL} is conversion factor for skilled labour
and CF_{LAB} is conversion factor for labour in general.

[d] Depreciation is revalued by CF_{Inv}

[e] Net surplus is GDP minus wages and depreciation.

The weights are the share of unskilled and skilled labour in total wage costs.

Source: Weiss (1985).

Table 11.5 Results of NEP studies

Author	Studies Country	Year of estimate	Unskilled labour	ACF	CCF	Parameters Construction CF	Electricity CF	Discount rate (%)
Adhikari (1988)	Nepal	1980–2	0.45	0.83	1.00	n.a.	0.90	9.0
Linn (1977)	Ivory Coast	1975	0.31	0.83	0.84	0.77	n.a.	10.0
			0.60$^+$					7.0–8.0$^+$
Mashayekhi (1980)	Turkey	1979	0.43(urban) 0.39(rural)	0.59	0.79	n.a.	n.a.	12.0
			0.57–0.60$^+$(urban) 0.56–0.60$^+$(rural)					5.0$^+$
Scott *et al.* (1976)	Kenya	1970–3	0.70$^+$(urban) 1.00$^+$(rural)	0.80	0.82(urban)	0.80$^+$	0.91$^+$	10.0$^+$
					0.94(rural)			
Lal (1980)	India	1973–4	0.56–0.73$^+$	n.a.	0.82–0.86	0.53$^+$	0.69$^+$	11.0$^+$
Schohl (1979)	Columbia	1978–9	0.59(urban) 0.58(rural)	0.92	0.94	0.84–0.87	0.96–1.10	11.0
			0.55$^+$(urban) 0.46$^+$(rural)					6.0$^+$
Page (1982)	Egypt	1979–80	0.47(urban) 0.56(rural)	0.96	1.12$^+$(urban)	1.67	3.32	10.0
			0.40$^+$(urban) 0.22$^+$(rural)		1.07$^+$(rural)			6.0$^+$
Weiss (1985)	Jamaica	1983–4	0.55	0.79	n.a.	0.73	0.74	10.0
Saerbeck (1988)	Botswana	1987	0.29(urban) 0.83(rural)	0.86	0.86	0.72	0.80	5.0
Castagnino (1981)	Paraguay	1979	0.50(urban) 0.43(rural)	0.73	0.76	0.65	0.29	6.0–12.0
Londero (1981)	El Salvador	1979	0.29–0.46	0.86–0.88	0.84–0.89	0.79–0.83	0.83–0.84	12.0
Donoso (1981)	Ecuador	1979	0.26	0.82	0.84	0.72	1.02	12.0
Morales (1981)	Barbados	1979	0.59	0.91	n.a.	0.81–0.85	0.89	12.0
Bid-Nafinsa (1987)	Mexico	1986	0.52	0.75	0.74	0.77	0.97	12.0

Notes

n.a. = not available

$^+$ refers to weighted estimates

systems improve, it may be possible to use ex-post data to derive firmer discount rate estimates.

SOME NATIONAL PARAMETER STUDIES

Some of the results of NEP studies are summarized in Table 11.5. Most use the SIO approach and all are in a world price system. Only results relating to a limited number of parameters are reported; these are the discount rate, a CF for unskilled labour, two aggregate CFs, the ACF and the CCF, and two CFs for the important non-traded activities, construction and electricity. In some cases, separate urban and rural estimates are available for labour and consumption. In a minority of the studies, weights for savings and consumption are incorporated in CF estimates, and in these instances the weighted estimates are shown for comparison with the efficiency or unweighted results.

It would be misleading to imply that there is a typical set of NEP, since the economic situation and policy of countries will determine their own parameter values. However, some generalizations can be made about the results in Table 11.5.

- There is a tendency for the average conversion factor (ACF) to be within a fairly narrow range. There are extremes of 0.59 for Turkey and 0.96 for Egypt, but both countries had their own peculiar features at the time of the studies. Turkey was relatively highly protected by an import licensing system which raised the domestic prices of import-competing goods and thus lowered the ACF. Egypt in the 1970s had a policy of subsidizing key goods, thus keeping their prices below world levels and raising the ACF. Excluding these extreme cases the range of the ACF is from 0.73 (Paraguay) to 0.92 (Columbia) with an average of around 0.80. As one would expect the more protected economies have lower values of the ACF.

- In many of the studies, the ACF and the CCF are close, implying that the former can be used as an approximation for the latter without much loss of accuracy. However, in Nepal and Turkey consumer goods have a considerably higher CF than the average for goods in general, so that for these countries failure to use the CCF could cause significant errors.

- There is a tendency for construction to have a CF below the ACF, due to its labour intensity, and generally the low shadow price found for construction labour. On the other hand, electricity, a capital- and fuel-intensive activity, tends to have a CF of both close to 1.0 and above the ACF. The exceptions are Paraguay, with a low electricity CF of 0.29, due to significant surplus capacity, and Botswana where electricity is partially supplied by imports from South Africa. In Egypt, the electricity CF of 3.39 is exceptionally high due to a heavy subsidy.
- In most studies, unskilled labour has a CF of well below 1.0. Where weights are not used the highest urban labour CF is 0.59 for Barbados and Columbia, and the lowest is 0.26 for Ecuador. There are differences between urban and rural labour, and in several cases where estimates for both are available the rural CF is higher.
- The discount rate is the parameter which shows the greatest similarity between the studies. The range is from 5% for Botswana to 12% for many countries. Botswana is in a peculiar position, being a net international investor, and if it is excluded the range is from 9% to 12%, with most estimates between 10% and 12%.
- Where weights relating to consumption and savings effects are used, for example for labour and the discount rate, the results differ significantly from the basic or unweighted figures. For unskilled labour use of weights raises labour's CF in the Ivory Coast and Turkey, but lowers it in Columbia and Egypt. In these latter cases the weight placed on the consumption gains of workers is sufficiently high, because of their low income to offset the consumption cost in foregone savings of their employment. The adjusted discount rate is in all cases below the unweighted discount rate.

CONCLUSION

The studies summarized above demonstrate that national economic parameters can be estimated for a range of economies. SIO analysis provides a means of deriving a consistent set of national CFs for use in project analysis. However, the rigour of the technique should not divert attention from the weak data that often goes into SIO tables and other problems in the application of the technique. Shadow pricing studies have come a long way from the early work in the 1960s and early 1970s but this is an area in which there will always be approximations rather than precise estimates.

APPENDIX 11.1 SEMI-INPUT–OUTPUT SYSTEM

Formally in matrix terms the calculation requires the Leontief inverse of the A matrix to give total produced inputs per unit of sector output. One must then post-multiply the direct primary factor matrix F by the Leontief inverse to give total primary factor inputs per unit of output, so that

$$M = F[1 - A]^{-1} \quad (11A.1)$$

where
M is the matrix of total primary factor requirements
F is the direct coefficient matrix of primary factors
A is the direct coefficient matrix of produced inputs
$[1 - A]^{-1}$ is the Leontief inverse.

Once sector output is broken down into only primary factors, for sector i producing commodity i

$$P_i = \sum_g c_{gi} . P_g \quad (11A.2)$$

where
P_i is the market price value of a unit of output i;
c_{gi} is the number of units of primary factor g per unit of i,
P_g is the value of a unit of g, at market prices.

The economic value of a sector is given as the sum of the primary factors that go into the sector, with each primary factor itself valued at opportunity costs. For sector i, economic value (V_i) is given as

$$V_i = \sum_g c_{gi} V_g \quad (11A.3)$$

where V_g is the shadow price of primary factor g, and c_{gi} is as in (11A.2)

As it is conventional to give information on shadow prices in the form of ratios, or conversion factors (CFs),

$$CF_i = \frac{V_i}{P_i} \quad (11A.4)$$

To derive a CF for a particular sector requires an economic valuation of the primary inputs into that sector. It can be shown from equations (11A.2), (11A.3) and (11A.4) that CF_i can be derived as a weighted average of the conversion factors of each of the primary inputs that go into i, so that

$$CF_i = \sum_g b_{gi} . CF_g \quad (11A.5)$$

where b_{gi} is the share of primary factor g in the value of output of i, where both g and i are at market prices, so that

$$b_{gi} = \frac{c_{gi} \cdot P_g}{P_i}$$

and CF_g is the conversion factor for primary factor input g.

The model is solved for the set of CFs by multiplying the total primary requirements for each sector by the CFs for different primary factors. Formally, in matrix terms M must be multiplied by the vector of CFs for primary factors, so that

$$P_n = P_f . M \tag{11A.6}$$

where P_n is the vector of final CF results
and P_f is the vector of CFs for primary factors.

However, in relation to the text example, this expression involves five equations in nine unknowns: P_n for $n = 1, \ldots, 5$ and P_f for f = 1, . . ., 4. It must be recalled that some CFs for the primary factors are themselves defined in relation to sectoral or aggregate CFs. In the text example, the CF for labour is related to the CF for the agriculture sector and the CF for operating surplus is related to the average conversion factor. Hence we have a further set of relations

$$P_f' = T P_n' \tag{11A.7}$$

where P_f and P_n are as in (11A.6), and P_f' and P_n' are their transposes, and T is a matrix summarising these interdependencies.

This provides a further set of four equations in the same nine unknowns for the text example. The combined model can be solved while assigning the value 1.0 to foreign exchange exogenously, in the world price system.

In summary, a full set of CFs is arrived at by simultaneous solution of equation systems (11A.6) and (11A.7); that is

$$P_n = P_f M$$

and

$$P_f' = T P_n'$$

with

$$P_f = 1.0 \text{ for foreign exchange.}$$

APPENDIX 11.2 WEIGHTED CONVERSION FACTORS IN SIO

Growth and distribution objectives can be incorporated numerically in the calculation of shadow prices and CFs using SIO analysis. The difference from the derivation of unweighted estimates lies in the treatment of primary factors. Once growth and distribution are incorporated, the additional income generated directly and indirectly in particular sectors must be adjusted by the weights for its savings and consumption components discussed in Chapter 10. The additional incomes captured in SIO analysis arise through the employment of workers at wages above their opportunity cost, the generation of surplus profits, and use of non-traded goods in fixed supply.

For primary factors valuation is now based on two components. First, their resource costs in normal SIO analysis; and secondly, the benefits and costs from the use of additional income for savings and consumption. With savings as the numeraire and all savings treated as equally valuable (and government income as equivalent to savings), only consumption effects need to be revalued by distribution weights. The example discussed below uses a savings numeraire at world prices.

The cost of additional consumption, in terms of a reduction in resources available for investment, is $\Delta C_i.CCF_i$,
where

ΔC_i is net additional consumption at domestic market prices to group i
and

CCF_i is the conversion factor to convert this to world prices.

Benefits of additional consumption to group i are

$$\frac{\Delta C_i.d_i}{v}$$

where

d_i is the weight on consumption to group i relative to average consumers,
and

v is the units of consumption to average consumers equivalent to one unit of savings.

The net effect of additional consumption is therefore

$$\text{Net cost of consumption} = \Delta C_i\, CCF_i - \Delta C_i \frac{d_i}{v} \qquad (11A.8)$$

$$\text{or} \quad \Delta C_i.\left(CCF_i - \frac{d_i}{v}\right)$$

This net cost of additional consumption must be incorporated in the valuation of primary factors. The main factor to be adjusted will be labour. There is now a new definition of the shadow wage, so that

$$SWR = M.CF_m + \Delta C_L\,.\,(CCF_L - d_L/v) \qquad (11A.9)$$

where the resource cost of employing labour is $M.CF_m$ (from equation 11.2) and

$$C_L\ (CCF_L - d_L/v)$$

is the net cost of additional consumption of workers (who are termed group L).

With this new valuation of labour all CFs will change, since they are related directly and indirectly to the valuation of labour in non-traded sectors.

Other income changes through surplus profits and use of non-traded goods in fixed supply should be treated similarly. Surplus profits have a zero resource cost, but additional consumption from the surplus will be treated as in equation (11A.8) with group i now referring to the recipients of surplus profits. Use of non-traded goods in fixed supply should be valued by willingness to pay for the goods concerned. In this form of SIO analysis, willingness to pay should be revalued by dc / v where d_c is the weight for the group of consumers involved.

The derivation of weighted CFs can be illustrated with the SIO example from Chapter 11. There are only four primary factors in this example, and since there are no surplus profits nor non-traded goods in fixed supply only labour requires adjustment. The original SIO table has no column and row for consumption expenditure. For this illustration these have been added so that a CCF can be calculated. The new table is given in Table 11A.1.

Table 11A.1 Revised SIO table – direct coefficients

	Industry	*Agri-culture*	*Services*	*Trans-port*	*ACF*	*CCF*
Industry			0.10	0.15	0.20	0.10
Agriculture					0.45	0.70
services	0.05		0.20	0.05	0.25	0.15
Transport	0.05	0.01	0.10		0.10	0.05
ACF						
CCF						
Transfers	0.30	0.09		0.10		
Foreign exchange	0.60	0.90	0.20	0.30		
Labour			0.30	0.30		
Operating surplus			0.10	0.10		
	1.00	1.00	1.00	1.00	1.00	1.00

The resource cost of employing a worker is $M.CF_m$
where $M = 0.5 \times MWR$
We assume that the increase in labour's consumption is 40 per cent of the market wage, so $\Delta C = 0.4 \times MWR$, and that $d_i = 1.50$ and $v = 2.50$.
With these assumptions the expression for the weighted shadow wage is

$$SWR = (0.50 \times MWR)\, CF_{AG} + (0.40 \times MWR)\left(CCF - \frac{1.5}{2.5}\right)$$

Dividing by MWR, the CF for labour is

$$CF_{LAB} = 0.50.CF_{AG} + 0.40\left(CCF - \frac{1.5}{2.5}\right)$$

$$\text{or } CF_{LAB} = 0.50.CF_{AG} + 0.40.\ CCF - 0.24$$

The full set of new CFs for sectors and primary factors are given in Table 11A.2. The new CF_{LAB} is now 0.55. In comparison with the original unweighted results in Table 11.3 the cost of employing labour has increased from approximately 45 to 55 per cent of the market wage. This raises the CFs for the non-traded sectors services and transport, but has only a slight effect on those for the traded sectors, industry and agriculture. Since these latter sectors dominate the economy the ACF also is only changed slightly from 0.78 to 0.79. This illustrates an important general point that this weighting system will have a greater impact on shadow prices in economies where non-traded activities have a major share of production.

Table 11A.2 Weighted full CF results

Sectors	Industry	0.6702
	Agriculture	0.9068
	Services	0.7245
	Transport	0.6812
	ACF	0.7913
	CCF	0.8445
Primary factors	Transfers	0.0000
	Foreign exchange	1.0000
	Labour	0.5512
	Operating surplus	0.7913

However, detailed application of this approach requires that additional incomes are specified in considerable detail through the use of several categories of primary factors, which can only be done with very detailed cost breakdowns at market prices.

Further Reading

The best introduction to SIO analysis is Powers (1981), which also has several useful country studies. The section in this chapter draws heavily on Weiss (1988) which discusses some of the limitations of SIO analysis. Other applications are Kuyvenhoven (1978), Schohl (1979), Page (1982) and Saerbeck (1988). Scott *et al.* (1976) is a very detailed discussion of the derivation of weighted CFs.

Illustrations of shadow wage and discount rate estimates for Jamaica are in Weiss (1985), chapters 2 and 4. For other examples, see Powers (1981), chapters 4, 5 and 6. Harberger (1972), chapters 3 and 6 discusses ways of estimating the opportunity cost of capital from macro data. Page (1982) and Mashayekhi (1980) illustrate use of a production function approach to the discount rate. For a discussion of a range of estimates of the discount rate for one country from alternative approaches, see Phillips (1986b) and Adhikari (1986), and (1988) chapter 4.

12 Limitations and Conclusions

The previous chapters have outlined and discussed the main features of project analysis, relating particularly to the economic analysis of projects. This has included a full discussion of the ways in which shadow prices can be applied in project analysis as well as the analysis of the distributional effects of projects and the estimation of national economic parameters. In all cases, the purpose is to arrive at better project decisions and to improve the effectiveness of investments.

However, these methods have some limitations which we briefly refer to in this chapter. A major problem, although not generally made explicit, is the value system underlying project analysis using shadow prices; questions arise as to whether such forms of project analysis are appropriate in all types of economy. A further problem is the static nature of most applications and the difficulties of including dynamic effects. Then there is the additional issue of the relationship between project analysis and programmes of economic adjustment taking place in many countries; do such programmes reduce the need for the economic analysis of projects? These questions will be discussed in turn, before the authors present their own conclusions on the continued role of project analysis in investment decision-taking.

THE VALUE SYSTEM IN PROJECT ANALYSIS

There remains a weakness in the value system which provides the basis for the economic analysis of projects. World prices represent the terms on which an economy can participate in foreign trade, and are therefore relevant when planning investments that either use or produce traded goods. However, border parity pricing means that even for traded goods there is a domestic component of value arising from the transport and distribution costs of moving goods to and from the border. For geographically large economies these non-traded costs can be a significant part of the border parity price, so that for such economies there is a greater divergence between economic value and cif or fob prices than in smaller economies. This illustrates the natural protection that inland projects in large countries enjoy in relation to import competition.

The main difficulty in the value system employed in project analysis lies in the treatment of goods whose use or production only affects their availability to domestic users. For such non-traded goods willingness to pay by the domestic user is the basis for value. Apart from the practical difficulty of measurement, willingness to pay indicators are derived from the existing distribution of income. If the fairness of the distribution of income is challenged, it will undermine the acceptability of this approach. To put the point simply, there is little logic in valuing all water supplied to households on the basis of what they are willing to pay to receive it. By this criterion all water supply projects would serve high-income areas.

One way around this difficulty is to use consumption weights to adjust the willingness to pay of different groups by the weight relevant for that group. In this way, the fact that higher incomes allow the rich to express a greater willingness to pay than the poor can be counter-balanced by a higher consumption weight given to the latter. However, this approach is limited by the difficulty in obtaining acceptability for a set of consumption weights and the fact that in practice this form of project analysis has not often been applied. Willingness to pay must be recognized as an unsatisfactory basis for value for some non-traded outputs, particularly those that are either major elements of consumption of the poor, such as low-income staple foods, or are part of social consumption, like education and health. For projects producing such goods valuation of benefits may not be possible, and project analysis will have to concentrate on meeting physical targets with the minimum cost in economic terms.

However, the problem is not limited to valuing some non-traded project outputs. It relates also to the valuation of non-traded goods and services that are in fixed supply and are direct and indirect inputs into other sectors. The more such goods there are, the more the valuation system will depart from the direct application of world prices to project inputs and outputs. As indicated already, this may be the case for locally oriented projects in large countries where a range of products, because of cost and quality, may be effectively non-traded. It may also be the case in small economies pursuing a relatively autonomous development path, or in countries faced by trade embargoes.

If in fact many economic sectors are not subject to international competition then world prices are not appropriate for valuing the outputs of those sectors. Valuation by willingness to pay, which is more difficult to estimate, will take a larger role in the analysis of projects. For economies that are either large or relatively autonomous, greater thought needs to be given to the sectors within which project analysis using world prices is most applicable and to operational means of estimating opportunity cost values for the many products not subject to world trade.

WORLD PRICES AND DYNAMIC EFFECTS

Use of world prices to value traded goods is sometimes confused with advocacy of an external policy of free trade. However, a number of situations can justify interventions in trade to promote or encourage new projects. The most significant of these are surplus incomes for others in the economy, and cost reductions and quality improvements over time through learning and technical change. In principle each of these possibilities can be incorporated in project analysis.

The treatment of surplus labour by valuing unskilled labour costs at a shadow wage below the market wage has been noted in Chapters 5 and 6. Incorporation of external benefits arising from a project's effect on incomes of others was discussed in Chapter 7. However, perhaps the most significant of these possibilities is the dynamic effects arising from learning and technical change, leading to reductions in unit costs or improvements in product quality over time. The existence of such dynamic effects is the basis for the infant industry case for protection, and there is evidence that they have been important in the industrial sector of several of the newly industralizing countries. These effects, whether internal to a project or spread to others as externalities, are additional benefits that should be included in a project analysis.

There is no difficulty in incorporating falling costs of production or higher revenue due to improved product quality in a project statement. The problem is in predicting if and when such changes will occur. Excessive pessimism can mean that potentially successful projects are not selected because initially their costs are high or their quality low relative to competing output on the world market. On the other hand, excessive optimism can mean that projects are selected on expectations of efficiency improvements that never materialize.

Relatively few guidelines are available for assessing whether favourable dynamic effects will occur. Developments in similar projects in a country or abroad are one indicator but the past cannot simply be extrapolated into the future. Evidence suggests that where such effects occur they are the result of conscious effort by project management and not simply an automatic by-product of the accumulation of production experience. The important policy issue here is that in project analysis for traded good projects domestic costs at shadow prices are compared with competitors' prices on the world market. If dynamic effects are not allowed for, this procedure will allocate investment only to activities that are currently competitive internationally, and will ignore the long-run dimension of changing efficiency over time. Omission of dynamic effects will thus be equivalent to the allocation of resources on the basis of an economy's existing not potential comparative advantage. However, identification and estimation of such effects at the project level is a major problem, towards which further research should be directed.

ECONOMIC ADJUSTMENT PROGRAMMES AND PROJECT ANALYSIS

As explained in Chapter 4, much of the details of project analysis methodology were developed during the 1960s, when many developing countries were characterized by heavy government involvement in terms of price and trade controls, as well as significant state investment and planning restriction over private sector activity. This government involvement was seen as a major factor in creating divergences between market prices and the opportunity costs to the economy of resources; so, for example, credit controls created a divergence between market interest rates and the opportunity cost of capital, and a fixed exchange rate policy caused a divergence between official and shadow exchange rates.

During the 1980s many developing countries introduced economic adjustment programmes involving reduced public sector activity. These programmes, involving a package of economic policy changes, have been oriented to shifting resources into the export sectors. In many cases, this has been attempted by providing direct incentives for export production whilst retaining many of the protection measures for other sectors. In others, it has involved removing many of the restrictions on the operation of markets for goods, services and other productive inputs. In the latter case, an important question is whether such liberalization measures that aim to bring market prices more in line with opportunity costs remove the need for the economic analysis of projects. If market prices reflect opportunity cost, conversion factors will tend towards unity and returns at market prices will hardly differ from returns at shadow prices.

Where reforms of this type are introduced this is likely to reduce the gap between market and shadow prices, but this gap will never be removed entirely. For example, taxes and subsidies will continue to be used by governments, although these create divergences between domestic market and world prices for traded goods, and between domestic prices and the opportunity costs of production for non-traded goods. Similarly, in all economies there will be some monopoly or surplus profits and undercapacity working, both of which will also contribute to a divergence between domestic market prices and opportunity costs in non-traded sectors.

Reforms in markets for foreign exchange, labour and capital are sometimes seen as bringing the official closer to the shadow exchange rate, market wages closer to shadow wages and interest rates closer to the economic discount rate. However, equality between market-determined prices for these factors and their opportunity costs to the economy will only obtain where an economy has no taxes and subsidies, and is perfectly competitive in the sense of having complete mobility and full employment of resources, and full information on their opportunity costs.

Economic adjustment programmes in a number of developing countries have reduced the scale of divergence between market prices and opportunity costs, and trade liberalization has been particularly important in narrowing the gap between domestic and world prices. However, divergences will persist; and in so far as such programmes are partial in their implementation, or rely more on an extension of incentives than a liberalization of markets, the economic analysis of projects will continue to have an important role in investment decisions.

CONCLUSIONS

It is important to recognize the limitations of project analysis, especially given the time and effort that is required to undertake an economic analysis of a project. However, there has now been extensive development of project analysis techniques and considerable experience of implementing them in practice. Moreover, the central purpose of project analysis as it has been discussed here, the analysis of investments from the point of view of national economic objectives, seems to be as important in the 1990s as in the 1960s, if not more so.

It will be important to retain and develop a technique whose role lies in assessing the trade opportunities open to an economy, since for projects producing traded goods benefits will be primarily in terms of foreign exchange and these can be compared with the costs needed to achieve them. What we have termed trade efficiency criteria will remain of critical importance to the vast majority of developing countries, with the growing interdependence of the world economy and the key role of the foreign trade sector in accumulation and growth. As noted above, problems remain in fully incorporating dynamic effects. However, with this qualification, analysis of traded sector projects should provide important information in determining where to invest in order to expand exports, and substitute for imports, and where to forego domestic production in favour of imported supplies.

In addition to foreign trade effects, for most governments the question of who gains and loses from projects will be of importance. The complex weighting system for savings and consumption has proved impracticable to implement. However, information on income changes for different groups arising from projects should be given in addition to the usual NPV and IRR indicators of economic worth, and this will incorporate the effect of divergences between domestic market prices and shadow prices. To this limited extent, and particularly for large projects, distribution analysis should be incorporated into project analysis practice.

If project analysis is to remain an important element in investment decision-taking then the task of the project analyst should be made as easy as possible. To this end it is convenient to have available a set of national economic parameters for use in project analysis. Not only does this make the analysis process easier, it helps in ensuring consistency across the analysis of different projects. The refinement of techniques to estimate sets of national economic parameters, and in particular evolving information systems for this purpose, would help to minimize the costs of estimation.

Finally, project analysis as a planning technique is capable of extension and adaptation according to changes in economic circumstances. In this spirit also, existing applications need to be joined to new applications. Two areas of current concern that have not been addressed in detail in this book are the effect of economic policy changes such as exchange rate and price changes on the financial viability of projects, and the incorporation of environmental effects into project analysis. Both these extensions relate to the sustainability of project investments, from the financial and environmental point of view, which complement the analysis of basic economic effects and hence project economic sustainability.

Further Reading

Weiss (1990) discusses some of the problems in the value system of project analysis, in relation to its application in socialist economies. Weiss (1986) and (1989) consider the implications of technical change and other dynamic effects for project analysis. Evidence on divergences between market and shadow prices, termed distortions, is in World Bank (1983), where developing countries are ranked in terms of a distortion index and details of economic reforms in Sub-Saharan Africa are in World Bank (1989).

Notes

2 Main Features of Projects, Project Resource Statements and Financial Statements

1. A change in relative prices can be illustrated as follows. Suppose that prices in general are expected to rise at 10 per cent per annum over the next ten years. This includes the main outputs and inputs of a project. At the same time, the government has announced a wages policy that would ensure that wages will not grow by more than 5 per cent per annum over the next ten years. In these circumstances, the price of labour in a project statement at constant prices should reflect the relative price change $(1 + 0.05)/(1 + 0.10)$ and should be reduced by 4.5 per cent per annum.
2. Other classifications or expressions can be used to describe different projects. For example, there can be rehabilitation projects which aim to restore pre-existing activities; however, they will generally involve some change in technology, output and organization, and frequently all three, and so are better described under the category up-dating.
3. The annual time period chosen may differ from case to case. Some resource statements are drawn up using budgetary periods, especially government funded projects; some are drawn up using calendar years.
4. This choice of initial period again relates to the process of discounting, which revalues resources to the time at which a decision is being made. This is explained in more detail below.
5. Commissioning a project refers to a short period after the main investment expenditures have been completed when the new investment is operated on an experimental basis, often at very low capacity, prior to normal working.
6. The technique of network analysis, when applied to a detailed statement of investment items, can be used in larger projects to identify the optimum sequence of investment activities and to find the minimum period which it will take to complete these activities.
7. The market life of the output refers to the number of years over which it is expected there will be a demand for the additional output generated by the new investment resources.
8. Here, the original investment costs are regarded as sunk costs which have already been committed. The best year for replacement cannot be determined without knowing at what rate to discount future costs and benefits, which is dealt with below.
9. Semi-variable costs can also be identified as those that vary in part with output, but are also partly fixed.
10. Projects sometimes involve internal benefits such as construction work or electricity production by the operating organization. Although the

costs of these activities will be recorded in project costs, the value of such internal production is generally not included in the benefit inflow, which relates to benefits delivered outside the operating organization. The benefit here is the reduced costs of not having to purchase such inputs from outside the project.

11. A modified discounting method has been proposed that aims to adjust the discounting procedure so that benefits (and costs) occurring in later years are not discounted so heavily (Kula, 1988). The rationale for this is that the General Discount Factor in the text discriminates against future generations by assuming they will have the same discount rate as present decision-makers and that benefits (costs) occurring to them should be discounted to the present, and not to the moment at which future generations become purchasers/users of project outputs. The argument relates particularly to infrastructure projects with very long lives. Under the modified discounting method the discount factors for future years do not fall so sharply as under the conventional treatment. This approach has been the subject of considerable controversy, however.
12. A common expression is the opportunity cost of capital. However, the discounting process is applied to all resources in a project, not just investment resources, so the more general expression in the text is more accurate.
13. Where there is a perfect capital market that reflects accurately the future returns on different projects, the subjective rate of time preference should be the same as the opportunity cost of capital. However, this is hardly likely to be so in practice.

3 Project Criteria

1. There are several project criteria using undiscounted values of benefits and costs. For a brief introduction to Soviet practice see Wilczynski (1977).
2. At some discount rate, higher than illustrated on Figure 3.1, the BCR lines for the two resource statements will cross. These lines are, of course, non-linear. They will cross because of the different pattern of benefits and costs between the two projects. The NPV curves of Figure 3.2 also cross at a relatively high rate of discount. For these examples, this occurs where both NPVs are negative. The meaning of this crossover point is explained below.
3. For some project resource statements, the NPV curve may cross the horizontal axis more than once, see below.
4. This process of trial and error is greatly enhanced by the use of computer spreadsheets to set up a project statement and perform the discounting; for the estimation of an internal rate of return when such a tool is not available, see Appendix 3.1.
5. Any project proposal can involve a large number of permutations of alternatives in design details. However, for decision-taking, each has to

be represented by a full project statement. There will only be very few alternatives for which a full project statement is constructed, depicting the major choices within a project.

6. This may be because the savings rate from domestic income has recently fallen, or there has been a flight of domestic capital to other countries, or declining economic conditions have reduced the willingness of foreigners to invest in new projects in the country.
7. This problem of capital rationing can apply at the corporate, sector or national level. In general at the national level, there are few instances where there is no opportunity at all of obtaining additional investment funds, either through borrowing or grants. However, some of the potential funds may be project specific and not relax the general investment fund constraint.

4 National Economic Returns and the Use of Shadow Prices

1. Similarly, prices of products may be kept above their full costs of production where the government wishes to encourage such production; or below their full costs of production where the output is a basic purchase, for example, basic foodstuffs. Such project outputs should be revalued to omit the effect of government price controls.
2. These types of indirect costs and benefits are conventionally termed 'external effects' as they accrue to activities outside the project that generates them. This is pursued further in Chapter 7.
3. Trade opportunity cost is not the only principle on which an alternative set of prices can be based, but it is the most widely used on an operational basis. Unsuccessful attempts have been made to base prices on the labour inputs directly and indirectly embodied in different products, based on a labour theory of value. There are instances also of opportunity cost values (for labour and for foreign exchange) derived from the dual solution of a linear programming model of an economy. These attempts to establish alternative sets of prices will not be discussed here, as they have not been made operational on a wide basis.
4. A conversion factor is also sometimes called an accounting price ratio (APR) or simply an accounting ratio.
5. Where land has no market price, and does not appear as a cost at market prices, the CF cannot be calculated. The shadow price value of the land has to be entered directly in the project statement. The text illustrates the customary procedure of starting from a project statement at market prices and converting it to shadow prices. However, project statements can be derived directly through the use of shadow prices.
6. This objective is sometimes referred to as maximizing net national income at world prices, where opportunity costs refer to the direct or indirect foreign exchange effects of outputs and inputs.

7. For simplicity, other effects such as handling and transport and monopoly pricing are ignored here.

5 World Price System of Economic Analysis

1. A formal definition of a non-traded good is one where domestic costs are below import prices, but above export prices, so that there is no incentive for trade to occur.
2. Little and Mirrlees (1968), made this suggestion.
3. Calculation of marginal revenues requires knowledge of the price elasticity of export demand, that is the degree to which demand changes in response to price. This is generally known only approximately, so that the adjustment made to the export price will be fairly crude. The formulae for marginal revenues and costs are

$$MR = WP_{fob}\,(1 + 1/e_d)$$

$$MC = WP_{cif}\,(1 + 1/e_s)$$

where

MR and *MC* are marginal export revenue and marginal import cost, respectively,

WP_{fob} and WP_{cif} are world prices, *fob* for export and *cif* for import, respectively,

e_d and e_s are the elasticity of export demand and import supply respectively.

In the conventional case, where the elasticities are assumed to be infinite

$$MR = WP_{fob}, \text{ and } MC = WP_{cif}$$

4. Theoretically, to be valid for intermediates this requires perfect competition in all markets of the economy.
5. Much of the discussion on shadow wages assumes that agriculture will be the labour-supplying sector, and that often more than one worker will migrate for every job created by new projects. Multiple migration can be handled readily by rewriting the shadow wage as

$$SWR = n.\sum_i a_i.m_i.CF_i$$

where *n* is the number of workers who migrate per job.

Such ideas, however, arise from 1960s evidence on rural–urban migration patterns, and with falling real urban wages and improvements in the rural–urban terms of trade in many countries in the 1980s this view may no longer be accurate. Often at least some of the workers for new urban projects will come from those already in the urban labour force.

6. A consumption conversion factor (CCF) can be interpreted as a weighted average ratio of world to domestic prices for a bundle of consumer goods, with the weights given by the share of goods in additional consumption expenditure. Strictly, world prices should be border parity prices including transport and distribution costs to the consumption point. There can be a set of CCFs for different income groups, as well as a national average figure.
7. This follows since, where

$$MWR = \sum_i a_i m_i$$

then $SWR = MWR.\ ACF$

and $CF_L = \dfrac{SWR}{MWR} = ACF$

8. In this example it is assumed that at the time of the year when farmers are engaged in cotton cultivation there is an opportunity cost of their time, given by the value of the other export crops they could be cultivating.
9. CF_q can be a ratio of separate conversion factors for the net return and the capital stock. The ACF may be used for the former and an investment conversion factor (ICF) for the latter, so that $CF_q = ACF/ICF$.
10. In a world price system, equation (5.7) must be at world prices. The foreign interest rate is already in foreign exchange so no adjustment is required. A domestic interest rate should be interpreted as ratio showing the return on consumption postponed. Both sides of this ratio need to be multiplied by a conversion factor for consumption to move from domestic to world prices. However, as the same conversion factors should be used for both sides of the ratio, this is identical to using a conversion factor of 1.0.

6 Domestic Price System of Economic Analysis

1. Where import trade is heavily subsidized or exports taxed, domestic prices may be below border parity levels. Such cases are relatively rare.
2. Using equation (6.2) the ACF will be the inverse of the conversion factor for foreign exchange, provided the same goods i and j are compared and the same weights a_i and a_j are used. Therefore

$$ACF = \sum_i a_i . \frac{WP_i}{DP_i} + \sum_j a_j . \frac{WP_j}{DP_j}$$

3. These elasticities are the import price elasticity of demand (f_i), and the export price elasticity of supply (f_j). The former is the percentage change in import quantity demanded divided by the percentage change in import price, and the latter is the percentage change in export quantity supplied divided by the percentage change in export price. A rise in import price, for example caused by a devaluation, will normally lead to a fall in import demand, so that f_i is negative, whilst a rise in export supply normally follows a devaluation, so that f_j is positive.

   Assuming the country concerned is a price-taker on the world market, the weights a_i and a_j can be derived from the trade elasticities for i and j, so that

$$a_i = \frac{-M_i.f_i}{\sum_j X_j.f_j - \sum_i M_i f_i}$$

and $$a_j = \frac{X_j.f_j}{\sum_j X_j.f_j - \sum_i M_i.f_i}$$

where

f_i and f_j are the trade elasticities for import i and export j,
M_i and X_j are the initial values of i and j in foreign exchange,
and
$\sum_j X_j.f_j - \sum_i M_i.f_i$ gives the total change in exports plus j i imports resulting from an exchange rate change.

As f_i is negative, $-\sum_i M_i.f_i$ will be positive.

4. In the treatment of electricity in a world price analysis in Chapter 5, the ACF is taken as 0.90. Following the equality $SER/OER = 1/ACF$, the CF for foreign exchange is 1.111.
5. Which of these alternatives is more accurate will depend on whether a CCF or ACF gives a more accurate conversion factor for the non-traded output. The second approach is equivalent to using the ACF to value these goods in a world price system. If the crops are foodstuffs, provided there is some substitutability with traded goods, one would expect a CCF for an appropriate group of consumers to be more accurate than the ACF, which is a general parameter.
6. As with unskilled labour, the difference in result follows from the use of a CCF not the ACF in the original world price example. If the ACF had been used to convert the local consumption of Rs500 to world prices both results would be identical.

7 Non-traded Outputs and External Effects

1. Where benefit valuation along the lines described here is not applicable, it will be necessary to fix output targets to be met within a

planning period. For such activities project analysis becomes concerned with the least-cost means of meeting these targets.

2. This additional consumer surplus is only a net gain to the economy if the cost of providing the water Q_l has fallen. If unit costs remain unchanged, but price is reduced, the gain to consumers is a transfer from producers, rather than a net saving in resources.
3. In principle, there will be different CCFs for different groups of consumers differentiated by income or region. In practice, however, use of a single national average CCF may be all that is feasible.
4. In principle one could also envisage a willingness to pay approach where demand for transport by road users captures the economic value of additional output. However, in practice in this type of situation one encounters the difficulty of specifying a demand curve by new users, who may have little idea of the potential benefits to be derived from access to transport facilities.
5. This procedure of excluding the water tariff is appropriate provided that the operating costs of water supply are included as separate costs in calculating the return to the irrigation project as a whole.

8 Uncertainty

1. With random selection of values for each variable the different values of the NPV are equally distributed around their expected value. Moreover, the closer to the expected value, the more likely a specific NPV value is to occur. Most samples, or generated distributions with more than twenty observations will approximate to the normal distribution, where the proportion of all results lying within a specified range from the expected value can be clearly calculated. It is this which allows us to calculate the probability of a project decision being wrong.
2. Strictly, these percentages are sample estimates (from a sample of 100 observations) of the true values. For simplicity, these proportions can be taken to represent the probability that a decision will be wrong, which is high at both market and shadow prices. The full connection between the 'best estimate' NPV value and its expected value, and between the proportion of negative (positive) NPV values and the probability of a decision being wrong, is not articulated here.

9 Income Distribution Effects of Projects

1. Following the procedure used in Chapter 2, terminal values of capital assets and working capital are included as benefits in the investment and working capital cost rows.
2. The formula for a regional multiplier is $1/1 - e$ where e is the proportion of income, which when spent results in additional regional income. For a backward region e is likely to be low; for example, with $e = 0.10$, the multiplier will be 1.11, $(1/0.9 = 1.11)$ meaning that every

extra unit of income in the region, when respent, will generate an additional 0.11 units for the region. Strictly, one can only rule out a regional multiplier if there is a fixed regional budget so that if the funds involved are not spent on one project they will be spent on another in the same region.

3. If foreign loans are involved it will be a foreign interest rate that must be compared with the economic discount rate.
4. This treatment assumes an equal rate of profit and repatriation of this profit in whatever project the foreign investment funds are committed to. This is clearly an over simplification, but the theoretically correct alternative of estimating incremental profit outflows on project alternatives is normally too demanding to be applied in practice.
5. Transfer prices are those charged on transactions between subsidiaries of the same parent transnational. Such prices are set in the interest of the corporation's global profit strategy and can differ from commercial prices.
6. Here it is linkages between a project and non-traded suppliers that will be relevant. Where traded good inputs are involved it is assumed that additional demand from a project will affect the balance of payments not domestic supply.

10 Savings and Income Distribution

1. UNIDO (1972) uses private consumption at domestic prices as numeraire and Little and Mirrlees (1974) use government savings at world prices. Strictly, the Little and Mirrlees definition is uncommitted government income at world prices, that is income in general, but since it is conventional to value government income by the returns from government investment, it is government income that is saved for investment purposes that is the real basis for their numeraire.
2. The present value is the annuity of 0.10 multiplied by the annuity factor at 5 per cent over twenty years, of 12.462
3. This involves estimating different returns on public and private investment (q), propensities to save out of these returns (s), and for private investment the share of returns that accrues to the government as taxation.
4. Squire and van der Tak (1975) adopt this approach when examining national parameters such as v, but argue that it can be misleading at the level of specific projects with major income effects on the private sector. Logically, if this equality between government savings and consumption and private savings is adopted, not only will there be a single economy-wide v, but the equations for v need to be modified so that s is now the proportion of income not consumed privately; this is higher than the marginal propensity to save, so that v will increase.
5. In a world price system v is defined as

$$v = \frac{(1-s)q}{i-sq} \cdot \frac{1}{CCF}$$

where CCF is the consumption conversion factor and all items are as in (10.3) except that q is here marginal returns at world prices. In a world price system a unit of savings (or government income) at world prices must be compared with consumption received by consumers at domestic prices. Division by CCF will convert the consumption $(1 - s)q$ to domestic prices.

6. Use of a constant elasticity formula means, for example, that a 10 per cent increase in the consumption level of recipients creates the same proportionate fall in the weight, whether the increase is from 100 to 110, or from 1000 to 1100. Strictly, equation (10.5) is relevant only for small changes in consumption. A considerably more complex formula is required for large changes; see Squire and van der Tak (1975, pp. 65–6.)
7. This suggestion comes from Squire and van der Tak (1975). Equation (10.5) uses average consumption ($\bar{c}$) as the reference point. An alternative approach to weighting identifies a base level of consumption. Here the government judges that additional consumption to individuals at this level is just as valuable as income to the government. This approach is put forward in Little and Mirrlees (1974), and implies that $\bar{c}$ is a subjectively determined parameter rather than actual average per capita consumption in the country.
8. A formula for ARI with a savings numeraire is

$$ARI = sq + (1 - s)q.\frac{d}{v}$$

where

q is the return on the marginal project

s is the proportion of this return that is saved

v is the weight on savings relative to average consumption

and

d is the weight on consumption to the beneficiaries of the marginal project relative to the average consumers.

Conventionally, the beneficiaries of a marginal project are taken to be average consumers, so $d = 1.0$. ARI will therefore be below q, the efficiency discount rate, as long as $v > 1.0$.

11 National Economic Parameters

1. An estimate of willingness to pay for additional units of the good concerned is required (although in practice this is often approximated by the prevailing domestic market price), and this will be converted to shadow prices by a consumption conversion factor.

2. If the transport cost for export is greater than for domestic use this net cost should be included in the transport row with a negative sign, since it will be a saving created by the diversion of agricultural output to the home market.
3. Since all foreign exchange effects will be measured at world prices already, there is no need for any further adjustment, hence the CF of 1.0. If the calculations use a domestic price system the CF for foreign exchange is given by the ratio of the shadow to the official exchange rate
4. This and the example below come from Weiss (1985).
5. A more sophisticated version of this approach involves a statistical relation, termed formally a Cobb–Douglas production function, to link capital inputs with net output. Here national income is determined by a constant, covering technical change, and two aggregate inputs labour and capital, so that

$$Y = A.L.^{a}K^{b}$$

where
Y is national income
A is the constant
L is labour
K is capital

and with constant returns to scale $a + b = 1.0$.

If one assumes that all markets are perfect, a equals the share of profits in national income, and the marginal product of capital at domestic prices will be given by $a. Y/K$.

Bibliography

Abouchar, A. (1985) *Project decision-making in the public-sector* (Massachusetts: Lexington Books).

Adhikari, R. (1986) 'National Economic Parameters for Nepal', Project Planning Centre Occasional Paper no. 9 (Bradford: University of Bradford).

Adhikari, R. (1988) *Manufacturing Industries in Developing Countries: An Economic Efficiency Analysis of Nepal* (Aldershot: Gower).

Adler, H. (1987) *Economic Appraisal of Transport Projects* (Baltimore: Johns Hopkins University Press for the World Bank).

Bacha, E. and Taylor, L. (1971) 'Foreign Exchange Shadow Prices: a Critical Review of Current Theories', *Quarterly Journal of Economics*, vol. 85, no. 2.

Balassa, B. (1971) *The Structure of Protection in Developing Countries*, (Baltimore: Johns Hopkins University Press).

Balassa, B. (1974) 'Estimating the Shadow Price of Foreign Exchange in Project Appraisal', *Oxford Economic Papers*, vol. 26, no. 2.

Baldwin, G. (1972) 'A Layman's Guide to Little and Mirrlees', *Finance and Development*, vol. 9, no. 1.

Beyer, J. (1975) 'Estimating the Shadow Price of Foreign Exchange: An Illustration from India', *Journal of Development Studies*, vol. II, no. 4.

Bid-Nafinsa (1987) *Los-Precios de Cuenta en Mexico, 1986* (Mexico DF: Inter-American Development Bank and Nacional Financiera).

Brent, R. (1990) *Project Appraisal for Developing Countries* (Hemel Hampstead: Harvester Wheatsheaf).

Bromwich, M. (1976) *The Economics of Capital Budgeting* (Harmondsworth: Penguin).

Bruce, C. (1976) 'Social Cost–Benefit Analysis: A Guide for Country and Project Economists to the Derivation and Application of Economic and Social Accounting Prices', World Bank Staff Working Paper no. 239 (Washington DC: World Bank).

Castagnino, E. (1981) 'Paraguay', in Powers, T. (ed.) (1981).

COMSEC (1982) *A Manual on Project Planning for Small Economies* (London: Commonwealth Secretariat).

Cook, P. and Mosley, P. (1989) 'On the Valuation of "External effects" in Project Appraisal', *Project Appraisal*, vol. 4, no. 3.

Cooper, C. (1981) *Economic Evaluation and the Environment* (London: Hodder & Stoughton).

Dixon, J. Carpenter, R. and Fallon, L. (1986) *Economic Analysis of the Environmental Impacts of Development Projects* (London: Earthscan).

Donoso, G. (1981) 'Ecuador' in Powers, T. (1981).

Fitzgerald, E. V. K. (1978) *Public Sector Investment Planning for Developing Countries*, (London: Macmillan).

Gittinger, J. P. (1982) *Economic Analysis of Agricultural Projects*, 2nd edn (Baltimore: Johns Hopkins University Press for Economic Development Institute of the World Bank).

Harberger, A. (1972) *Project Evaluation-Collected Papers* (London: Macmillan).

Harberger, A. (1978) 'On the Use of Distributional Weights in Social Cost Benefit Analysis', *Journal of Political Economy*, vol. 86, no. 2 (part II).

Harberger, A. (1984) 'Basic Needs versus Distributional Weights in Cost Benefit Analysis', *Economic Development and Cultural Change*, vol. 32, no. 3.

Irvin, G. (1978) *Modern Cost–Benefit Methods. An Introduction to Financial, Economic and Social Appraisal of Development Projects* (London: Macmillan).

Karatas, C. (1989) 'Third Bosphorus Bridge versus Bosphorus Road Tube Tunnel and Combined Alternative: An Economic Appraisal', *Project Appraisal*, vol. 4, no. 2 (June).

Kula, E. (1988) 'Future Generations: The Modified Discounting Method', *Project Appraisal*, vol. 3, no. 2, (June).

Kuyvenhoven, A. (1978) *Planning with the Semi-Input-Output Method* (Leiden: Martinus Social Science Division).

Lal, D. (1974) 'Methods of Project Analysis: A Review', World Bank Staff Occasional Papers, no. 16 (Washington DC: World Bank).

Lal, D. (1980) *Prices for Planning: Towards the Reform of Indian Planning* (London: Heinemann).

Layard, R. (ed.) (1972) *Cost–Benefit Analysis* (Harmondsworth: Penguin).

Linn, J. (1977) 'Economic and Social Analysis of Projects: A Case-Study of the Ivory Coast', World Bank Staff Working Papers no. 253 (Washington DC: World Bank).

Little, I. and Mirrlees, J. (1968) *Manual of Industrial Project Analysis in Developing Countries*, vol. 2, (Paris: OECD).

Little, I. and Mirrlees, J. (1974) *Project Appraisal and Planning for Developing Countries* (London: Heinemann Educational).

Londero, E. (1981) 'El Salvador', chapter 5 in Powers, T. (1981)

Londero, E. (1987) *Benefits and Beneficiaries* (Washington DC: Inter-American Development Bank).

MacArthur, J. (1978) 'Appraising the Distributional Aspects of Rural Development Projects', *World Development*, vol. 6. no. 2.

Marglin, S. A. (1967) *Public Investment Criteria. Studies in the economic development of India* (London: Unwin).

Mashayekhi, A. (1980) 'Shadow Prices for Project Appraisal in Turkey', World Bank Staff Working Paper no. 392 (Washington DC: World Bank).

McKean, R. N. (1968) 'The Use of Shadow Prices', in Layard, R. (ed.) (1972).

Morales, L. (1981) 'Barbados' in Powers, T. (1981).

Novozhilov, V. V. (1970) *Problems of Cost-benefit Analysis in Optimal Planning* (New York: International Arts and Science).

ODA (1982) *Appraisal of Projects in Developing Countries* (London: HMSO).

ODA (1988) *Appraisal of Projects in Developing Countries. A Guide for Economists*, 3rd edn (London: HMSO).

OECD (1989) *The Impact of Development Projects on Poverty* (Paris: OECD Development Centre).

Page, J. (1982) 'Shadow Prices for Trade Strategy and Investment Planning in Egypt', World Bank Staff Working Paper no. 521 (Washington DC: World Bank).

Pearce, D. and Turner, R. K. (1990) *Economics of Natural Resources and the Environment* (Hemel Hampstead: Harvester Wheatsheaf).

Pelt, M. van, Kuyvenhoven, A. and Nijkamp, P. (1990) 'Project Appraisal and Sustainability: methodological challenges', *Project Appraisal*, vol. 5, no. 3 (September).

Phillips, D. (1986a) 'Inflation, Income Distribution and Cost Benefit Analysis', *Project Appraisal*, vol. 1, no. 4 (December).

Phillips, D. (1986b) 'Pitfalls in Estimating Social Discount Rates: A Case-study', *Project Appraisal*, vol. 1, no. 1 (March).

Pouliquen, L. Y. (1970) 'Risk Analysis in Project Appraisal', World Bank, Staff Occasional Paper, no. 11 (Washington DC: World Bank).

Powers, T. (1977) 'Guide for Appraising Urban Potable Water Projects', Inter-American Development Bank. Paper on Project Analysis. no. 4 (Washington DC: Inter-American Development Bank).

Powers, T. (ed.) (1981) *Estimating Accounting Prices for Project Appraisal* (Washington DC: Inter-American Development Bank).

Price, C. (1989) 'Equity, Consistency, Efficiency and New Rules for Discounting', *Project Appraisal*, vol. 4, no. 2, (June).

Ray, A. (1984) *Cost–Benefit Analysis* (Baltimore: Johns Hopkins University Press).

Remenyi, D. and Nugus, S. (1988) *Lotus 1-2-3 for Financial Managers and Accountants* (London: McGraw-Hill).

Saerbeck, R. (1988) 'Estimating Accounting Price Ratios with a Semi Input–output Table: Botswana', *Project Appraisal*, vol. 3, no. 4 (December).

Schohl, W. (1979) 'Estimating Shadow Prices for Columbia in an Input–Output Framework', World Bank Staff Working Papers no. 357 (Washington DC: World Bank).

Scott, M. (1974) 'How to Use and Estimate Shadow Exchange Rates', *Oxford Economic Papers*, vol. 26, no. 2.

Scott, M. (1990) 'Social Cost–Benefit Analysis', chapter 13 in Scott, M. and Lal, D. (1990) *Public Policy and Economic Development* (Oxford: Clarendon Press).

Scott, M. MacArthur, J. and Newbery, D. (1976) *Project Appraisal in Practice* (London: Heinemann).

Sell, A. (1989) 'Calculation of Working Capital for Evaluation of Projects in Developing Countries' *Project Appraisal*, vol. 4, no. 3 (September).

Sen, A. K. (1972) 'Feasibility Constraints: Foreign Exchange and Shadow Wages', in Layard, R. (ed.) (1972).

Squire, L. and Tak, H. van der (1975) *Economic Analysis of Projects* (Baltimore: Johns Hopkins University Press).

Stewart, F. (1975) 'A Note on Social Cost Benefit Analysis and Class Conflict in LDCs', *World Development*, vol. 3, no. 1.

Thomson, K. J. (1988) 'Future Generations: the Modified Discounting Method – a Reply', *Project Appraisal*, vol 3, no. 3 (September).

UNIDO (1972) *Guidelines for Project Evaluation* (New York: United Nations).

UNIDO (1978a) *Manual for the Preparation of Industrial Feasibility Studies* (Vienna: United Nations).

UNIDO (1978b) *Guide to Practical Project Appraisal* (New York: United Nations).

UNIDO (1980) *Practical Appraisal of Industrial Projects* (New York: United Nations).

Walsh, C. and Daffern, P. (1990) *Managing Cost–Benefit Analysis* (London: Macmillan).

Weiss, J. (1976) 'UNIDO Guidelines Case-Study Expressed in a Little and Mirrlees Framework', PPC Occasional Paper no. 2 (Bradford: University of Bradford).

Weiss, J. (1978) 'Problems in the Use of World Prices in Social Cost Benefit Analysis', *Institute of Development Studies Bulletin*, vol. 10, no. 1.

Weiss, J. (1979) 'Project Selection and the Equity Objective: The Use of Social Cost Benefit in Pakistan', *Pakistan Development Review*, vol. 18, no. 2.

Weiss, J. (1980) 'Cost–Benefit Analysis of Foreign Industrial Investment', *Industry and Development*, no. 5 (New York: United Nations).

Weiss, J. (1985) 'National Economic Parameters for Jamaica', Project Planning Centre Occasional Paper no. 7 (Bradford: University of Bradford).

Weiss, J. (1986) 'Industrial Projects and the Importance of Assumptions about Learning and Technical Change', *Project Appraisal*, vol. 1, no. 3 (September).

Weiss, J. (1988) 'An introduction to Shadow Pricing in a Semi Input–Output Approach', *Project Appraisal*, vol. 3, no. 4 (December).

Weiss, J. (1989) 'Assessing the Technical Impact of New Investment Projects in Developing Countries', *Journal of International Development*, vol. 1, no. 4.

Weiss, J. (1990a) *Industry in Developing Countries* (London: Routledge).

Weiss, J. (1990b) 'Some Comments on the Use of Cost–Benefit Analysis in Socialist Economies', *Project Appraisal* vol. 5, no. 2 (June).

Wilczynski, J. (1977) *The Economics of Socialism*, 3rd edn (London: Allen & Unwin).

World Bank (1973) *Compounding and Discounting Tables for project evaluation*, Economic Development Institute (Washington DC: World Bank).

World Bank (1983) *World Development Report 1983* (Washington DC: World Bank).

World Bank (1989) *Sub-saharan Africa: from Crisis to Sustainable Growth* (Washington DC: World Bank).

Yaffey, M. (1988) 'Layout and Structure of Computer Spreadsheets for Project Planning', *Project Appraisal*, vol. 3, no. 2 (June).

Index*

*Compiled by Jackie McDermott.